COMBAT HANDGUN SHOOTING

COMBAT HANDGUN SHOOTING

JAMES D. MASON

Small Arms and Ballistics Consultant
San Diego County Sheriff's Department
San Diego, California

CHARLES C THOMAS · PUBLISHER
Springfield · Illinois · U.S.A.

Published and Distributed Throughout the World by
CHARLES C THOMAS • PUBLISHER
Bannerstone House
301-327 East Lawrence Avenue, Springfield, Illinois, U.S.A.

©*1976, by* CHARLES C THOMAS • PUBLISHER
ISBN 0-398-03461-3
Library of Congress Catalog Card Number: 75 12787

*With THOMAS BOOKS careful attention is given to all details of manufacturing
and design. It is the Publisher's desire to present books that are satisfactory
as to their physical qualities and artistic possibilities and appropriate for their
particular use. THOMAS BOOKS will be true to those laws of quality that assure
a good name and good will.*

Library of Congress Cataloging in Publication Data

Mason, James D.
 Combat Handgun Shooting

 Bibliography: p.
 Includes index.
 1. Pistol Shooting. I. Title.
 GV1175.M37   799.2'02833   75-12787
 ISBN 0-398-03461-3

Printed in the United States of America
BB-14

This book is dedicated to those vigilant souls, past, present, and future, who toil in the cause of the citizen's right to keep and bear arms . . . on such individual initiatives are based all political rights, freedoms, and fundamental securities.

William W. McMillan (Lt. Colonel, USMC, Ret.)

Colonel McMillan, who has written the Foreword for this book, is one of America's foremost competitive marksmen. He has competed in five Olympic Games, three Pan-American Games, and five World Championships. Between 1958 and 1967, he won three Gold Medals for pistol marksmanship, including the exacting International Rapid Fire event. He was a World Pistol Champion in both .22 and .38 caliber in Caracas, 1954. He was five times All Marine Rifle and Pistol Champion. He has actively coached Marine Corps shooting teams over an extended number of years.

Since his retirement from the Marine Corps in July, 1974, he has been Weapons Training Coordinator for the San Diego (California) County Sheriff's Department. In this capacity he directs small arms training for over 500 full-time and reserve deputies, designing training programs, supervising range operation, and evaluating tactical weapons and systems.

FOREWORD

Combat handgun shooting is a welcome challenge to anyone who has ever fired a pistol. It incorporates all of the fundamentals of marksmanship with the physical requirements of an athlete. For Law Enforcement and the Military, combat handgunning skills hold many practical applications.

My first encounter with combat handgun competition came in the early 1960's. By this time, I had successfully competed in three Olympic Games, a Pan American Games, and three World Shooting Championships. Names like Thell Reed, Ray Chapman, Elden Carl, and Al Nichols were familiar to me, but not their brand of shooting. When several of these friends invited me to a combat shoot, I jumped at the chance.

Following my earlier triumphs, I was confident of "cleaning house" and dazzling the troops. I was wrong. The competition was tough and the style of pistol shooting was quite different from anything I had done before. It was an unexpected experience peering over pistol sights while balancing on a log, or shooting a rapid-fire string after completing a 100 yard dash. It was a whole new ball game.

Combat handgunning is not for everyone. To excel in competition is a real test of skill, requiring a cool head, good physical condition and coordination, fast reflexes, and mastery of marksmanship fundamentals. But, while not everyone will become a top-notch competitor, the discipline will improve significantly any shooter's skills. Incidentally, this style of handgunning should not be confused with the less challenging PPC events.

Jim Mason's superb, unbiased writings on combat handgunning will be of interest to all pistol marksmen. There is something in this book for every handgunning interest. Law enforcement agencies in particular will be assisted in decision making for issue handguns, types of ammunition, and what courses of fire are best suited to their needs. This book is "must" reading for every police rookie and experienced veteran patrolman.

Military organizations should review combat shooting positions and courses of fire that can stimulate a renewed interest in effective tactical handgunning. Although military missions differ from those of law enforcement, this book will prove beneficial to many service marksmanship units.

I congratulate the author on filling a major "missing link" in handgun journalism. This volume is a unique and valuable addition to the literature. Certainly it will benefit those of us in the small arms instructional field, providing an excellent reference manual for teaching and shooting the "short gun."

—Bill McMillan

PREFACE

Combat handgun shooting has matured during the past decade into a full-fledged sport and martial art. Handling skills, combat shooting techniques and performance standards with handguns have changed dramatically in this activity that remained virtually unchanged for nearly a century. The shifts away from more traditional military and target shooting concepts are so remarkable that a separate treatment of the subject is called for. From the wealth of information developed over the past 10 to 15 years, only a few attempts have been made to include in a single volume a comprehensive overview of the subject. The particular advantage of such a volume lies in its ability to expand individual shooting capacity for all levels of marksmen, rather than to preach a fixed doctrine or method directed primarily at the novice.

Although a solid set of basic procedures has developed, combat handgun shooting is still a fluid field for experimentation. For this reason the sporting applications are emphasized although police and military organizations will find the material equally pertinent. This book can be either a main text or supplementary reading for policemen or military personnel as well as aspiring civilian combat shooters. Combat shooting instructors will find the text most flexible and adaptable to their own teaching approach. The book serves to sharpen student interest in classwork and to build positive identification with the learning activity. Class time is more effective in reinforcing learning and helps students acquire higher levels of skills within the course duration. The text serves also to instruct in the home defense use of handguns. With appropriate skills, not only will homeowners be more controlled and confident in gun handling during emergencies, but shooting accidents will be reduced sharply when handguns are manipulated by trained, competent people. The key to understanding is a point of view; a way of looking at combat shooting aimed at individual development and performance, not merely prescribed shooting techniques. The plan for the book includes discussions of the human and mechanical firearms systems, as well as the interface of the two. Creating images in the reader's mind of what goes on during effective shooting activity equips the combat marksman to analyze his own strengths and weaknesses; to capitalize upon that which he does well and to correct his deficiencies. Too often, the approach to shooting mastery is by rote application with little understanding of the total processes that produce good marksmanship.

The chapters each deal with key aspects of combat shooting. Each chapter is written to stand alone while still having continuity with the other material. While it is preferred that chapters be read in sequence, reading can be done at random, depending on a person's needs and interests. The book is written so that it will continue to serve the needs of the shooter over several years. Areas that do not completely make sense to the novice shooter will have special meaning later, after more experience is acquired. The book can be reread many times to reinforce what the shooter has learned from actual practice; the reader is encouraged to project his capacities beyond the bounds of the text. Many technical sections such as those dealing with pistolsmithing, ballistics, and handloading assume some requisite skills on the part of the reader. While they are not meant to be "how-to" material, readers with basic mechanical skills will find ample information in the text so that they can tune their own pistols or reload and evaluate their own ammunition. Finally, it is hoped that an objective presentation of the fundamentals of this challenging shooting sport will serve to overcome some of the misinformation and prejudicial thinking abroad in our society today, especially in regard to handgunning activities.

J.D.M.

ACKNOWLEDGEMENTS

For starters in combat shooting, I was particularly blessed to have two of the finest Combat Masters for teachers. Elden Carl shaped my early fundamental experiences; he must be regarded not only for his superior shooting skills, but for his instructional ability as well. Elden maintains a pervading interest in his students' accomplishments and provides a continuous, vital leadership so essential for effective teaching.

Al Nichols groomed my performance for competition. A perfectionist with strong competitive drives, Al's example sets standards that inspire confidence and the desire to excel. His knowledge of the intricacies of each match reflects his own superlative achievements. He has won the Southwest Pistol League crown five times. For the background and guidance given by these two outstanding people, I am deeply indebted.

My thanks also to Lieutenant Colonel Bill McMillan, who reviewed the manuscript and wrote the Foreword for this book. His outstanding qualifications are noted opposite the Foreword.

For the graphic layout and handsome appearance of this volume, Stan Hodge lent his taste and good judgment as design consultant. Stan has been an award winning graphic art director in industry, and now teaches at San Diego State University.

Dr. William Eppler generously reviewed the physiology material contributing insights and understandings to those references.

My colleague, Professor John Peters, counselled regarding psychological aspects of the manuscript. His comments and questions helped shape a useful group of statements out of complex basic material.

Artist Paul Johnson produced the outstanding pen and ink anatomy drawings which should help create reader imagery. Carolyn Houston typed both the rough draft and final copies of the manuscript.

For their time and consideration, thanks go to gunsmiths Dan Dwyer and Paul Blazejowski, Irv Stone of Bar-Sto Precision, Jerry Krasne and Tony Schmidt of Triple-K Manufacturing Company, John Bianchi and Richard Nichols of Bianchi Leather Products, Ron Bittner, of Ron Bittner's Gun Shop, Escondido, California; Blaine Hutchison and Dennis Johnson of Hiram's Gun Shop, El Cajon, California. Thanks also to Rick Middlested, Dave Hadley, and Burt Quick, as well as Wayne and Maudie Simmons, all of whom graciously posed for illustrations.

For permission to use material previously published in magazines and annuals, appreciation is due John Amber, Editor of *HANDLOADER'S DIGEST*, and Jerry Rakusan, Editor of *GUNS* Magazine.

An author's position in these matters is humble, indeed. While giving credit due for all of the right things in the book, errors or omissions fall squarely on the author's shoulders.

The final nod goes to the reader. Since the book is intended to help the combat shooter, it is necessary to know what kind of a job it does. Comments and criticisms are welcome.

J.D.M.

CONTENTS

COMBAT HANDGUN SHOOTING

CHAPTER I

COMBAT HANDGUN SHOOTING— SPORT OR MARTIAL ART?

H OW CAN AN activity that prepares people for mortal conflict be called a sport? In the minds of many casual observers, the spectre of combat handgun shooting as a martial art tends to overshadow its sporting possibilities. But, there are a number of individual sports that draw their antecedents from martial applications; it takes little imagination to see the origins of the javelin throw developing from spear throwing contests among primitive tribal warriors. These sports served to keep warriors practiced in the arts of combat and encouraged the expansion of individual and group war making skills as an instrument of tribal survival. Moreover, the pageantry of competitive sporting contests built tribal unity (patriotism) and a general tribal identity with martial skills. These social values in turn inspired young tribesmen (and women) to acquire competence in the arts of survival.

SURVIVAL PLAY

Man is no different in this respect from other animals. Even the domestic cat plays games as a kitten that subtly build the capacity for hunting and defense. Indeed, the evolution of team sports in man's culture emphasizes the need for cooperation and interdependence in order to "win the day." The subtle survival effects of these cultural activities really cannot be measured, but we see evidence of the character building aspects of competitive sports activity in the lives and accomplishments of many of our foremost leaders as well as ordinary citizens.

Swordsmanship is closely akin to combat handgunning in many respects. The sport of fencing was developed as a means of teaching swordsmanship in the days when the rapier was a common sidearm. While the purpose in carrying or using the rapier had mortal significance, the sport or "play" activity of fencing had only indirect overtones. Protection of face and torso and the blunting of foil tips are mute testimony to the sporting intent. The dueling sports conditioned mind and body to the martial aspects of this activity, but were no substitute for actual combat. Most people who trained in the sport never used the blade in anger. Today fencing, like most sports, still transfers much cultural value to its adherents, while it would be laughable to overly ascribe morbid connotations to the motives of sporting swordsmen. No amateur swordsman is going to make shish kebab out of his fellow citizens, yet the contribution of this sport to the total development of the individual is unmistakable.

And so it is with combat handgunning; a sport grown out of a martial skill that places premiums on eye and hand coordinations and total body movement. In traditional one-handed target shooting, the object is precision bullet placement to a particular point of impact. In combat shooting, two hands are used, usually, to manipulate the gun to deliver multiple shots into a prescribed area within short time limits. While the Martial applications of this skill are evident, the targets are paper and the object of the sport is "to shoot" not "to kill."

MILITARY ANTECEDENTS

Combat handgunning draws considerable background from its military antecedents. Originally, handguns as such were scaled down and shortened long guns with a hand grip instead of a butt stock. Flintlock or early percussion handguns were single shot affairs used for short range defense. They lacked sufficient fire power to be anything other than supplementary to the sword and dagger. Some of these early single shot muzzle loading pistols contained integral knives for close combat. The contemporary concept of the pistol was that of a single-hand weapon, literally. It was common to carry two pistols, one in each hand, to increase fire power. The pistol was a primary shooting iron for mounted troops and had to be shot from one hand, the other hand holding the horse's reins.

The idea of using the pistol in one hand only was persistent. As this kind of weapon took over from the sword for personal duels,

The traditional one-hand stance used in formal handgun target shooting. This is an anachronism left over from pistol dueling days, and has little relevance to current dynamic combat shooting modes. This style is still useful, however, to teach and perfect fundamentals of marksmanship.

a single handed stance was perfected and stylized. To minimize the profile presented to a dueling opponent, and to protect the heart from penetration of the ball, each shooter turned sideways raising the exposed arm to fire. There was no possibility for using the idle hand to support the gun without exposing more body area. Since the duelist had only one shot, he had to make it count. Deliberate aim was taken to hit a vital area, usually the head or mid-chest cavity. This duelist stance was practiced widely as a sport in its day and became the basis for our current, traditional form of handgun target shooting; a sideways body position relative to the target with the shooting arm outstretched.

FIRE POWER

Rapid fire techniques were developed by the military and frontiersmen to increase firepower. Reloading a single shot, muzzle

Sam Colt, the inventor of the revolver, reshaped the role of the handgun. It has taken over a century to fully develop the potential of "modern" repeating handguns.

Captain Sam Walker's personal Whitneyville Colt, #1010. Walker was instrumental in obtaining the purchase of these Model 1847 percussion revolvers. The order firmly established Sam Colt in the gun business and revolutionized tactical handgun applications.

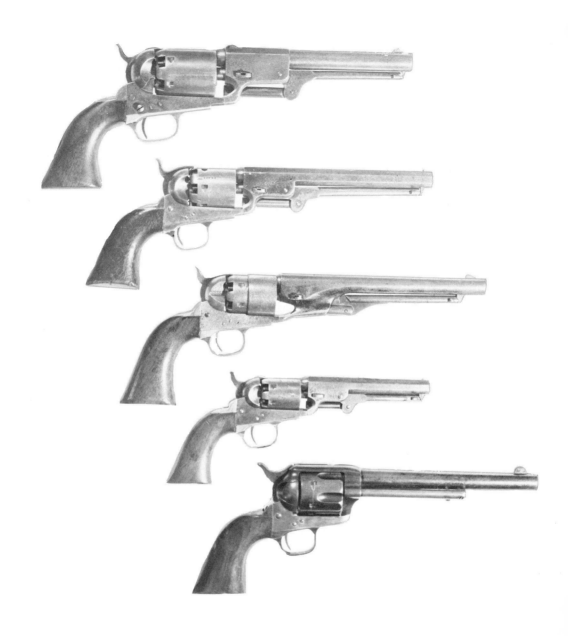

Colt's designs expanded rapidly to meet a burgeoning demand. From top to bottom, the Model 1848 Dragoon, 1851 Navy, 1860 Army, 1849 Pocket Model. The Model 1873 Single Action Army revolver (bottom) was Colt's first production revolver designed for self-contained ammunition. This gun is still manufactured today.

loading pistol from horseback was no mean feat. Later, the innovation of the Colt revolver (1836) was the beginning of a new era for the handgun. Short range intensive fire delivered from horseback revolutionized cavalry tactics. Using early model Colts, tactics were developed first during the Creek and Seminole Indian Wars. The revolver came of age during the Mexican War with the design of the 1847 Walker (Whitneyville) Colt. Although the bulk of these revolvers arrived late for service in Texas and Mexico, the Walker model established Sam Colt in the revolver business. Performance of those revolvers that were available in Texas and during the Mexican campaigns demonstrated the full meaning of handgun fire power.

Carrying two revolvers in belt holsters and two more in saddle holsters, Texas Rangers (commissioned as the United States Mounted Rifles during the Mexican War) had 24 rounds available to fire. The Walker Colt took a charge of 50 grains of black powder behind a 220 grain conical bullet. This load exceeded 950 fps (feet per second) and was considered the equal of a rifle at 100 yards and superior to a musket out to 200 yards. Later Colt production guns adapted the Walker configuration to the Dragoon series that was made from 1848 up until the Civil War. During the same period, other smaller, handier cap and ball models were brought out, such as the 1851 Navy (.36 caliber) and 1860 Army (.44 caliber). Following the Mexican War, the revolver had "arrived" as a tactical military weapon and elevated the importance of the horse cavalry to its apex; this position was short lived, however. Development of artillery technology and barrage tactics during the U.S. Civil War and the Franco-Prussian War in Europe, along with the advent of the repeating cartridge rifle ended much

Frederick Remington's famous painting, "Cavalry Charge on the Southern Plains," (c. 1907) depicts the role of the revolver as it applied to cavalry tactics. Notice the necessity of the one-hand hold for mounted six guns. Cavalry played out its epic role in the Indian Plain Wars; advances in individual and barrage weapons made cavalry obsolete in the latter part of the 19th Century. (Photo courtesy The Metropolitan Museum of Art, Gift of Several Gentlemen, 1911).

of the combat significance of full-scale horse cavalry operations during the last quarter of the 19th century.

THE OLD WEST

Following the Civil War, the Westward Movement brought in a unique era regarding the nation's development as well as the role of the handgun. The advent of self-contained cartridge ammunition inspired a proliferation of revolvers. The Colt Single Action Army revolver was introduced in 1873, along with the .45 Long Colt cartridge. Remington and Smith & Wesson introduced cartridge handguns in the large caliber series also, and helped supply the burgeoning demand for personal sidearms during that period.

With revolvers so universally available in the Old West, it was inevitable that they would affect social processes of a nearly law-less, competitive, and highly individualistic era. While much of the image we have of the Old West is more than slightly tinged by sensational journalism and Class B western movies, the free-style for gunfighting in those days is unmistakable. The image of the gun-fighter grew as a kind of folk hero. The fact that most of these men were psychopathic drew little note from a population largely deprived of entertainment and diversions from a hard and not too rewarding life.

The traditional nature of the gun duel was greatly altered in the Old West. Confrontation was more informal and free-style, although the motives for gun fighting might have been unchanged. In the best "High Noon" tradition, holstered six guns were drawn and fired with the fastest and most accurate shooter winning the day. More often, shooting was done from ambush. The "dry gulch" required a high degree of adapt-

Other makers also marketed single action revolvers during the period Colt dominated the market. This S&W Schofield in .45 Long Colt was available. The Russian and American models of this same basic revolver were quite popular.

Hammer fanning involved coordinated use of both hands to fire the SA revolver rapidly. Colt's large hammer spur made this technique a natural. Fanning was a specialized technique that was hard on the revolver lock work.

able skill to spell survival for the intended victim. Many fights involved more than two adversaries or were shot at distances, or under conditions, where more than a single round would have to be fired.

Multiple shot techniques originated where hammer "fanning" could empty the SA cylinder with the speed of a modern self-loading pistol. (This technique was quite hard on the revolver lock work.) Thumbing the hammer was a more effective means of delivering well placed shots, and executed with two-handed coordination, it was almost as fast as hammer fanning. The two-handed thumbing technique called for gripping the revolver handle securely with the shooting hand, while cocking the hammer with the thumb of the other hand. The idle hand was cupped around the shooting hand for stability. Thumbing did not put undue strain on the lock work and did not require unusual modifications of the gun. Another interesting observation on thumbing techniques was that both hands were used in a coordinated manner to control the pistol.

EVOLUTION OF DOUBLE ACTION

But the gunfighter's equipment and techniques were things to read about and marvel over; practical handgun shooting remained a one-handed, traditionally oriented technique for both the military and civilian shooter. Fire power was severely limited because hammer cocking was commonly done with the thumb of the shooting hand, requiring a repositioning of the gun handle for each shot. Advent of the double action revolver did little to change things, even though evolution of the DA solid frame design gave potential for greatly increased fire power (hammer cocking was accomplished by the long DA pull of the trigger). Most actual shooting with combination DA's was done using single action hammer cocking well into the first half of this century.

Few shooters accepted the discipline of DA shooting for target and recreation, preferring the easy, precise single action pull used in formal target shooting. Most people who did develop good double action techniques were more talented members of police organizations.

SCIENCE AND ART OF GUNFIGHTING

Many of these outstanding shooters were trained as members of the United States Border Patrol, an elite group of lawmen highly trained and motivated in the use of

One of the pioneers who advanced combat handgunning into what it is today, Bill Jordan, is well known and respected as a lawman and exhibition shooter. The lanky Texan served with distinction in the U.S. Border Patrol and is author of the combat shooting book NO SECOND PLACE WINNER.

handguns and all firearms. The Southwest border area developed a lot of gun play, so mastery of gun handling crafts was a way of life. The influences of the gunfighter era were still fresh in the Southwest border area in the late 20's and 30's. Since that time, such men as Charles Askins, Tom Threeperson, Walter Walsh, and Bill Jordan developed DA revolver skills into a combat shooting system.

Equally important were the books and publications of ardent civilian pistol shooters like Ed McGivern and Elmer Keith. Developing the sport of handgunning, these shooters and experimenters broadcast the results of their activities to the public and influenced the shooting activities of thousands of other handgunners. During the 1930's, law enforcement activity was much publicized with the "war against crime." FBI handgun training reinforced public interest in combat shooting skills with emphasis on draw and fire techniques and simulated combat courses of fire. All during this time, the revolver was King with little attention given to autopistols.

EXPANDING SPORTING INTERESTS

Public interest in handgun shooting sports grew rapidly in the 1950's. In the West, especially, quick draw contests developed into an organized sport complete with formal judging and electronic timers, including an impressive array of specialized equipment and techniques. Fast time out of the holster was the whole object of the draw and fire. This emphasis soon made the sport so specialized that competitors were firing blanks the instant the muzzle cleared leather, with no regard to where the bullet impact might be. Quick draw contests later became lead bullet shoots where the winner had the shortest time to hit a prescribed target (a balloon or gong). Under these conditions, it was soon observed that some of the fastest pure quick draw competitors were not able to hit a balloon in anywhere near the time that they could clear the holster under the old blank firing rules.

Later, more formalized courses of fire were designed to incorporate much of what was known and had been learned about combat pistol shooting. Growing numbers of DA revolver shooters entered these activities with timing handicaps given to SA shooters on reloading phases. A very few people used autopistols, usually the .45 Government Model. By the early 1960's, rules in the Southwest Pistol League (Southern California area) threw out all handicaps on loading time limits, and introduced power factors for various loads; this completely cut out the SA shooter and severely handicapped the DA shooters. Following these changes within a period of two years, the .45 Government Model became the dominant handgun. For the first time, the autopistol got a serious airing of its particular advantages as a combat arm.

Along with this hardware change, new shooting techniques developed, such as the two-hand hold. Courses of fire were designed or modified to create spiraling challenges to handgun shooting capacity. The Southwest Pistol League became the hub of combat shooting development. Largely under the early influence of Jeff Cooper, retired Marine officer and Handgun Editor for *GUNS & AMMO* Magazine, the League and affiliated clubs became an arena for regional shooters to develop and test combat shooting skills.

COMPARISON OF COMBAT AND FORMAL TECHNIQUES

From out of years of pistol activities, certain charactersitics for this sport have developed that contrast significantly with the older, formal target pistol shooting. Combat events call for dynamic gun handling. Starting positions are from the holster; drawing the pistol is an integral part of all events. Shortened time periods and the most effective two-hand holds demand total body coor-

dination. This contrasts rather markedly with the static body poise of formal target shooting. The martial purposes of combat shooting demand the most effective and flexible defensive fire with a handgun, while formal target shooting is the practice mode for pistol dueling in the old traditional sense. The object of the traditional mode is to deliver deliberate single shots to a designated point. Combat shooting emphasizes delivery of multiple shots to prescribed areas within short time periods. Combat shooting also embraces a spectrum of firing modes and conditions all the way from long range slow fire to short range rapid fire at single and multiple targets.

The demands on equipment and shooting

SA revolvers had to be cocked manually to be fired. This was usually accomplished with the thumb of the shooting hand (top picture). The process was slow and clumsy. Thumbing techniques were used which required two-hand coordination (bottom picture). Two hand thumbing was nearly as fast as fanning, was quite flexible, and allowed accurate bullet placement. The latter technique was not in general use, however.

skills are such that combat handgunning provides a challenge unlike any other shooting activity. It is with that challenge in mind that this book will discuss the conditioning of the human and mechanical systems that are responsible for effective performance.

Combat handgunning provides a challenge unlike any other shooting sport. Cultivation of a dynamic, well-coordinated style builds gun-handling confidence and poise. Competitive aspects of this shooting game are limitless.

CHAPTER II

AUTOPISTOLS VS. DA REVOLVERS

NEARLY EVERY FIELD of activity has its controversies and pistol shooting is no exception. One of the most famous dichotomies among handgunners is the autopistol vs. DA revolver debate that dates back to the turn of the century. It was during this period that the double action revolver was evolving into what would be called the "modern" solid-frame configuration. About 75 years ago, the self-loading pistol was the latest advancement in the application of propellant energy to operate breech loading arms.

AMMUNITION EFFECTIVENESS

The base of the controversy has been laid as much on cartridge ballistics for revolver and autopistol ammunition as it has on the mechanical features of these two handgun configurations. Through the years, *aficionados* of both kinds of arms have extolled the virtues of their favorite while lambasting the opposing point of view. There seems to be a lack of good objective material compiled for both kinds of guns, where authorities have no particular axe to grind in promoting one type of gun over the other.

To further complicate the matter, there was a minor scandal in Army ordnance that arose just at the turn of the century and figured prominently in decision making for selection of a new U.S. military sidearm. The old Single Action Army revolver, Model 1873, had been replaced officially in 1892 by a Colt double action revolver in .38 caliber. Later in the decade, the United States assumed the protectorate of the Philippine Islands at the conclusion of the Spanish-American War. Shortly thereafter, an insurrection broke out among the Moros, groups of Muslim Maylay tribes in the Southern Philippines, who opposed the rule of the new government.

The Moro warriors were fanatical on occasion, performing opium-laced rituals just prior to attacking Army positions. Many defensive positions were overrun by groups of hopped-up Moros who lived long enough to carve up our troops with long machete-like knives after receiving multiple .38 caliber wounds.

Here are three self-loading pistols eminently suited for combat shooting. (l. to r.) .45 ACP Government Model, 9mm Combat Commander (steel frame) and the Browning Hi-Power 9mm with 13 round magazine. All these guns incorporate the Browning recoil system for self-operation.

This lack of "knock-down" power of the .38 cartridge was overcome by reissuing mothballed SAA .45 Colt revolvers which dispatched the attacking Moros before they could overrun the defense perimeter. The ineffectiveness of the .38 cartridge in the Philippine campaigns led to the Thompson-LaGarde ordnance investigations during the early 1900's. Following extensive testing on human cadavers and livestock, the committee report recommended pistol cartridges of no smaller than .45 caliber for military use. This set of circumstances has had recurring influence on the "debate" through the years since that time.

DEVELOPMENT OF SELF-LOADING PISTOLS

During this same period, John M. Browning had been developing his short recoil mechanism for self-loading pistols. Work was begun in 1905 that culminated in the .45 Automatic Colt Pistol (ACP) cartridge and a gun to shoot it. Ordnance competitions insued that led ultimately to the adoption of the Model 1911 pistol and its now famous .45 caliber cartridge. This satisfied the military, and the police were left with the .38 revolver. Ballistics for the smaller cartridge improved with the introduction of the .38 Special round in 1898, which significantly enhanced terminal performance over the older .38 caliber military loading. And since there were no hopped-up Moros on American city streets, the police were happy with the new standard service revolvers and the ammunition, which represented a considerable improvement over previous arms and ammunition used for urban law enforcement.

Since that time, various authorities and protagonists have wrestled with the dilemma over which type of sidearm was most effective. With few exceptions, the split still remains with the military favoring self-loaders and the police using the DA revolver. But the debate still goes on, fueled by articulate and opinionated writers whose own biases often tend to be the guiding light of their logic. Indeed, strong cases can be drawn in favor of both kinds of arms, and it is in this light that we shall approach the subject.

LIMITATION AND TERMS

Since this discussion relates to combat shooting, the consideration of firearms and ammunition should be limited likewise. Serviceable combat revolvers in .38 Special or .357 Magnum with barrels not over 4-inches in length are defined. For autopistols, the field is narrowed effectively to the .45 ACP and its standard variations (Government Model, Commander, .38 Super, etc.), and

medium frame autopistols in 9mm Parabellum (Model 39 and Model 59 S&W, Walther P-38, Browning Hi-Power, Colt Commander). Large, heavy frame revolvers are generally considered to be too clumsy for combat use, although they cannot be ruled out for powerful, large-handed shooters where cartridge loads are reduced in power. Recoil from full-power .41 or .44 Magnum loads is excessive for adequate control and recovery in combat shooting. Pistols shooting ammunition lighter in power than .38 Special fall into a separate class of secondary importance. Handling these light loads effectively takes special techniques. So, where pocket pistol calibers are concerned (.380, .32, .25, .22 Long Rifle), they will be considered as a unique class of arms.

The past ten to twelve years has seen the autopistol come into its own as a combat shooting piece. Cursed by three generations of soldiers, the M1911 .45 ACP has, in the

The Smith & Wesson Model 19 Combat Magnum revolver is the most popular and effective gun of its type used by combat marksmen. This handgun's dimensions, 35 oz. weight, and favorable grip shape plus an impeccable DA trigger pull make it ideal for sport or duty use.

last decade, become known as the most effective combat handgun in the world. In the hands of specialists, the .45 Government Model has captured virtually every combat shooting championship. It is used by eight out of ten combat marksmen.

The current trend in some shooting circles seems to be to knock the revolver and boost the autopistol for a variety of reasons. This does not overcome the inherent and overwhelming conservative choice of the revolver by the vast majority of police organizations in this country. Neither point of view by itself seems to shed much light on the comparative virtues or faults of both types of handguns. An analysis of the strong and weak points of each design is necessary in order to draw effective conclusions.

AUTOPISTOL

The choice of an autopistol is made for reasons of fire power and reliability. Stopping power and ease of operation (e.g. magazine release and thumb safety) are particularly desirable features in the case of the .45 ACP. Self-loading operation of an autopistol, coupled with fast reloading, means that more rounds can be delivered over a given period of time compared to a revolver. Reloading the autopistol is about twice or three times faster than the same operation in a revolver. It must be considered, though, that where reloading is not a factor, the DA revolver can deliver aimed shots as fast as the autopistol.

The .45 ACP round is one of the best stoppers of any pistol cartridge without getting into the Magnum class. Contrary to popular myth, a hit in a little finger will not knock an adversary off his feet. .45 ACP bullets do transfer more energy with hits in solid or vital areas than do most bullets from smaller calibers that travel at approximately the same velocity. The factory 230 grain loads for the .45 ACP, for example, are formidable and they must be considered very effective in terms of stopping power.

RELIABILITY

Autopistols have been criticized for being unreliable. Quite to the contrary, operating parts are simpler, fewer in number, more rugged, and less liable to failure in autopistols compared to revolvers. Normal dirt and residues are more easily digested by properly fitted self-loaders. However, if tolerances between critical parts are too tight, malfunctions can occur. Precision fit slides and barrel bushings of target-type autopistols are notorious for jamming under adverse combat conditions.

Stoppages can arise in automatics from failures to feed or fire due to ammunition irregularities or damaged magazines. When this kind of interruption occurs, however, the recovery time with an autopistol is usually much longer than that of a DA revolver where the shooter needs only to pull the trigger again to by-pass a faulty round. The use of factory hardball (full metal jacketed) ammunition all but eliminates feeding stoppages in autopistols. Proper bullet nose shape and solid gilding metal jackets all contribute to smooth and reliable feeding. Handloads are another story. Lead and softnose jacketed bullets tend to drag on the feed ramp or catch on the lower rim of the barrel breech opening. Polishing the feed ramp and reshaping the lower breech opening all aid in overcoming feeding difficulties with reloaded ammunition. Cast lead bullets should be made from relatively hard alloys, should be seated to correct depth, with proper case mouth tension in order to assure reliable functioning. If proper bullets are used, then failures to feed in an autopistol will probably occur only from a damaged magazine. The best remedy for this problem is a new magazine. But a faulty magazine can put an autoloader out of service in an emergency.

ACCURACY

Autopistols have been criticized for their lack of accuracy. From a practical point of

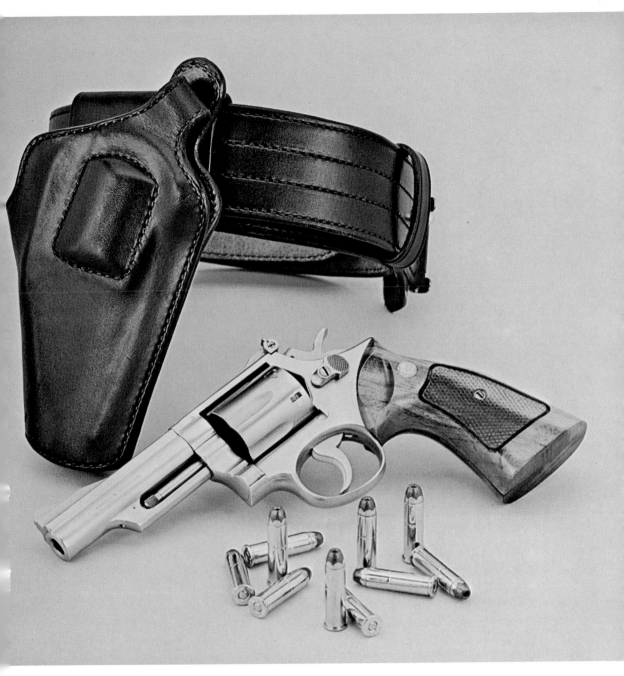

S&W Model 66 stainless steel Combat Magnum, caliber .357 shown with Bianchi's #2800 front opening holster.

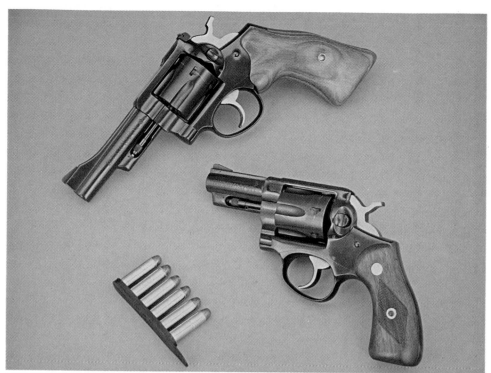

(Top) Ruger's Security Six in .357 magnum is shown with the short barreled Speed Six version. (Bottom) The author's Match conditioned .45 ACP's fitted with low-lock Colt Match barrels and full-house refinements.

S&W's Model 59 autopistol — 14 round magazine capacity.

(Top) A trio of 9mm autopistols. Colt's Combat Commander, Browning's Hi-Power, S&W's Model 39. (Bottom) Short barreled guns on the combat shooting scene — S&W's Model 60 stainless steel, Model 19 2 1/2-inch barrel, Ruger's Speed Six.

(Top) Representative pocket automatics. Going clockwise from twelve o'clock, S&W Model 61 Escort in .22 LR, Mauser HSc in .380 ACP, Walther PPK-S in .380 ACP, Mauser 1910 New Model in .32 ACP, and Mauser 1910 New Model in .25 ACP. (Bottom) Two basic combat revolvers — S&W's Model 19 and Ruger's Security Six.

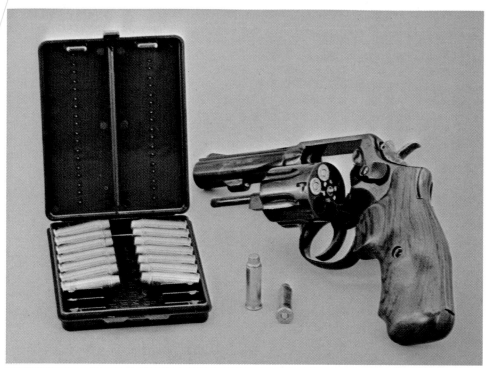

(Top) The Model 10 Heavy Barrel revolver by S&W makes and ideal general purpose combat gun — MTM ammunition wallet, Super Vel International Police loads. (Bottom) The old and new handle shapes from Ruger. The original stainless Security Six handle shape is on top. The new police frame is on the bottom. The new frame shape and fatter stocks makes Ruger's handgun especially well suited for combat shooting.

A premier pocket defense gun Walther PPK-S in .380 caliber imported and distributed by Interarms. Guy Hogue cocobolo grips.

(Top) Colt's small frame combat revolver is the Diamondback. Nickel finish is functional but sights must be blacked. (Bottom) Colt's Combat Commander is a formidable carrying gun. Anderson's "Corso" model combat rig is shown.

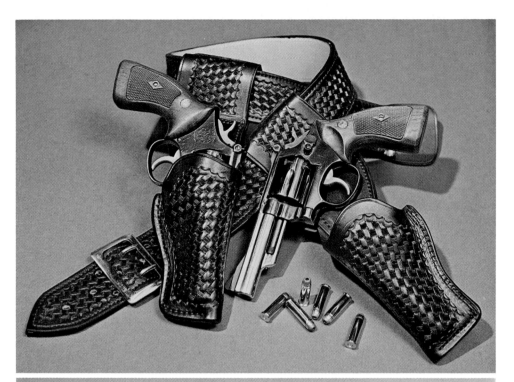

(Top) Elden Carl's matched set of tournament guns — S&W Model 9's with chromed barrels. Triple K forward rake holster set was designed by Carl. (Bottom) These look-alikes are identical except for sights and other minor differences. Dan Wesson's Model 15 revolver with 5 3/4-inch barrel is matched to High Standard's Mark III Sentinel.

(Top) Big magazine capacity has become more popular in recent years. These two guns are currently available — Model 59 S&W on top, and Browning's Hi-Power are illustrated here. (Bottom) Small frame revolvers shoot better with heavy barrels. This 3-inch heavy barreled J-frame S&W sports a Hogue diamond-profile combat grip.

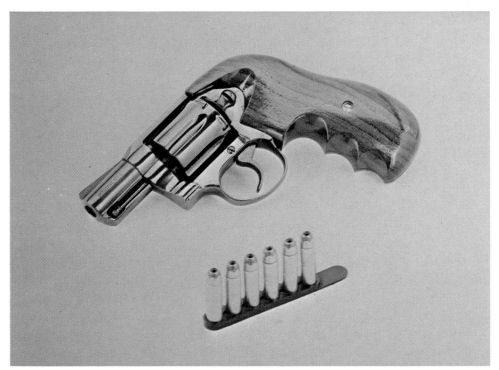

(Top) Colt's Detective Special becomes a formidable light frame competition gun when fitted with J-R grip. (Bottom) Favored pocket autos with combat capability are available in .380 ACP. The Mauser HSc (left) and Walther's PP are distributed by Interarms.

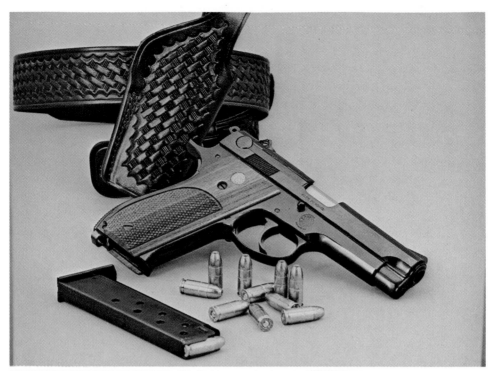

(Top) One of the best DA autos is the Model 39 S&W, shown here with Bianchi's Model 19 holster and the very effective Remington 115 grain JHP ammunition. (Bottom) A .22/45 conversion on the Government Model frame provides good and inexpensive practice shooting.

The standard of excellence in combat automatics is the Colt Government Model. This Anderson rig is typical of top quality leather used by combat shooters. Lead bullet reloads feature the #68 H&G bullet.

(Top) Shooting short-barrel guns is a challenge. Two of the best combat shooters are the Model 19 S&W and Colt's Detective Special. Guy Hogue concealment combat grips grace the frames of both guns. (Bottom) A stainless steel duet of combat revolvers is Ruger's Security Six (left) and S&W's Model 66 Combat Magnum. Super Vel 137 grain JSP loads are effective for combat use.

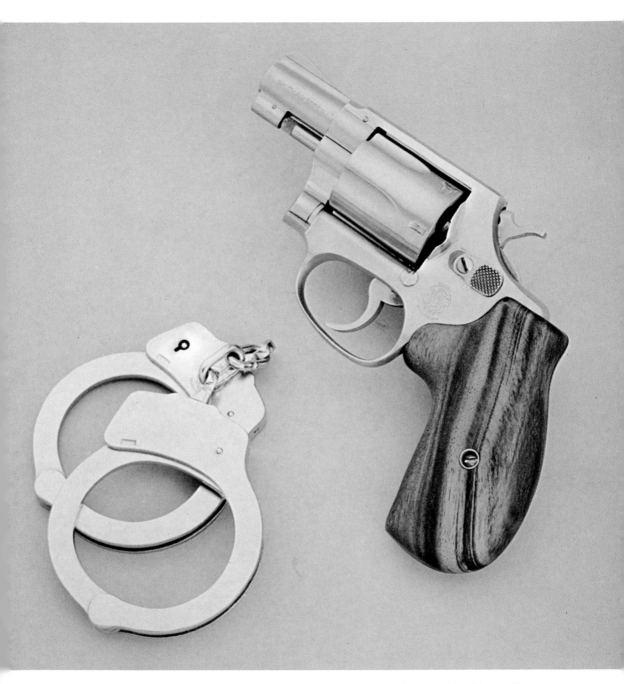

S&W's Model 60 is the stainless steel version of the Chief's Special. This small frame gun shoots with marvelous control using the Hogue combat grip. Most people will recognize the S&W bracelets.

A long-time standard for target shooting excellence is the Colt Python. Long, heavy, six-inch barrels provide stability during rapid fire but tend to be somewhat slower handling than 4-inch barrels. Shown is a Triple-K Model 5 holster, belt, and cartridge pouch.

view, automatics shoot as accurately as need be for combat purposes. As a defense gun, any pistol that can group inside four to five inches at 25 years is adequate. Most standard first-quality factory self-loaders will shoot this well.

However, target grouping capability can be built into self-loading pistols by reducing tolerances between critical operating parts. Close fitting parts in turn can reduce reliable operation under field conditions. Most combat shooters who use the Government Model reach a compromise by simply reworking the trigger for a 4½ pound pull, installing and fitting a National Match barrel with a lapped precision barrel bushing. The .45 ACP can be made to shoot 2 to 3 inch groups at 25 yards with these basic alterations. And these selected changes have a negligible effect on the reliability of the handgun.

Reworking of Walther P-38, Model 39, or Model 59 S&W handguns is somewhat more

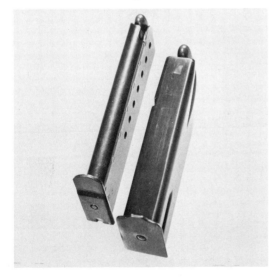

Big magazine capacity with enhanced fire power has become more popular in recent years, especially for 9mm handguns. Compare here the regular single column 9-round magazine with the Browning double column 13-round magazine. The Browning Hi-Power has been available with this big magazine since 1935. Recently, S&W has offered their M59 with a 14-round capacity box.

involved and results in less dramatic improvement in accuracy. These guns shoot fairly well as they come from the factory and may not justify reworking effort. Rather extensive modifications are being made to Browning Hi-Power pistols with justifiable results. These modifications are extensive, however, and most combat shooters who go to this trouble and expense are devotees of the Hi-Power, 9mm ammunition, and large magazine capacity. Availability of the aluminum framed M59 S&W offers another attractive 9mm, large magazine alternative. Large magazine capacity is of dubious value in combat shooting except for mass attacks in military situations.

Most combat shooters shy away from aluminum framed autoloaders especially in heavy calibers. There are several reasons for this. Light weight is no advantage, since recoil effect is increased; control and recovery time become problems, particularly with full loads. Aluminum framed guns tend to shoot loose sooner than pistols with steel frames, even though endurance tests show that aluminum frames can withstand several thousand rounds of full power loads without functional failure. This one factor becomes significant for ardent combat shooters who may consume 500 rounds every weekend. But the fact remains for pistols requiring a little shooting and a lot of carrying (probably 90% of the cases) the light aluminum frame makes sense.

SAFETY CONSIDERATIONS

Safety is a major consideration in the use of a handgun. Handling speed of autopistols largely depends on carrying the gun loaded with the hammer cocked and the safety locked. Special holsters provide safety straps to block an improbable but possible accidental hammer fall. Getting such a handgun into action is another matter. Holster safety straps must be released before the pistol can be drawn; the safety lever must be depressed before firing, but after the pistol clears leather. A poorly trained or uncoordinated shooter could very well send a stray round high or low during this procedure. If, for safety reasons, the autopistol is carried in a holster without a round in the chamber, the slide must be retracted manually before the gun can be fired. Such an arrangement nullifies the first-round speed advantage over the revolver.

DA AUTOPISTOLS

Since the early 1930's, there have been a few double action autopistols on the market (Walther and Smith & Wesson presently make the only combat sized DA self-loaders) that allow the handgun to be carried safely with a loaded chamber and the hammer down. The first shot is fired double action, like a revolver, but each succeeding shot is fired single action, with self-actuating operation. This feature virtually eliminates most

of the safety problems in getting an autopistol into action.

Combat shooters do not favor double action autopistols, however. The main objection is that the first shot is not much quicker than manually charging an autopistol, and not nearly as fast as a cocked and locked self-loader. The second round from a DA auto is fired single action after the mechanism has cycled. This second shot is more apt to go wild, since there is a pronounced change in coordination needed to touch-off the trigger after the initial long, double action pull. The difficulties of this change in coordination require a good deal of practice to overcome for most shooters, and many never really master the transition.

The double action feature is very good, however, on "everyman's" autopistol. For the average shooter who is not an accomplished pistoleer, the safest features and techniques are the best, even if they detract

These two DA autopistols combine the virtues of self-loading operation with the safety of a double action first shot. The S&W M39 is on the left. The German Walther P38, also chambered for the 9mm Parabellum cartridge, has an aluminum frame in current production, the same as the S&W M39/59.

from some of the gun's speed and effectiveness. After the first shot, however, the DA self-loader is as dangerous as any autopistol.

The outstanding virtues of the autopistol as a defensive gun are realized only through practice. Mastery of the various coordinations for shooting a self-loader is an art which can be accomplished by most people who possess above average manual dexterity and the determination to excel. Training is the key to proficient and effective use of the autopistol. In the hands of an accomplished shooter the autopistol, and notably the .45 ACP, becomes the most over-all effective combat handgun. In the hands of a novice or unaccomplished shooter, self-loading handguns have serious drawbacks.

DA REVOLVERS

For several years now, it has been the vogue among some gun writers to relegate the revolver to the boneyard. While there

Carrying the .45 ACP cocked and locked in a holster with special fly-off safety strap allows for a fast first shot.

has been an expanding interest in autopistols, many unique virtues of the DA revolver still make this handgun a formidable contender for popularity.

BASIC RECOMMENDATIONS

The strongest recommendations for the revolver relate to its simplicity and safety of operation. Nearly anybody can manipulate a revolver with passable results. The grip hold on a revolver is much less critical than that needed for autoloaders. Although a well aligned grip is best, position of the revolver relative to the hand and arm can vary considerably without adverse effect on shooting scores.

The revolver is not seriously affected by a misfire. If a round misfires, the next cylinder can be positioned by pulling the trigger again. The revolver has a versatility in the use of handloaded ammunition. Many bullet and loading combinations can be tried that would not work satisfactorily in autoloaders. Special bullet designs and weights can be used for unusual tactical purposes without regard to functional reliability of the arm. Revolvers are not hard on brass and recovery of spent cases is easy except where fast reloading phases are encountered.

Accuracy from first-line revolvers in factory new condition is better overall than that of a production line autoloader. Nothing can be done easily or inexpensively about revolver accuracy, however, if the gun just happens to be a sour shooter. Refitting is called for by an experienced pistolsmith. Most revolvers shoot more accurately than the marksman can hold, so the question becomes academic.

CONCEALMENT

Revolvers in the round butt configuration have an advantage over combat automatics regarding concealability. This feature is most valuable to policemen who may wish to cut down the bulk of their off-duty sidearms.

Concealment is a factor of handgun choice, especially for off-duty police officers or plainclothesmen. Round butt revolver handle shapes are easy to hide although the thickness of the cylinders add some bulk. Overall length of the gun is not as critical as other concerns.

Many shortened or otherwise abbreviated versions of autopistols have been experimented with in order to improve concealability of the self-loaders. The square end of the autoloader's handle still protrudes more than the graceful contour of a round butt revolver handle regardless of how the gun is carried. Reduction of size in an automatic means reduction in weight, which increases recoil disturbance. In the heavier autopistol calibers, notably the .45 ACP, recoil can become a serious problem for control and recovery with the modified and abbreviated low-bulk versions of self-loading handguns.

BALLISTIC EFFICIENCY

Revolvers are criticized for the gap between the cylinder and the barrel as a point where inaccuracies can initiate through misalignment. It is true that a revolver takes more handfitting and timing at the factory than autopistols, but revolver design and production in recent years also has benefitted from more advanced machining and fabrication techniques and the closer parts toler-

ances that can be held. If handfitting does not drop in quality, today's production run revolvers are better than ever from the standpoint of alignment and accuracy. Ultimate accuracy in a revolver probably will never equal the potential of an accurized autoloader, but the practical differences are negligible for combat shooting.

The gap between the cylinder and barrel also comes under critical review because of the loss of chamber pressure and subsequent reduction of ballistic performance. With the fast burning powders used in straight cased pistol cartridges, it is doubtful whether this is an overly significant factor in .38 caliber or larger bores. The larger the bore the lower the relative loss in ballistic performance because of this leakage. Any differences in performance level are easily made up with increases in the power of modern revolver cartridges, in particular the .357 Magnum, with combat loads. Power potential is more than adequate to meet any defensive needs.

The many moving parts in a revolver make it vulnerable to wear and misadjustment. Dropping a revolver on a hard surface may possibly call for complete retiming if it is to operate reliably. Close movement and

The gap between the cylinder face and the barrel earns criticism for revolvers. Its importance in ballistic performance is not as pronounced as some critics claim.

interdependence of parts, many frictional surfaces, and multiple lever systems make revolvers especially susceptible to malfunction from sand or dirt encountered under field conditions. Such conditions are mostly experienced under military circumstances, however. Urban police and most civilian shooting environments would not adversely affect functional reliability from foreign matter entering the mechanism.

MANIPULATION

Reloading the DA revolver requires superlative manual dexterity; even with the Hunt multi-loader or other efficient charging systems, the operation takes about three times longer than the automatic. For all practical purposes, however, the absolute difference in time is most important only to competition shooters. While automatics can be reloaded in about one second, the revolver takes only three seconds. A study of reloading procedures shows many more critical operations that have to be performed to put fresh rounds in a revolver cylinder compared to inserting a fresh magazine into an autopistol. Revolver reloading is made even more difficult under adverse light or temperature conditions. But the speed of reloading an automatic assumes availability of loaded spare magazines. Without these preloaded spares, reloading a revolver would have the time edge. Critics of the revolver overlook the possibility of cold hands dropping a loaded magazine. In such a predicament, the magazine could be lost or damaged; with no magazine the automatic is just another piece of hardware.

Training is a big factor in getting the most out of any handgun. While the novice is safer and more proficient with a revolver from the beginning, some of the sixgun's best virtues are not realized until more skill is attained. Effective employment of double action shooting technique is one of these skills. The particular arm and hand coordinations necessary for effective DA perform-

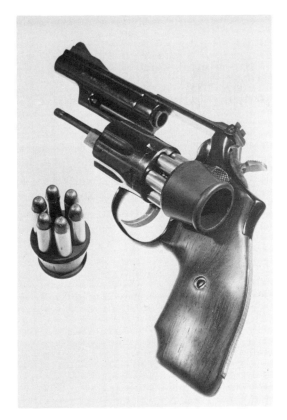

Reloading a revolver is greatly simplified by using a multiple loading device. The Hunt Multi-Loader, shown here, holds six rounds for easy insertion into the cylinder. Once rounds are chambered, the flexible neoprene holder is peeled off the rims and discarded.

ance are not easily attained by all shooters. Mastery is not difficult but requires concentration. While an autoloader will deliver more rounds over long strings, the first six rounds fired double action by a proficient revolver shooter are as fast and effective as the first six rounds out of the automatic. And, this is especially true if the automatic is carried with an empty chamber. The revolver may be better suited to most all shooters who have not or will not pursue an effective training program. But for those individuals who want to get the most out of either handgun, a positive program for improvement of personal shooting skills is necessary.

CARTRIDGES AND HANDGUN CHOICE

Choice of handgun calibers is more important than is generally thought. Many shooters think in terms of cartridge power in the same way they would buy an automobile with a big engine. This kind of thinking can be disappointing in the shooting game. The best caliber is one that comes within the power limits for combat handguns and does not create a negative mental set on the part of the shooter. Most of the time this means a 9mm autopistol or .38 Special revolver, usually a .357 Magnum firing .38 Special ammunition. Muzzle blast and recoil developed by more powerful loads or calibers, such as the .45 ACP, can be disturbing to a novice.

If early shooting experiences are negative, a person can become discouraged or develop bad shooting habits, such as flinching or tensing of muscles in anticipation of the report. In regard to effective fire power, it is better to hit consistently with a .38 Special or 9mm than to miss with a Magnum or .45 ACP. Most shooters must condition themselves gradually into the use of heavier calibers, and some marksmen find that the .38 Special or 9mm Parabellum is all the power they can ever handle effectively.

In the final analysis, the question of which is better, a DA revolver or an autopistol, really depends upon the individual shooter. There is really not enough evidence to completely recommend one or condemn the other; but there is some circumstantial concern as to why one design or the other receives the most promotion.

BIASES FAVORING THE AUTOPISTOL

One strong reason for the autopistol being so universally used in combat shooting competition is its acceptance and publicity gained

These cartridges form the group of effective combat loads presently used in competition shooting (l. to r.) 9mm Parabellum (Luger), .38 Super ACP, .45 ACP, .38 Special, .357 Magnum, .41 Magnum, .44 Magnum. The .38 Special and .45 ACP are the most usual loads seen at matches, followed by 9mm Parabellum. Choosing the correct cartridge for combat shooting is important. Most beginners fare better with the .38 Special or 9mm Parabellum. Control with more potent rounds such as the .45 ACP or .41, .44 Magnums comes with practice. Some shooters are never overly bothered by disturbance from the big bore loads and shoot them effectively from the beginning.

One distinct advantage for autopistols of the M1911 configuration is the push button magazine release. This feature allows an empty magazine to be dropped using the shooting hand only. Autopistols that have the magazine release located in the butt require both hands to extract the empty magazine; this doubles or triples the time for reloading.

through its use by championship shooters. One pragmatic reason for the champions using the autopistol and in particular, the .45 ACP, is that present combat scoring systems and many courses of fire tend to favor the automatic.

The .45 ACP is considered to be more difficult to shoot than the .38 revolver, so a power rating is applied to scores shot with the various caliber guns. A .38 Special has power rating of 1.0. As guns are rated more difficult to shoot, they receive a higher power rating. The .45 ACP receives a power rating of 1.3 (the highest rating is 1.5 for the .44 Magnum). So, if a trained shooter can fire nearly identical scores with either a .45 ACP or a .38 Special, he is a fool not to use the bigger bore, since he will have 1.3 times as many competition points for the same match scores. Largely because of this point subsidy, it is regarded as nearly impossible to

win a competitive championship today in combat shooting with any other handgun but the Government Model .45 ACP.

Another very real advantage to the champions' choice of the .45 ACP comes during rapid fire shooting strings. The speed and ease of reloading offered by the Government Model makes it clearly superior to other autopistols or revolvers in closely timed competitions. The placement of the magazine release and the subsequent ability to dump an empty magazine with the shooting hand (while grasping the replacement magazine with the left hand) allows the reloading cycle to be completed in under one second by proficient combat shooters. Autopistols with the magazine release located in the butt of the handle take longer to reload than a revolver with a multi-loader device.

Autopistols are also favored in the current prestigious combat quick-draw shortrange competitions. Rules for the Leather Slap favor speed alone and do not reflect realistic draw-and-fire circumstances. Current fast-draw open front leather rigs are little more than shelves to support the gun on the shooter's hip. If the shooter bent forward to pick up something off the ground, his gun would fall out of the "holster." Presently, during the fast-draw, a shooter's open hand can be held just above the gun butt. On signal, the competitor just closes his hand, thrusts the pistol forward and fires at his balloon. The first hit wins.

If holsters for these quick draw events were made to more closely resemble practical service rigs, and shooters were made to draw from an arm-raised position, many knowledgeable people claim that the revolver

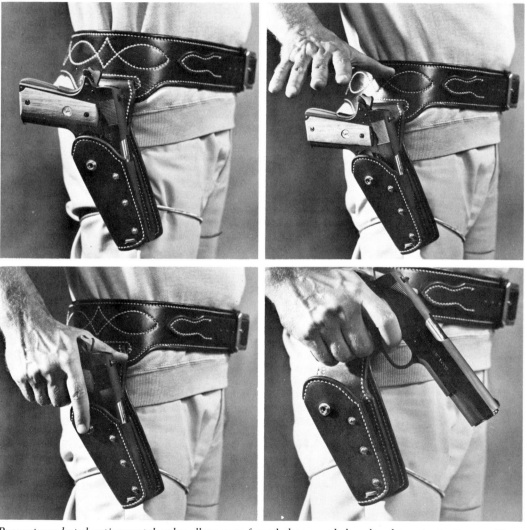

Present combat shooting match rules allow open front holsters and close hand-to-grip starting positions. Many shooters feel that this ruling is unrealistic. The close hand hold assures a good positive grip on the .45 ACP handle, essential to accurate shooting of this type of gun. More standard closed front holsters and raised arm starting positions would make competition more realistic and would diminish the autopistol edge over the revolver for quick draw events.

would take the quick draw events a majority of the time. While this may seem conjectural, one way to find out if it is true is to change the rules to allow for the conditions mentioned above. The development of courses of fire and competition rules has been strongly influenced by autopistol proponents. It becomes clear that many biases in competitive shooting rules have tended to favor the autopistol. In reality, not so solid a case can be drawn for the self-loader when all the facts are in.

FINAL JUDGEMENTS

Before deciding too hastily either for or against the autopistol or the revolver, try to look rationally at some of the considerations put forth here. Each shooter should examine his own needs and abilities before choosing. There are unique roles for both types of handguns and the circumstances of shooting will continue to support their use by different shooters well into the future. We have not seen the end of the evolution of either type of handgun.

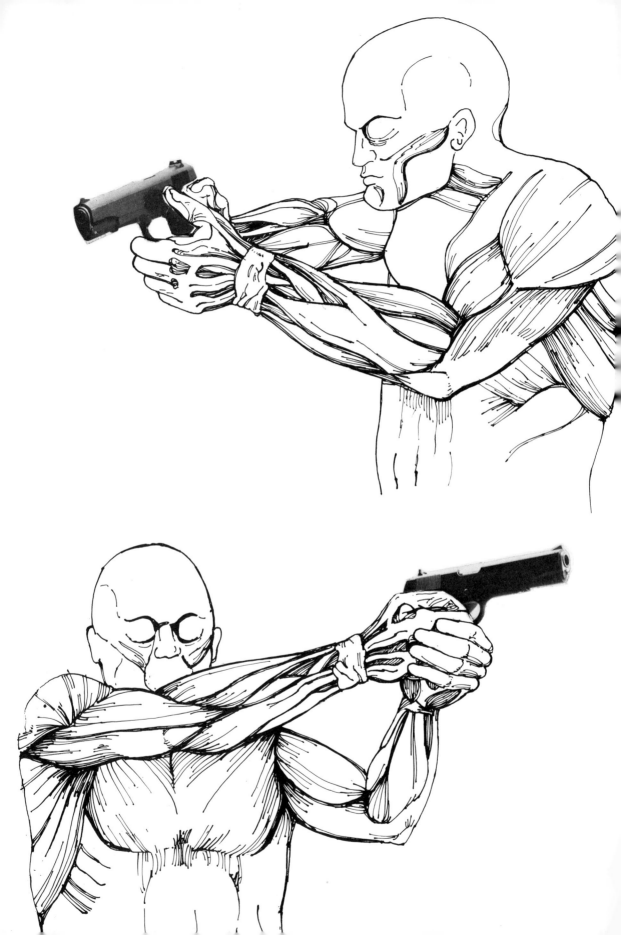

CHAPTER **III**

PHYSIOLOGY FOR HANDGUNNERS

As PART OF THE total shooting system, the human body is of paramount importance to effective marksmanship. Control of the body relates directly to effective manipulation of the firearm. For this reason, the handgunner needs a basic understanding of the human body, how it functions, and most important, how and why it fails to perform effectively.

The purpose here is not to make physiologists out of handgunners. Such a goal is beyond the scope of this book. Rather, the intent is to develop a nontechnical imagery so the shooter becomes aware of body functions, thinks about them, and improves his understanding of motor processes. So informed, a handgunner should be able to adapt a shooting style suitable to his own individual capacities, in keeping with the free-style philosophy of the sport.

THE HUMAN COMPONENT

Most often, it is the human component of the shooting system that fails to respond effectively, contributing the biggest potential shooting errors. Army ordnance tests have established a human error factor of 15 mils dispersion for an average G.I. using the .45 Government Model. This "average" man is relatively untrained with the handgun. In contrast, however, the mean dispersion of the handgun when shot from a machine rest is only 5 mils. (A mil is an angle of rotation that subtends one inch over one thousand inches of range.) It can be demonstrated that the gun usually is capable of much better accuracy than the shooter. Improvements in the control of the body will contribute more to better shooting scores and overall performance than any other single factor.

So many body functions are taken for granted that we rarely think about them. The capacity to observe and analyse body functioning will aid any shooter in perfecting gun handling techniques. The boney processes of the body relate to physical poise, efficient maintenance of balance and coordination, and a steady support for the shooting position. Using triangulation and beam principles, the leg bones support body weight, distributing muscular stresses evenly so as to minimize imbalances and strains. Proper foot placement forms a base that accommodates the center of gravity within a wide range of stable upper body positions. Arm and shoulder structures form a stable triangle that supports the handgun when hands are joined on the gun handle.

NEUROMUSCULAR SYSTEM

But, bones are passive parts of physiology, responding to forces created by contractions of muscular tissues. The muscles, in turn, are controlled through a network of nerve cells that transmit electrochemical pulses to and from the brain. Muscular tissue is nourished and energized through the circulatory metabolism. Neuromuscular relationships are vital to shooting effectiveness. Muscles are like motors to the various body sections; muscles most often are positioned in opposing pairs, to effect flexion or extension, abduction or adduction of body parts. Being attached to bones either directly or through tendons,

contraction of flexor muscles, such as the biceps in the upper arm, causes the forearm to rise. Contraction of extensor muscles (e.g. the triceps) in the backside of the upper arm causes the forearm to straighten.

Compound movements of limbs are achieved by complex, coordinated actions of different sets of muscles. Simply drawing a large "O" on a chalk board brings into play over a dozen muscles that must contract and then relax in coordination with one another in order to produce the figure. The same muscles will produce a square instead of an "O" if the coordinational pattern is changed. It is helpful for any athlete to develop an awareness of which muscles are used for a given moment and to analyse the coordinations necessary to achieve effective results. Normally, we do not notice muscular action in other people or ourselves, so we have to make an effort to acquire these skills of observation.

Muscles are tissues composed of many millions of individual cells organized in long

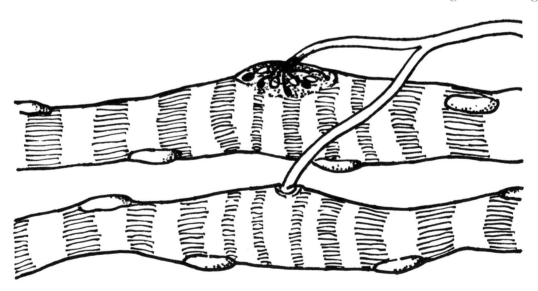

Nerve endings in muscle strands fire cells making them contract as is represented here. Short muscle segments contract during light exertion, long segments during heavy exertion. In each muscle, many thousands of reactions such as those shown here take place during coordinated movements.

strands. These strands are bundled and joined by fibrous tissues. Muscle cells are designed to contract in size by up to 50 per cent when triggered by biochemical processes. In and around the muscle cells are many thousands of capillaries that carry glycogens (sugars) from the blood stream to energize the cells. Nerve endings in the tissues fire the cells, making them contract. Individually, the cells are either relaxed or completely contracted, in keeping with an "all or none" theory. Relative degrees of contraction of the whole muscle is controlled by the percent of individual cells that are fired at a given time. Nerve endings can fire just a few cells during light exertion or many cells during heavy exertion.

Contraction of the muscular cells converts glycogens into heat and lactic acids, which must be carried away from the cell for it to continue to contract efficiently time after time. Rapid accumulation of lactic acids during heavy or repeated exertions inhibits cell contractions and induces one form of fatigue. Lactic acids eventually find their way back into the blood stream where they are either oxidized or converted back into sugars by the liver.

Of particular importance to handgunners is the locomotion of shoulder, arm, and hands. The large muscles in the girdle of the shoulder position and support the cantelever of the arm(s). They also figure prominently in the process of drawing the handgun and elevating it to the shooting position. As abductor muscles raise the arms away from the body, adductors (muscles that pull limbs toward the body) contract slightly to counter upward movement. In this way, some muscles that may work independently to achieve simple single movements of limbs, also become synergistic when they work with other muscles to accomplish a smooth, controlled gun movement. Without this counter tension of muscles, the gun could not be rapidly and precisely elevated for sighting. Again, ele-

ments of coordination in the neuromuscular system spell the difference between effective shooting techniques and miscoordinated "purpose tremors." Because of miscoordinated movements, the novice shooter many times goes through a series of small oscillations (purpose tremors) before settling on the target. This inefficient action is time consuming and contributes to tenseness and various kinds of handling and judgemental errors.

HAND AND WRIST FUNCTIONS

The hand is one of the most complex parts of the body from an anatomical viewpoint. In order to achieve flexibility, strength, and precision of movement, the hand contains many separate bones, joints, muscles, ligaments, and tendons. Employment of the hand in pistol shooting is relatively simple and direct, however. Flexor power is used chiefly for holding and stabilizing the gun. The shape and size of the gun handle, how well it fits the hand, can significantly affect shooting scores. Full flexoral strength and coordination is attained when all fingers are curled and all flexor muscles in the hand and forearm can coordinate. Distention or distortion of the fingers on a poorly shaped grip causes a loss of gripping power and coordination. The wrist also must be straight before the hand can attain maximum power. Cocking or canting the wrist will reduce gripping strength; bend the wrist down and see how fingers lose power and control.

The wrist itself is critical to shooting stability and control. It is not much of a joint, being made up of eight separate bones, grouped in a flat plane, that are designed to slide against one another. This arrangement provides great flexibility but not a lot of strength in any configuration other than rigid and straight. A band of ligaments surrounds the boney set and stabilizes the joint. Some fifteen tendons pass over the joint and pro-

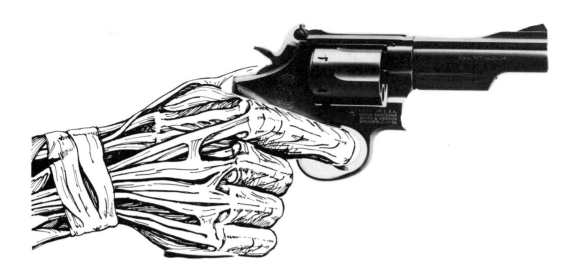

The union of the human and mechanical systems is critical for effective handgun shooting. A firm grip on the gun handle, wrist set, and trigger finger control are necessary. A straight wrist is needed for maximum strength and stability. Shape of the grip must conform to hand and finger dimensions for best results.

vide exceptional strength and rigidity when all are contracted. The flexor muscle sets in the lower forearm close the fist and provide the main reinforcement. But the extensor muscles in the topside of the forearm can also be set in opposition to the flexed fingers. This action will not open the hand, but it will serve to stiffen the wrist and provide the maximum stability for the shooting hand. Notice, again, that the wrist must be in a straight position in order to be set to near maximum strength. This kind of coordination where muscles set against one another is called isometrics; this kind of set differs in the way it is applied and controlled as compared to isotonic movements, where muscles set against an external force (e.g. as in lifting weight). Close observation of the finesse and efficiency of isometric movements can reveal subtle areas for both the improvement of shooting scores and reduction of reaction times required for precision gunhandling.

VISUAL FUNCTIONS

The eyes and vision rarely are given concern by people unless something ails their sight. Many people with a minor defect adapt to the inconvenience; it then becomes "normal" to them. Usual daily living habits do not tax vision enough to show up many minor limitations. However, shooting, particularly handgun shooting, can be adversely affected by a number of otherwise marginal visual problems. Normal to superior vision correlates highly with successful shooting performances.

As the primary receptor for light stimulation, the eyes must accomplish a complex variety of responses. Visual acuity or the "sharpness" of the focused image is important in acquiring the target and maintaining a well defined sight picture. Where targets are small or poorly defined, deficiency in the ability of the eyes to focus sharply will result in poor performance.

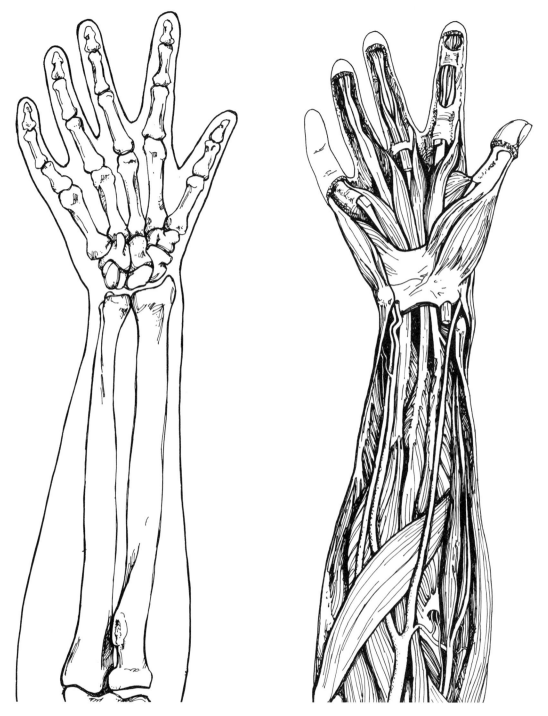

Hand, wrist, and forearm compose the human interface with the gun. Flexor muscles in the lower forearm work through tendons and with fascia tissues in the palm to grip the gun handle. Forefinger control must coordinate separately to manipulate the trigger; this action is especially important for DA revolver shooting. The wrist is stabilized by a cuff of ligaments surrounding the joint. The wrist becomes strong only when straight and when flexor and extensor muscles in the forearm are set in coordination.

Eyes have considerable effect on body movements, especially in aligning the shooter's posture to the target. The tissue lining the interior wall of the eyeball is the retina. Composed of millions of light sensitive cells, this tissue receives light stimulation transmitted through the ocular lens, transmitting responses to the brain where they are decoded into images. In the center of the retina, the receptors are concentrated in a small area called the macula (MACK-you-lah). In the center of the macula is a pin point area called the fovea (FOE-vee-ah). Vision is most acute at the fovea; acuity falls off dramatically just outside the macula. We see general objects with the macula, specific details with the fovea.

Because of this fact, the eye always tends to center on an object for critical viewing. This foveal aiming phenomenon will result in compensating head movements to allow the eyes to hold center position in their sockets. The body then usually responds by facing the object. This results in a natural, total bodily lock on the target, which is desired posture for consistently high shooting scores.

Target acquisition is affected by variable retinal sensitivity. Most photo sensitive materials such as photographic film have a consistent, predictable reaction to given light levels. The retina of the eye does not react in this way. The retina adjusts its sensitivity according to levels of illumination; a portion of the light sensitive cells do not function in normal light. When illumination falls *below* a given level, these cells begin to fire. Walk out of a dim-lit room into noontime sunlight. The iris closes, but it cannot adjust enough for the high sensitivity of the retina that has adjusted to the darker illumination. Within several seconds, the retina gradually adjusts sensitivity to the increased ambient light level by "shutting off" a portion of the receptor cells. By returning to the dim-lit room, the retina must then adjust again to increase its sensitivity to the lower light level. Drastically changing light conditions can affect target acquisition adversely.

When very critical sight pictures must be drawn, especially in long range shooting, the marksman may experience "floaters" in his vision. Some of these worm like images are opacities that populate the jelly-like center filler of the eyeball. Being behind the lense, floaters cannot be focused, registering instead as shadows cast on the retina. They can be experienced most usually when looking at a light colored, uniformly illuminated surface such as the sky. Passage of a floater over the gunsight picture can cause a momentary or partial loss of visual image, due to the shadow cast on the retina by the opaque body. Sometimes, imperfections in the retina can cause similar problems. Any gross or persistent problem of this nature should be checked out by an ophthalmologist.

VISION AND OBJECT PERCEPTION

Another very useful property in the eyes is called motion parallax. This is one of the most effective cues for judging the relative distance of objects in the visual field. This sense of depth perception helps significantly in target acquisition. Close one eye then move the head from side to side. Notice that near objects appear to move opposite to head motion. They also move to a greater relative degree than distant objects. We learn to read these movement differentials so as to first perceive and then localize objects in our visual field.

Once a target is acquired, visual cues trigger motor activity to raise the gun to shooting position. Eyes must then refocus on the plane of the sights. This taxes the ciliary muscles of the eye that squeeze the lens to change its shape so it will focus on the near object. Middle-aged eyes have a tough time making this accommodational change due to the increased stiffness of the lens material. Even young

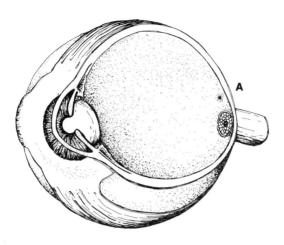

The human eye is incredibly complex and amazing in its adaptability as a light receptor. Light entering the eye is controlled by the iris opening (pupil) and the adjustment of retinal sensitivity. The light is focused on the retina by the ocular lens, through action of ciliary muscles surrounding the lens. The macula (A) is the area of maximum retinal sensitivity; in its center is a pin head sized depression called the fovea, where the most sharply focused images are registered.

eyes may lack ciliary muscular strength to make the focus changes quickly and precisely. In this case, a trip to an ophthalmologist for an eye examination is in order. Many times vision problems of this kind can be aided or eliminated by exercises. Otherwise, they can be corrected by prescription lenses.

In fairly bright illumination, the iris of the eye closes down so many minor sight problems are minimized. Depth of focus of the lens increases, somewhat relieving accommodational demand on the eyes. In poor light, however, the eye must work harder to accomplish its vital tasks. A shooter should always be aware of the effects of light on eyesight and the image of the gunsights. Many times, where nothing can be done to correct light conditions, compensations can be made to better adapt to shooting conditions. These little tricks of the shooting game can help to maintain better performance than otherwise might be the case under adverse lighting conditions.

One example is where shooting is done in the early morning when light is in the shooter's eyes and the targets are in the shade. Light glare in the eyes stops down the iris, reducing the amount of light entering the eye. The targets are in the shade, however, and require the iris to open wide for maximum illumination of the object. This conflict leads to marginal levels of object illumination, poor or inconsistent sight alignment, and correspondingly poor scores.

Novice shooters confronted with this situation often get rattled and fire more rapidly to compensate for their visual confusion. Moderately experienced shooters may slow up, trying to adjust for fading target visibility; on a closely timed string, the result can be shooting past the clock. Under these circumstances all handgunners suffer eyestrain, frustration, and loss of efficiency. Shading the eyes, shooting from under a covered position, using haze cutting yellow lens glasses will all help, but will not eliminate the need for adaptional techniques to compensate for adverse shooting conditions.

VISUAL FEEDBACK AND BODY COORDINATION

Visual feedback is necessary for precise movements needed to shoot consistently well. Hip shooting, where the gun is kept out of the visual field, is not consistent or accurate except at very close ranges. Moving the gun into the visual field increases the predictability of hits and reduces the overall time needed for consistent scores. When sight pictures must be made for very precise shooting at longer ranges, the visual image guides and verifies what the shoulders, arms, and hands are doing. When the sights are aligned and positioned to the target, the eyes transmit the cue that sets off the psychomotor reactions leading to trigger release. How well the eyes "see" and how realistically the brain perceives the images, helps determine the degree of control and precision in shooting. This is the essence of eye and hand coordination. Poor employment of visual feedbacks and/or incomplete control of motor processes will lead to disappointing and ineffective results.

KINESTHETIC SENSE

Another kind of feedback comes from the muscles themselves. This kind of information is vitally important to coordinated and precision body movement. The muscles contain many free nerve endings that deliver sensations to the brain according to the distortion of muscular tissue. That tingling feeling of a slow stretch after a nap, the strain of a sudden or intense muscular contraction, "gas" pains from indigestion, or the ache of a tendon under heavy stress are all evidences of this nerve network. We are not always aware of the more subtle forms of feedback from the muscles. When we walk, trot upstairs, push a key into a lock, clasp in a hand-

Point shooting requires development of kinesthetic senses. Feedback from muscles and the visual field tells the shooter whether or not the gun is aligned with the target. A little practice at seven yards lets the shooter establish the kinesthetic "feel". By thinking "center", the hits soon strike in the upper center of the target without conscious effort.

shake, how often do we have to look down to verify the precision of the movement?

Kinesthesis is the name applied to this kind of feedback. It tells us what work the muscles are doing and where our limbs are located relative to body position and the visual field. Kinesthesis plays a key role in effective body coordination. Developing sensitivity to the body's kinesthetic messages will accelerate any athlete's development and elevate the level of accomplishments. Many kinesthetic sensations go unnoticed only because we are not aware that they exist. Because these sensations are relatively weak, closing ones eyes during slow motion practice of shooting stances and movements

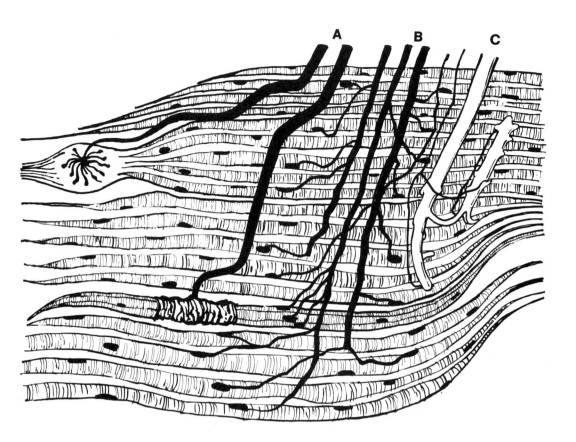

Muscle action is complex. In this typical cross section, we see nerves that sense muscle movement and tension, then send impulses to the brain, (A). At (B) motor messages reach the muscles from the central nervous system, cause foreshortening of the muscle cells. Blood circulates through the vessels (C) to supply sugars and carry away lactic acids produced by the firing of muscle cells.

helps develop the feel for kinesthetic reactions. Knowledge and imagery of neuromuscular functioning gained by this technique helps eliminate the frustrations of learning by rote, repetitious exercises. Each individual comes to internalize his understanding of the bodily functions needed for effective shooting. Eye and hand coordinations are paramount to success in most all sports and especially in combat handgun shooting. And kinesthesis offers one of the most effective avenues toward building competent eye and hand coordinations.

Muscular coordination is more important than strength in shooting sports. This is not to play down strength, since capacity and endurance play important roles, especially in competition. It is common to see tyros practicing stiff, clumsy movements with the handgun. It is obvious to a critical observer that the shooter's mental set is devoid of body imagery. Overworking of the large muscles inhibits efficient use of the small muscles that modulate movements and contribute to precision gun handling. Large muscles should be set to achieve a funda-

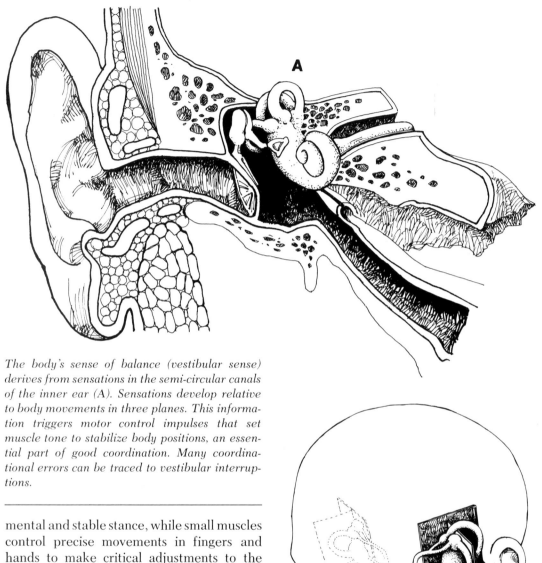

The body's sense of balance (vestibular sense) derives from sensations in the semi-circular canals of the inner ear (A). Sensations develop relative to body movements in three planes. This information triggers motor control impulses that set muscle tone to stabilize body positions, an essential part of good coordination. Many coordinational errors can be traced to vestibular interruptions.

mental and stable stance, while small muscles control precise movements in fingers and hands to make critical adjustments to the sight picture and trigger release.

One does not have to become a physiologist to develop an imagery of body movement. Knowledge of the functions and locations of muscles can be developed by observing body movements in a wall mirror and by finger touch. Once an understanding of basic functions is acquired, the novice can accurately observe accomplished shooters to help develop his own style. A sensitive kinesthetic feel will gradually develop so the shooter can identify his own deficiencies and strengths in stance and economy of movements. The object of training is to produce an effective shooting posture with the simplest coordinations. Efficiency of movement is achieved with the least stresses, the simplest, consistent coordinations, with all effort concentrated on the essential task. Inefficient movements are characterized by superfluous stresses that distract from the essential shooting task; ineffective movements result in tension and strains, erratic body poise, overcorrections and purpose tremors. Continued practice or reinforcement of inefficient body movements will develop negative mental attitudes that can seriously hamper development. A strong intuitive body imagery shortens the learning period, contributes to long term development, and aids the shooter to perform well even under physical and competitive strains.

VESTIBULAR SENSE

Located inside the inner ear are semicircular canals. Inside these canals are small hair-like sensory endings; movement of fluid on these endings gives sensations of motion and inclination of the body. A highly developed vestibular sense contributes to body stability by controlling compensating muscular tone to achieve positions of balance and equilibrium. Highly sensitive vestibular functions feed back information through the nervous system to trigger reflexes that correct for instability and disequilibrium in the shooter's posture. This feedback is very important for static types of formal target shooting, but it is crucial in dynamic sports like combat shooting. It can spell the difference between a tense, ineffective shooter and a graceful, adaptable style. Small muscle contractions can maintain body equilibrium more effectively than tense, rigid muscle tone. Tension in neck muscles and tendons reacts unfavorably on vestibular efficiency. Any positions that require unnatural or strained head and neck positions tend to detract from stable posture, and efficient eye and hand movements. Light, minimal,

economical muscle movements create a condition that is receptive to beneficial vestibular influence. Gross, over-controlled big muscle movements tend to override the weaker, stabilizing reflex pulses transmitted through the nerve pathways from the inner ear.

Since combat handgunning is a more dynamic sport as compared to formal pistol shooting, emphasis is on total body involvement. These demands are opposed to the set body poise predominate in conventional pistol shooting. The ability to hit quickly and consistently with a handgun is directly related to development of dynamic body poise. Lack of achievement of this dynamic poise tends to be a barrier to learning in many combat courses of fire. Learning how to use kinesthetic and vestibular processes of the body will increase efficiency and reinforce the most effective shooting habits. In order to realize this state, however, total body conditioning is essential.

PHYSICAL CONDITIONING

Formal gymnastic programs are unrealistic for all but the most dedicated individuals. However, most sedentary jobs do not provide enough activity or exercises of the necessary types to condition body reflexes for shooting. Individuals vary as to the amount and kinds of exercises needed to maintain good muscular conditioning.

Building cardiovascular strength is primary to total body conditioning. It does little good to exercise muscles only to get winded or to have an elevated heartbeat disturb critical sight pictures. Twenty minutes a day of swimming or jogging is a good program for general body conditioning during competitive seasons. Exercising every other day works well for some people or for competitors in the off-season. No one should begin a physical conditioning program without seeing a physician for a thorough check-up. Start out slowly and work up to the maximums; "train don't strain."

Supplemental exercises of the upper body using dumbells and barbells tone muscles and condition psychomotor pathways. Repetitions are more important than maximum weight limits. A moderate weight with 20 to 30 reps done rhythmically and without strain does more for circulation than four or five reps at maximum weight limits. Gymnastics and sitting-up exercises condition synergistic muscle sets. Shoulders, arms, hands, and abdomen are especially important for combat shooting. Certain isometric exercises can be done at work or taken briefly during a break time. The hand grip of both the master and weak hand can be exercised using a rubber ball kept in a desk drawer. Shoulder and chest muscles are toned by interlocking fingers and applying tension, or by placing palms together and compressing. Total body

Combat handgunning demands dynamic body poise. This shooter is advancing and firing during the Mexican Defense Course. It is imperative that upper and lower body movements coordinate, otherwise erratic shooting scores result.

motion is conditioned during games such as catch or throwing at a target. A shooter might take up knife throwing, a related sport, for off-time exercise. The relationship to scoring on a target reinforces mental sets transferrable to shooting.

Maintenance of body mobility is important as a goal in any physical exercise program. Exercises such as heavy weight lifting, put no emphasis on flexible body bending. The more muscles work together to control complex, supple body motions, the better coordinated all movements become. Movements should be accomplished with minimal muscular tension. Swimming, gymnastics, or various games like tennis, that require coordinated upper and lower body movement tend to reinforce this skill. People who tire easily may not lack stamina; they may be overly tense, using too much energy to accomplish movements in their sport.

Building physical endurance and capacity also reinforces positive mental sets and self-confidence. Undertaking the discipline of a regular, if not rigorous, conditioning program helps temper and harden personal resolve. Learning and shooting performance are improved. Focus on and commitment to performance goals is enhanced.

CONDITIONS ADVERSE TO SHOOTING

Anything that distracts or detracts from physical performance will cost in terms of shooting scores. Fatigue from overwork, overexertion, or illness takes its toll in mind/body coordination. Some people have enough reserve to continue performing well under adverse physical strain. Performance under these conditions heavily taxes the body, however, and the risk of error is still high.

Physical conditioning helps eliminate or modify tensions and anxieties attendant with shooting competition. One's personal life and health bear heavily in this area. Emotional pressures tend to interrupt concentration and modify psychomotor processes. Physicians can prescribe mild drugs that help control such conditions. However, heavy doses have detrimental effects, particularly if tension levels are lowered to where normal excitation is impossible. Aside from aspirin for the "blahs" most drugs are detrimental to overall performance. Too much tension, though, is bad for shooting skills. But, it is better to work on tension over the long-run, through living habits, physical conditioning, and rational, systematic development of skills.

Alcohol and tobacco seem to elevate the senses in the short run, but depress them over time. Alcohol works to inhibit or scramble the central nervous system, slowing reaction times and damping personal resolve. People who seek the bottle to suppress tension most probably will pay in terms of shooting scores. The old adage "alcohol and gunpowder don't mix" is still valid. Long term, heavy use of alcohol leads to a number of cardiovascular and neuromuscular conditions that hamper shooting efficiency. Tobacco stimulates formation of blood sugars, giving a lift during and shortly after the time of smoking. Long-term, steady use reduces pulmonary efficiency and taxes cardiovascular processes among other things. Some people's psychomotor efficiency is badly affected by habitual smoking.

A balanced diet, high in protein and low in fats, with ample carbohydrates will suffice to sustain health. Overeating leading to overweight taxes hemostatic processes. Irregular eating, no breakfast, small lunch, and huge evening meal is not optimal. If some imbalance is preferred, the large meal should be in the morning to fully serve body needs. Carbohydrates can be emphasized in the morning rather than in the evening before inactive hours. Ample and regular sleep is important to peak physical condition. The amounts and timing for sleep vary. Some recommendations are for about six hours at night with a one or two hour nap in the afternoon, if this can be arranged. This sleep schedule extends the working day well into the evening. Sleep patterns significantly affect personal feelings of well-being and can help control anxieties or tensions that develop from inadequate rest.

Light, temperature, and noise in the ambient environment can have subtle effects on performance. Hot days dehydrate the body, and replenishment of water alone may not reinstate efficient body functioning. Mineral loss through perspiration can fatigue the body. Taking salt tablets with water intake is effective; such prepared solutions as Gatorade® replenish salinity and reduce total effects of dehydration.

Shooters should rest in areas well-removed from the firing line. Long-term exposure to muzzle blast, even with appropriate ear protection, is fatiguing. Shooters build up a high tolerance for muzzle noises, but prolonged exposure is tiring. Reflex thresholds to flinching are lowered to a point where subtle distractions are possible. Design for courses of fire should take this factor into consideration by providing enough space between shooters.

Sun glasses should be worn on bright days to reduce fatigue from eye strain. Ultra-violet light diffuses vision. The attendant glare suppresses operation of a percentage of cells in the retina. All these conditions can adversely affect visual acuity both as to target acquisition and sight picture refinement. The effects can be quite subtle. Sitting in shaded areas and avoiding glare is one of the best ways to reduce fatigue. Otherwise, wear haze-cutting glasses and shade the eyes with a hat brim when glare cannot be avoided.

All of these items are mostly matters for common sense. They do not offer panaceas for how to become a pistol champion. They are directed toward maintaining physiological efficiency, so shooting efforts can be directed wholly toward performance. While an awareness of the body's functions is necessary, the shooter should also be aware of the role of the mind and the nervous system in controlling the body.

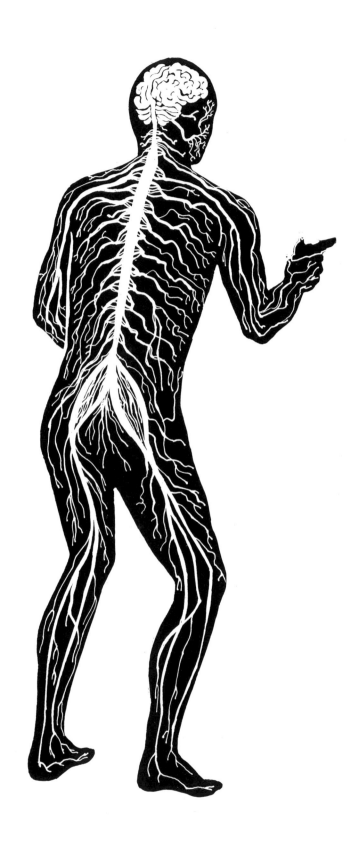

CHAPTER **IV**

PSYCHOLOGY FOR THE HANDGUNNER

A NUMBER OF IDEAS from psychology are useful in combat handgunning. This information deals with how voluntary motor movements and involuntary (emotional) responses are controlled. Understanding psychic processes goes hand-in-glove with knowledge of body physiology; development of gun-handling skills and performance control can be accelerated and carried to higher levels of achievement than would be the case with less informed shooters.

Understanding can be developed on both an intuitive as well as a rational plane. But the object is to make the knowledge work for the shooter; no attempt is being made to make shooters into psychologists.

NERVOUS SYSTEMS

Control centers of the body are divided into two systems: the central nervous system (CNS) and the autonomic nervous system (ANS). The CNS is comprised of the brain and spinal cord with branching networks or nerve ganglia. Voluntary movements and the conscious sensations are handled by the CNS.

The ANS centers at the base of the brain (hypothalamus) and automatically regulates basic body functions. ANS nerve impulses arrive through separate networks as well as from interaction with the CNS ganglia. The ANS has two major divisions: the sympathetic and parasympathetic systems. ANS nerve fibers are separate from those of the CNS, but both occupy the spinal column. The sympathetic network emerges and branches from the middle-back region innervating and controlling such processes as the viscera, blood vessels, glands, and pupillary dialation of the iris of the eye.

The parasympathetic system emerges from the cranial and sacral regions of the spine and controls more directly the operation of the heart, breathing, digestion, and elimination. While the ANS is split into two parts, both sections interact. While the sympathetic system is designed for alarm and arousal of the body ("war" responses to danger, threats), the parasympathetic ganglia affect "peaceful" activities, including modulating an overstimulated sympathetic response. For instance, while sympathetic nerves dialate blood vessels, parasympathetic processes constrict the vessels. Without many modifying influences of the parasympathetic system, the body would have no way of controlling arousal to violent actions.

Nerve tissues carry messages from the CNS to the motor areas of the body (efferent nerves) and transmit information from receptors to the CNS (afferent nerves). Pulses from efferent nerves of the CNS merge with the parasympathetic nerve ganglia in the mid-back area. Through synaptic unions, much moderating control can be imposed on the ANS by the consciousness of the CNS and vice-versa. For example, while the regular heartbeat is controlled by the parasympathetic network, the sympathetic nerves can cause the heart to beat faster in emergencies. Digestion is initiated by the parasympathetic ganglia, but can be shut down by the sympathetic system when it prepares the body for a "warlike" status.

Overreaction of the emotion producing sympathetic system can cause lowered efficiency for coping with an emergency. The "wisdom" of the subject in identifying overreaction can alter body behavior to modify the severity of emotions, so as to maintain more effective levels of performance. Caution is called for, however. Anxiety induced by trying willfully to suppress normal emotions can reinforce the reaction, making it worse. Conversely, when a fatigued subject is underperforming, the mind/body link can stimulate reactions by lifting parasympathetic moderation. We can direct our emotions to a great degree by conscious control of bodily behavior, but we must know what performance goals we seek and how to modulate (not control) the autonomic nervous system. All of this relates to our maturity as personalities and as handgunners.

How important is all this to shooting performance? It is interesting to note at combat matches that young shooters who have the quickest reflexes, the best eyesight, and comparatively good muscle tone, never seem

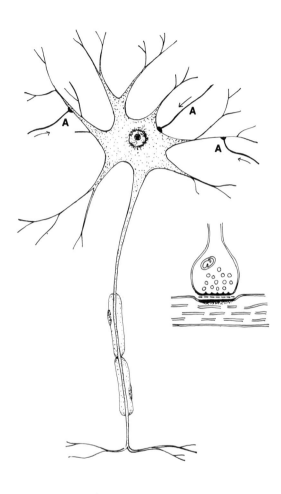

The typical nerve cell functions as a switch board for messages from interconnecting cells. The union of cells at the synapses (A) is critical to the speed and accuracy with which messages are transmitted. Illness, toxicity, or fatigue can interrupt communications by electro-chemical interference at the synaptic joint (see detail inset). If enough critical impulses are slowed or lost in the system, poor concentration and poor coordination most likely will result.

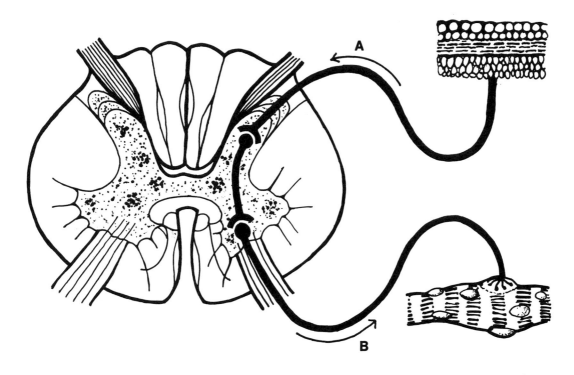

Not all sensory impulses go directly to the brain. "Knee-jerk" reflexes result from stimulation of receptor nerves that send messages directly through the spinal column (A), which are transmitted through synaptic connections directly into the motor nerves that activate muscular contractions (B). Such reflexive actions can be cultivated to decrease reaction times and improve responses in some types of shooting situations.

to perform consistently well. A good many Class A and Champion shooters seem to be in the "over thirty" group. Is it because these older shooters have more time and money for practice? Maybe. But, it could be due to their maturity in being able to consciously modulate "hyper" sympathetic nervous responses and to stimulate body reactions as they become fatigued.

SOR CONCEPT

The chain of body responses can be understood through the S-O-R (Stimulus-Organism-Response) concept, also. In this concept, the introduction of a stimulus is perceived by the organism; the organism then processes the essential data and picks an appropriate reaction which is translated into motor responses. The chain is invariable but the speed and characteristics of reactions can vary between individuals, or from time-to-time in the same individual.

In combat shooting, stimulation usually comes either from light (sight receptors) or sound (audio receptors). The quality of stimulation varies according to the source. A light bulb will create a slower response than a strobe light; the intensity of the stimulus will affect reaction times. Condition of the receptor will also vary. A shooter who has hearing loss in his left ear, and who is the last man on the right side of the firing line, will not respond as readily to a whistle signal as if he were close to the whistle with his normal right ear turned toward the signal.

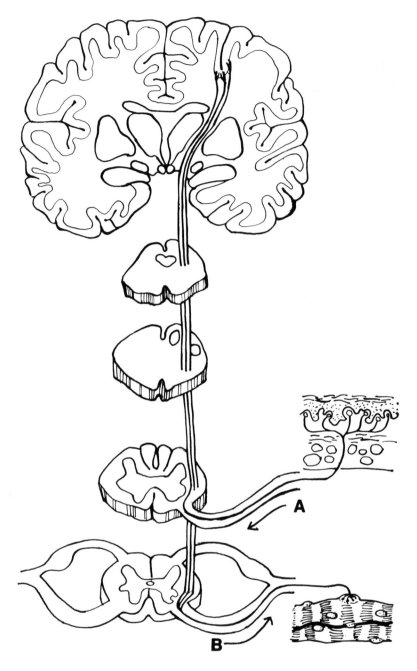

SOR reactions produce voluntary motor responses. Here stimulation takes place at the receptor with messages traveling to the CNS (A) up to the appropriate areas of the brain that control bodily response. Motor responses travel down to the muscles (B) to actuate the response. The organism's reaction processes shown here are relatively constant, but the response can be made quicker by mentally concentrating on the motor action. Such a practice eliminates distracting rational decision making that tends to lengthen reaction time.

Assuming the stimulus threshold is exceeded, the organism begins to interpret the data as afferent nerve fibers carry the signal to the brain. Efferent messages are transmitted through the CNS to the appropriate muscles (motor functions). Primary cues have already stimulated the sympathetic portion of the ANS, and adrenaline begins to flow, heart beat increases, digestion stops, etc. Efferent messages from the CNS are transmitted through the parasympathetic ganglia that begin to modulate the primary ANS reactions into appropriate levels of response. In this moment the body is ready to physically respond. The hand closes on the gun butt, the arm withdraws the pistol from the holster, raises it to sight, aligns and fires.

The shooter's responses can be affected by such things as the level of motivation, relative health, toxic influences, general level of excitation or motivation prior to stimulation. If the subject is overly tense or distracted, responses will not be as quick or as accurate as when the subject is highly motivated, confident, in normal health. What constitutes an optimum level of mental or emotional "set" for action is individual. Merely being aware of the need for this optimum should help the shooter to observe his reactions and develop an intuitive moderation of emotions that will aid performance.

REACTION TIMES

While the shooter can condition himself to discriminate keenly thresholds of stimulation or to groom a motor reaction to perfection, little can be done to change the reaction time factors of the organism itself. The reaction time is measured from the moment of stimulation to the beginning of the response. Electrochemical pulses travel at nearly the same speed through the nervous system, between .15 and .20-seconds, depending on heredity and condition of the synapses. The "O" of SOR theory is relatively constant. But, the shooter can slow down a total response

time noticeably by being overly conscious of the organism's recognition signs to stimulation. Put in a positive meaning, total response time can be significantly improved by "short circuiting" the organism factor of the SOR chain, making the reaction more nearly reflexive.

Beginning shooters and many accomplished handgunners are prone to listen closely for the whistle start signal, especially in a closely timed event. In effect, they are saying to themselves, "Don't miss that whistle." By listening so intently for the start signal, they distract themselves from the stimulus when it sounds. Then they say, "There's the whistle, now the pistol must be drawn." With this kind of linear process, each step in the SOR chain inhibits the next sequence. The result is slow total response timing for the event.

Since little fundamental change can be made in the organism's transmission time, the shooter should shunt around this factor by developing a highly sensitive discrimination of the stimulus and use this to trigger the response factor by reflexive action. While this technique does not eliminate the organism's reaction time, it does reduce the inhibiting effect of thinking about it. In essence, the shooter should "think response" concentrating on the action "set," keeping the threshold for the stimulus very low. While developing this technique, many people "jump the gun" at first, triggering the response even if someone in the gallery coughs or sneezes. This is because the discriminatory techniques are not tuned to the precise stimulus (the whistle) but to any auditory stimulus. With practice, the "think response" technique can cut 40 to 60 percent off total response times for many competitors in draw and fire events.

Human reaction times vary according to the type of stimulus. Experiments with light, sound, and electric shock showed light stimulation elicits the slowest average reaction time. Electric shock resulted in almost the

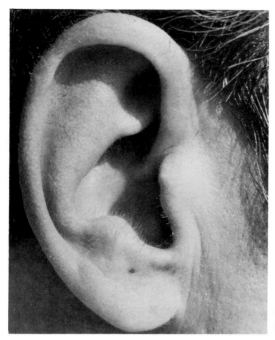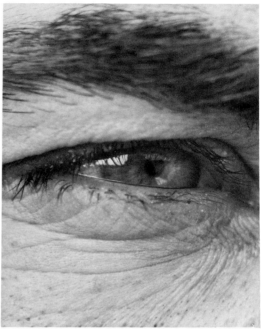

Reaction times differ depending upon the kind of sensory stimulation. Audio-cues cause the quickest reaction. Light stimuli take the longest of the common receptors used in combat shooting. Good hearing is essential to good reaction times.

same reaction time as a sound stimulus. It appears the delay time for receptor stimulation is longer in retinal tissue of the eye than in skin and auditory receptors. Various combinations of stimuli produced interesting results. For instance, a sound and light stimulus caused the same reaction time as sound alone. This indicates that the effect of light is cancelled in combination with sound. The organism has reacted to the fastest sensory stimulation (sound) before the light stimulation has an effect. The following table is from Todd's experiments showing reaction times to stimuli in milliseconds (.001-second).

STIMULUS	AVERAGE REACTION TIME (ms)
Light	176
Shock	143
Sound	142
Light and Shock	142
Light and Sound	142
Sound and Shock	131
Light, Sound, and Shock	127

Bear in mind that experimental evidence is drawn from controlled conditions where relatively pure stimuli can be used. In real time situations, multiple stimuli are present. The shooter's ability to discriminate from among conflicting sounds. sights, smells, etc., will affect response time. The individual's motivation, training, skill, health, luck, etc. also will shorten or lengthen the relative response time. Learning improvements can be achieved over time with knowledge and application in people who possess the necessary neurological equipment and determination to excel.

CONDITIONED RESPONSES

Through the learning process of conditioning, the shooter cultivates and organizes the skills needed to score consistently well. The repetition of segments and sequences of effective shooting routines builds confidence and, if properly reinforced, forms a positive self-image as a combat marksman. Reinforcement comes in many forms. Being able to successfully learn basic skills and show improvement in scores and/or time is one of the chief reinforcement techniques in a training program. Praise and recognition of progress are other means.

Negative reinforcements, such as harsh critiques, exercises that extend far beyond the developed ability of the shooter, or too slow a pace in advancement all tend to have detrimental effects on the novice shooter. Competitions that are introduced too early or before adequate skills are developed tend to discourage learning, also. A set of learning goals designed to structure fundamental skills can be most useful for development. These objectives can be spiralled upward in challenge and complexity, allowing individual shooters to advance at their own pace. Any set of goals should always provide continuous reinforcement of the basic shooting skills.

LEARNING OBJECTIVES

Since shooting is a psychomotor activity, a summary set of learning objectives is useful in planning individual goals. The shooter needs to picture the task in terms of what is expected for effective performance. As a first step, the shooter will have to know what sensory stimulation will begin the process. Chapters three and four of this book are designed to help understand the body processes involved. Hearing and sight are the chief receptors involved in shooting, but tactile sensation through the hand on the pistol grip is of great importance, also. Kinesthetic sensation is vital to coordinated performance. Without a thorough understanding of the sensory basics, the shooter will not develop mature perceptions of the contest. It will be more difficult to determine and discriminate effectively among cue selections. The shooter will tend to be awkward in translating stimulation into smooth, accurate movements resulting in good consistent scores. Consistency is especially important even if scores are not above average. Upon consistency is based confi-

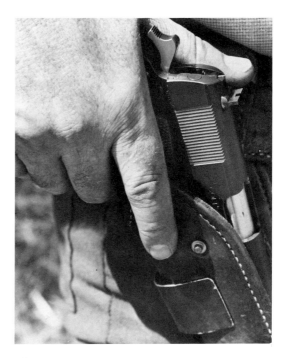

Alignment and consistency of the grip is important to shooting top scores. The tactile senses of the hand on the grip tells the shooter if the hold is good without his looking. Practice this sensory exercise often to establish good first-time gripping, especially needed on the autopistol.

dence in the ability to develop and improve techniques.

The mental and emotional sets of shooters are important because they reflect the individual's degree of readiness to perform the necessary tasks demanded in the sport. Mentally the shooter prepares the body to perform. Emotionally the organism builds the *willingness* to respond, suppressing or neutralizing inhibitions that would otherwise cut efficiency of operation.

It is important to divide the learning task into manageable segments that do not overtax ability and at the same time provide adequate challenge to assure continued development and avoidance of boredom. Guided response activities introduce the shooter into efficient, effective techniques either by imitation of other shooters, or by trial and error performance. He can test his capacities, discover appropriate responses, and develop rationales for skill combinations ("this works better than that because. . .").

Soon, learning advances to a stage where a complexity of skills becomes habitual. Confidence and a polished degree of skill are evident. The shooter begins to "put it all together." Then, learning formal courses of fire helps the shooter to order and discipline his skills and to exercise the mechanism of the sport.

Complex responses become evident as the shooter reaches the upper levels of development. At this developmental level, basic skills of gun handling are so natural, they are performed without hesitation and with narrow variations in standards. Any performance uncertainties are resolved and required sequences are performed in combination with confidence and without confusion. Performance becomes automatic on cue and is characterized by finely coordinated skills with ease and economy of muscular control.

SHOOTER'S TRAITS

Many people wonder exactly what makes a top flight handgunner. What particular combination of characteristics increases probability of success? A number of fallacies creep into observations due to biases and human error. One such fallacy relates to the "big man" theory, wherein large men arbitrarily make the best pistol shooters. This would seem to preclude small and medium sized males and women from success on the shooting field. No definition is given of what "big man" really means in terms of height, weight, frame size, body type, etc. Indeed a casual survey of several combat matches revealed a physically mixed bag within the top ten shooters. The one thing they all had in common was better scores than the other sixty shooters at the match.

One speculation is that the "big man" idea comes in part from the fact that many combat shooters are policemen, and these men as a group tend to be picked for above average height and stature. Another casual survey of top-grade shooters showed a tendency for the group toward above average height and weight, mesomorphic (athletic) body type, excellent eyesight, strong arm and hand strength, exceptional endurance, agility and coordination, and high native intelligence. However, absolute body size tended to be the biggest single variable in the group of fifteen shooters observed.

A self-picture as a competent, competitive shooter is also high on the list of characteristics of top-flight pistoleers. While everyone has a "bad day," the best shooters recover and perform consistently well over time. The self-image is very important to development for success in any activity. "You are what you think you are," is one way of putting it. This attitude needn't reflect an unrealistic viewpoint in a developing shooter who sets high goals. While high performance expectations usually indicate high motivations, realistic goals need not be destructive to the development process. Strong ego is important to superlative achievement as long as the self-image is in line with real capacities. Otherwise, the individual just might be projecting superiority feelings (boasting, setting unrealistic goals) to cover underlying fears of inadequacy.

PERSONAL MOTIVATIONS

Various mental sets of the individual shooter should be examined. What basic attitudes and motivations do people have that attract them into shooting? The Freudian psychosexual dogma is pretty well known, but quite exaggerated in the public mind. Psychoanalysis assumes personal motivations to be based on abnormal experiences in childhood during one of the three major periods of personality development. The gun (expecially the handgun) is suppose to have phallic significance. The shooting public withdraws from this negative kind of analysis and for good reason. Surely if a maladjusted person takes up the gun to relieve frustrations, it does not follow that all people who shoot have similar personality problems. It has been pointed out that Freud was a cigar smoker and that psychoanalytically the cigar is high in phallic symbolism. When confronted with this connection by a colleague, Freud replied, "Sometimes, a cigar is just a cigar."

Most Freudian analysis is concerned with abnormal adjustments; the "sick" side of personality. Unfortunately, even if the implications are true, there is nothing that can be done about them. Modified aspects of psychosexual symbolism draw the relationship to power. Certainly the gun is a power symbol. There's a certain romance to the gun. It has a magical fascination even for many people who never pursue shooting. To be able to control any violent, powerful instrument can give a sense of mastery, especially when it is done in sport where no one will be hurt. One's identification with power to reinforce ego or to maintain personal security is not abnormal as long as it is directed within rational bounds. We see the same motivational patterns in other aggressive, competitive sports such as boxing, fencing, autoracing. But, the dueling aspect of combat pistol shooting is considerably more abstract.

Sports of any kind can be an effective vehicle for personal development and the reestablishment of reality between ego and the outside world. Reinforcement of such factors as motor skills, independence, goal setting and achievement expands the sense of human awareness and the identity with reality. All game activities are not merely regressions, they create conditions for personal growth. Shooting provides such a vehicle for human expansion and, for the vast majority of participants, the games foster a sense of human awareness.

What is most discouraging to see, however, is the individual who walks onto the shooting range seeking self-realization through the gun. Some pistoleers have this mental set and it shows up in a number of behavior patterns. One notable pattern is a callous disregard for

gun safety and courtesy to other shooters, the treatment of the handgun as a plaything. Another syndrome can be the quiet, withdrawn person, wrestling with complexes, who wants to shoot to fulfill the wish for manhood, recognition, or control over worldly circumstances. Fantasies such as these may creep into thought patterns of any normal person, but when the individual begins to *believe* them, the situation becomes a little frightening. To the extent that these motivations lead to expansion of human capacities, they are constructive. Irrational behavior can be on the threshold of personal growth. To the extent that fantasies consistently reinforce hostility, alienation, or personal inadequacies, they are neurotic. Shooting sports do not differ from other activities in this regard.

This discourse is not given to be harsh or to criticize unduly, for combat shooting will crystalize legitimate personal goals for people who pursue it seriously, regardless of their initial motivations. But, individuals should learn to recognize their personal needs and motivations in order to assure a constructive, worthwhile experience in combat shooting. To this end, shooting, like all sports, should build and exercise the human character. Put on a very basic level the exercise of human capacities relates to the larger questions of what we *are*, what we would *like* to be, and what we *could* become.

GUN SAFETY

While we are in a psychological vein, it is productive to talk about gun safety. So often, shooting safety is discussed as a mechanical set of procedures, a list of do's and don'ts that will eliminate the possibility of accidents. What is not discussed is that safety is a state of mind. The callous, inconsiderate individual may very likely harbor overly aggressive traits that relate to unresolved personality problems. If shooters could realize how uncomplimentary poor gun etiquette can be, how it reflects ill on their personalities, we could eliminate a major cause of shooting incidents. To this end, handgun shooting safety can be a gauge of the maturity of an individual.

Safe gun handling is an integral part of mastery of combat shooting. It also reflects favorably on the general maturity of the individual. People who are trained to the mastery level in handgun shooting, who have experienced personal development through shooting sports, will be unlikely to have gun accidents or to use an arm imprudently or to project its use in anger. The confidence in gun handling exhibited by the trained shooter will eliminate the need to prove his prowess, openly or irrationally. The policeman trained to the mastery level is much less likely to exceed undue force doctrines. When it becomes necessary to use the side arm, deadly force will be used effectively with less danger to the officer and innocent citizens.

CONCENTRATION

The mental set and self-picture will have a great deal to do with the shooter's concentration and span of attention. The capacity to focus one's attention on a given task, to call up physical and mental reserves spells the difference between superlative and mediocre performance. Essentially, when an accomplished shot "falls apart" during a match, as everyone does occasionally, blame lapse of concentration rather than lack of ability. Lapses in concentration may be due to psychic causes. The possibilities are so varied, it is beyond the scope here to follow. Other

The mental set and concentration of the shooter have a great bearing on marksmanship. Controlling a violently discharging arm need not break concentration or cause flinching. It takes a lot of shooting experience to build and maintain consistent control. Even so, shooting masters will have their off days.

physical causes, such as thirst, a full bladder, or a painful lesion may interrupt the complex interactions of psychomotor processes. Failure to perform results from either missed sequences in a reaction chain or overriding (inhibiting) of the CNS at a critical moment in time.

Trying to reconstruct failure is difficult to do; it is more effective to try to avoid failure in the first place. Conditioning theory gives us many pointers for competitive preparation. Analyzing a detailed check list of the items needed for a given shooting event builds confidence in simply *knowing* what has to be done. Any failure that can be traced to a procedure should be added to the list. Beware of lists, however. They can become compulsive, a place to hang one's faith rather than to accept full responsibility for performance.

Many psychic failures come from not having taken appropriate expected actions. For example, as a shooter refines his sight-picture on a long-range shot, he may suddenly remember that he did not prepare match-grade ammunition the day before as he should have. This lapse can cause a miss or a drop in points that demoralizes the shooter for the rest of the match. The capacity to recognize lapses and analyze their effects is the first step in shoring up one's ego, moderating emotions, and getting one's "stuff" together again. In a match, many shooters fall apart to some degree and the ability to recover from errors and reach a new peak in efficiency can mean the critical difference in performance. It is very bad psychologically to quit a competition before it ends either by physically leaving or mentally forfeiting the effort. This self-destruction of image will do more damage to future performance than the worst drubbing at the hands of competitors. It takes a special kind of courage to lose in a way that results in personal growth. The competitor who thoroughly understands why he is not performing well is not apt to repeat his errors in another match.

A physical warm-up period before or between stages of a match controls tension, builds positive mental sets and sharpens psychomotor responses. A number of transfer skills related to eye and hand coordinations are helpful. Simply playing a game of catch or throwing stones at a stump (for the solitary warm-up) is useful. A person so occupied is less liable to let subconscious, inhibiting thoughts invade and affect conscious behavior. He is able to "psych-up" without building gut-wrenching fear. Appropriate attention should be given to physiological needs, also; in other words, eat, drink, rest, and eliminate as needed.

The self-picture of the shooter as a competitor should take the task as a challenge without the need for Mittyesque self-aggrandizement. Judgement should dominate the gun, not the other way around. Competition should be directed toward individual standards first, then outwardly toward fellow competitors. Like all sports, the character of the combat handgunner is on the line when he performs. With motivations well understood, pursuit of this challenging activity will make a significant contribution to personal growth.

CHAPTER V

COMBAT HANDGUN STOCKS

ONE OF THE MOST important considerations in basic handgunning is the physical interface between the human and the mechanical systems. Where the hand meets the gun grip influences shooting scores as well as the pattern of development for combat shooters. It is not so much a question of finding the "perfect" grip as it is of eliminating factors that distract from shooting abilities.

What makes a good and effective grip shape is an individual matter. Our concern is not so much with recommending specific grips as it is with analysing the functions of handstocks to provide criteria for evaluating their shapes and functions.

Rising popularity of handgunning has opened a fertile market for custom handgun stocks. For whatever reasons, factory frame shapes and grip designs have always been abysmal. Evidently, the people who design these features must not be shooters, since the best combinations are only adequate, while most factory designs have several undesirable or unacceptable features.

EVOLUTION OF COMBAT GRIPS

Over the years, a number of commercial grip features have come out that correct to some degree the deficiencies of factory stocks. Up until recent years, most of these designs were made to conform to NRA formal target shooting needs. The grips had numerous ridges, flanges, and contours, made to reconstruct the shape of the hand and to promote deliberate shooting techniques. The large thumb rest on traditional target stocks is one such feature along with assorted ridges and grooves designed to consistently position the hand. These grips are wholly unsuited for combat shooting, since many cannot be holstered or manipulated rapidly.

There has been a steady process of "dehorning" going on for the past few decades as enlightened grip makers and demanding shooters sought to improve the breed. The biggest changes have come in revolver grips, since autopistol handle shapes are more nearly dominated by frame configuration. In fact, autopistol factory stocks (especially for .45

Government Model frames) are regarded by many shooters as being the most adaptable and effective. Still, many of the principles involved in revolver grip design pertain as well to self-loaders.

BASIC FUNCTIONS

Two chief considerations affect functional grip designs. One deals with the fit in the hand; comfort, and accomodation of physiology are paramount. The other factor concerns the positioning of the hand to the gun so as to minimize recoil effect and maximize recovery mode. All of these factors enhance double action shooting. Both considerations are interdependent; deficiencies in one will detract from the other.

Factory revolver frames are notorious for being too narrow at the top and wide at the bottom. Exactly why this bell-shaped frame design was started is not known, but manu-

The bell-shaped flare at the bottom of revolver frames creates problems for acquiring an effective grip hold.

facturers have clung to it through the years. This configuration is all wrong for the physiology of the hand. The narrow upper portion is where the long middle finger engages the handle, while the wide, bell shaped bottom section must be negotiated by the short little finger. Displacement of the little finger is a source of discomfort with the corresponding loss of gripping power. Not only is little finger pressure diminished, but it will adversely affect coordination of all muscles of the hand to some degree. Loss of little finger gripping pressure is made more serious because of its potential leverage on muzzle recoil rise. When a properly fitted grip is on the handgun, an estimated 15 to 20 pounds additional little finger pressure contributes to comfort, confidence, and stable control of the handgun.

DESIGN IMPROVEMENTS

Addition of a filler block between the trigger guard and the front strap of the frame increases girth for the middle finger. This feature accommodates the middle and third fingers. Shape at this point should be moderately rounded, not being too fat or too thin or sharp on the front edge. Flat ledges at the saddle section serve to irritate the tender inside surface of the middle finger. The filler block also positions the middle finger lower than it would be on the bare frame contour. This provides a desirable degree of separation from the trigger finger and lowers the middle finger knuckle so it will not collide with the trigger guard during recoil.

The leading edge of the grip should angle in toward the bottom of the frame so as to decrease girth to accomodate the little finger. For some hands on some frame designs, this will require removing wood until the tip of the front strap is exposed. Some grip styles provide for this dimension by indenting a small radius groove at the bottom of the grip for the little finger. Since most combat grips extend the wood below the bottom of the frame straps, this feature is possible.

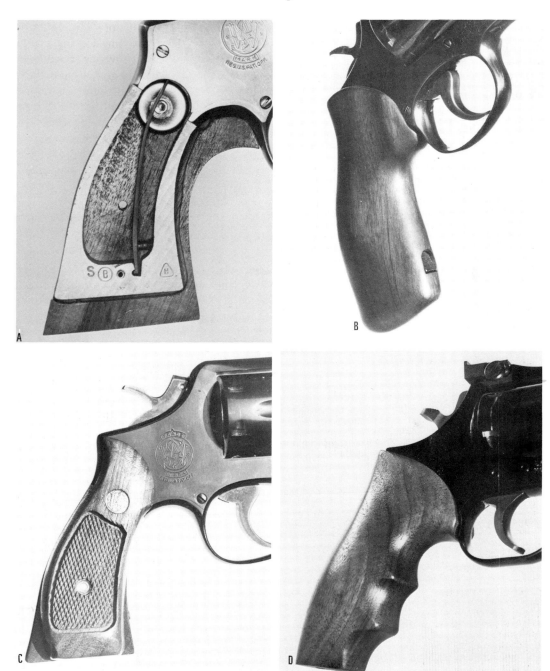

(l. to r.) Factory target grips provide a filler block behind the trigger guard (A) that helps position the middle and third fingers. Custom grips can be made to reduce the girth of the grip bottom as in (B) above where the front strap is exposed. S&W round-butt frame handles are nearly ideal in front strap contour. Notice in the third picture (C) that extra front strap material on a square-butt frame. Dan Wesson revolvers (D) have done away with the frame straps. The solid, one-piece grip is attached with a through bolt from the butt end. This system allows any kind of grip shape without interference from steel straps.

Other grip designs have gone so far as to require the diagonal removal of the bottom corner of the front strap to make room for the tapering of the grip base. This machining will harm resale value and is a "no-no" if metal cutting intercepts the serial number stamped on the butt. Properly done, this technique results in a rakish looking configuration that is considered well worth the effort by many shooters.

The round butt configuration of the Smith & Wesson K frame may be the best compromise. This round butt version has a straight drop contour on the front strap that makes proper grip fitting easy compared to the regular bell-bottom shape of the square butt

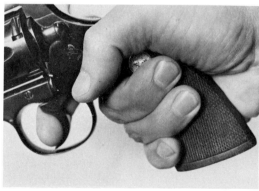

The correctly fitted grip (top) allows all fingers to engage the stocks fully with evenly distributed pressure. Standard frames (bottom) do not provide enough girth for the middle and third fingers, too much girth for a little finger.

frames. Colt's current D frame has an abbreviated handle that allows for considerable flexibility in the grip bottom treatment. Ruger's Security Six scales the handle to accomodate a variety of shapes. The Dan Wesson and High Standard Mark III revolvers have no handle frame straps and provide wood handles attached to the frame by a through-bolt. Stocks can be shaped to any style without concern for filling or inletting to the frame straps.

For combat grips, good design results from a form-follows-function rule. Shape and configuration should satisfy needs and superfluous features are eliminated. Grip length and girth should be dedicated in terms of the shooter's hand. Satisfying all individual needs is a tall order, and probably explains why factories have not supplied really well designed grips. Some factory grips have good singular features, and with minimal adjustments make passably good combat grips. The S&W Model 19 target grip can be sanded to straighten the front strap contour which narrows the bottom girth to help accomodate the little finger. It still takes fairly long fingers to negotiate this grip modification. Rounding of the sharp bottom edges of S&W target stocks also enhances comfort and functional qualities.

FUNCTIONAL STANDARDS

How does a shooter know when a grip fits his hand? Several tests can give positive indications. Place the grip in the shooting hand so it is aligned to the center line of the forearm. Check to see that all the fingers close securely around the grip. The middle finger should close to within ½ to ¼ inch of the mount of the thumb; the little finger should be no farther than 1½ inches away from the heel of the hand. The second knuckles of the middle, third and little fingers should align. If these knuckles are displaced outwardly, this indicates too big a girth at the butt to accomodate the little and third fingers.

No ridges or edges should be felt. Tightly gripping the handle should not produce sensations of prominences created by irregular pressures on the palm. Such sensations indicate contours alien to hand shape that will create distractions and possible movements of the grip inside the hand during recoil. Wood should not extend significantly below the bottom of the hand. Back strap contact with the center of the palm should be continuous without the sensation of prominences. Fit of the web into the recoil shoulder should be solid and full. There should be ample width in the recoil shoulder to blend with the natural contours between thumb and forefinger; this will avoid painful battering of the main joint of the thumb during firing. This thumb joint is a common spot where bruising takes place on the hand. A thickening process builds a kind of callous over the bone to protect this vunerable place. A well designed grip that fits the individual's hand will minimize this kind of bruising.

Thickness of grips will vary. The needs of combat shooting sometimes conflict with other standards. For a gun to be concealable (i.e. for the off-duty policeman or detective), many designers make the grips too thin to be practical for effective combat shooting. Grips that are too thin create pressure sensations in the hand at the front and back strap. Such grips usually lack the necessary thickness at the recoil shoulder and bruise the thumb joint during firing. Poor palm fit causes horizontal group dispersions that show up dramatically beyond 12 to 15 yards. Lack of comfort and confidence in the grip distracts the shooter's concentration and can cause further deterioration of scores. Careful compromises have to be made to produce functional, desireable service grips.

The gun handle should rest in the hand so the web rides high on the recoil shoulder. The object here is to place the hand as close to the axis of the bore as possible. This high position minimizes muzzle rise and recoil effect by transmitting thrust into the hand and wrist.

Straight-line recoil minimizes dislocation of the muzzle, promoting firing stability and fast recovery for the second shot. Grip design can facilitate this high-hold by providing the proper angle of the grip to the bore line. The test of a proper grip angle is how high the hand can be placed on the recoil shoulder without assuming unnatural proportions. This positioning factor varies among gun designs. Small frame revolvers provide a natural high-hold due to the small size of the handle. Medi-

The even gripping pressure possible on custom grips (top) provides for consistent hand holds and recoil control, with a confident feeling hand/gun union. Center knuckles of the master hand are aligned. Regular frames (bottom) tend to frustrate balanced gripping pressure, many times causing a shift in impact points with attendant poor recoil recovery.

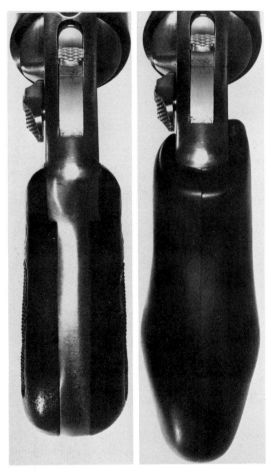

A fitted combat grip on a small-frame revolver can mean the difference between good or bad scores. Small frames are narrow and do not allow for good recoil control. Short length will not allow all fingers to grip properly. A custom stock overcomes most of the problems experienced with small frame guns.

um sized or large frames have a tendency to place the hand lower to the shoulder, particularly with the factory grips. This position accentuates muzzle hop during firing and provides poor support for the web of the hand. Recovery time is longer and DA shot strings tend to open up vertically.

Small frame guns also need special support at the recoil shoulder. Because of their light weight and low recoil inertia, full combat loads are hard to control. Grips usually require a broad recoil shoulder to fill the web and allow a very high hold. If hammer spurs are too long

to cock SA against the wood shoulder it is best to bob the hammer slightly to fit. The J-R combat grip allows an exceptionally high hold with a broad shoulder area to absorb recoil. Control is quite good and DA scores improve immediately with this unique design.

Trigger reach in a DA revolver needs careful examination. Average sized hands can adjust up to a 3-inch reach (as measured from the recoil shoulder to the midpoint of the trigger curve). A reach of 2.7 to 2.85-inch gives the best control for the vast majority of hands. On small frame guns, reaches run from 2.3 to 2.4-inches, nominally, and may be a bit short for long fingered shooters. Obtaining combat grips with an integral wooden recoil shoulder for these small guns is advisable. Since the shoulder is functional for recoil control, it also increases trigger reach.

However, ordering a custom grip with an integral recoil shoulder just to have it is foolish. Any features included on a grip should be functional. Use of a recoil shoulder increases trigger reach and makes DA shooting more difficult if this distance exceeds 3-inches. Medium frame revolvers commonly used in combat shooting (S&W K frame, Colt .41 caliber frame, Ruger's Security Six) have reaches that are just about right for most hands. If such guns are to be shot SA, deliberately in game hunting with full-bore loads a built-up recoil shoulder could be justified. Otherwise, unless a man has quite large hands with long fingers, it is best to order custom grips with the open back strap.

Palm swells should be carefully scrutinized on any custom grips. Some makers tend to accentuate the mound of the swell making the rest of the grip extra thin. This looks good but tends to create excessive pressure in the palm. This grip configuration will not give adequate recoil shoulder breadth to control lateral muzzle movement. The web of the hand can become quite sore when shooting heavy loads if not properly supported. Properly proportioned, a combat grip should distrubute recoil force over the major portion of the palm.

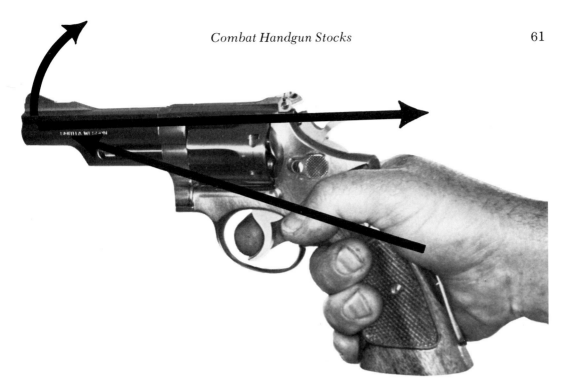

Recoil forces project along the bore line. Hand, wrist, and forearm resist the thrust. Since the bore is above the wrist, a resultant vector raises the muzzle. The higher the hand is positioned relative to the bore, the smaller the muzzle rise vector. The web of the hand should ride high on the recoil shoulder for this reason.

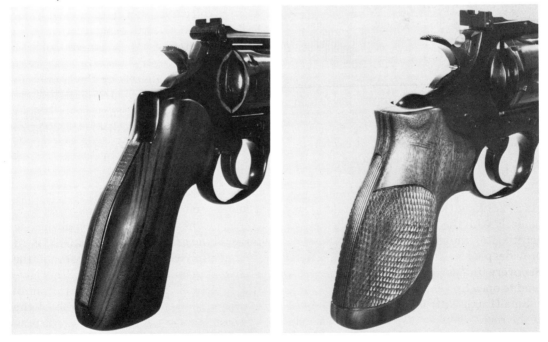

The open back strap style of grips is best suited for most combat handguns. Built-up recoil shoulders on custom stocks have utility, but should not be purchased without good reason. This feature can render a combat revolver less effective than it would be with the open back strap style grip.

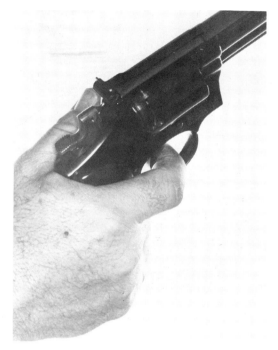
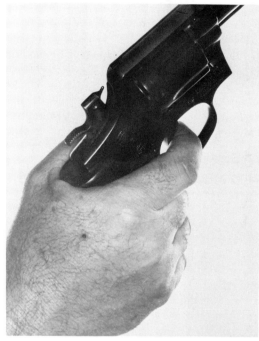

Trigger reach is an important consideration in choosing a combat revolver grip. Too long a reach strains DA techniques for many shooters. Addition of a recoil shoulder can lengthen the reach, making the gun harder to shoot in the DA mode.

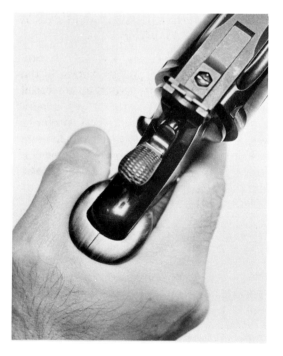

Many grip designs feature a flare on the bottom side contours. This has eye appeal if executed properly and some shooters think it helps position the hand in the grip. This feature tends to be out of context with the form-follows-function rule, however. Finger grooves, too, may help the novice learn a consistent grip, but their value is questionable. Most experienced shooters prefer a well proportioned grip that is plain. If finger grooves are ordered on a custom grip, they should be shallow and of a proper radius to fit the fingers. Finger separations should be rounded. One bad feature of finger grooves

Comfort and control of heavy field loads is a positive factor for using a built-up recoil shoulder. Field guns that are shot predominantly in the SA mode will not suffer from this feature. Also, shooters with very long fingers may want a shoulder to make the gun more comfortable to shoot in the DA mode.

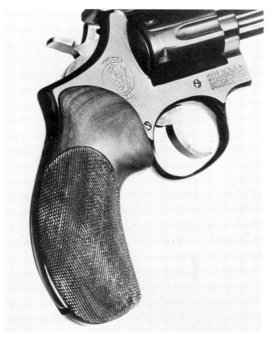

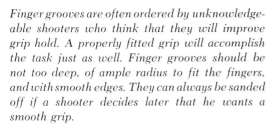

Finger grooves are often ordered by unknowledgeable shooters who think that they will improve grip hold. A properly fitted grip will accomplish the task just as well. Finger grooves should be not too deep, of ample radius to fit the fingers, and with smooth edges. They can always be sanded off if a shooter decides later that he wants a smooth grip.

Checkering is optional. A well-fitted grip does not need checkering to provide a secure hand hold. Shooters who prefer checkering should require that the whole palm area be covered with a fine line pattern as shown here. The grip is by Guy Hogue and the checkering was done by the incomparable Aaron Hogue.

is that during the draw, the fingers can clamp on the separations, causing an improper grip and corresponding poor scores. One nice thing about grooves or flares is they can be sanded off after the shooter matures and outgrows the need for these features.

Checkering is another feature taken for granted on custom grips. Aside from its esthetic value, the functional reasons for checkering seem obvious. Ideally, checkering fields should be generous enough to provide a textured surface to bite into the skin of the shooting hand to help stabilize the gun in recoil. If the gun does not move in the hand from one shot to the next, accuracy should improve. In truth, this feature does serve a useful purpose if virtually all palm surfaces are checkered. Small panels of

decorative checkering are just that. Decorative. And, if a grip is properly fitted to the hand, checkering is not necessary for recoil stability with sensible loads. Many experienced combat revolver shooters prefer a smooth grip, since it provides for cinching up the handhold for long-range shots or rapid-fire strings. Checkering can be irritating to the hand during a fast draw. Also, checkering can wear out clothing of a police officer.

DIAMOND PROFILE GRIPS

In order to solve certain DA shooting problems, the author undertook a project to refine a combat grip design. The design was to incorporate features and functions given above that corrected deficiencies in other custom grips that were available. The program was

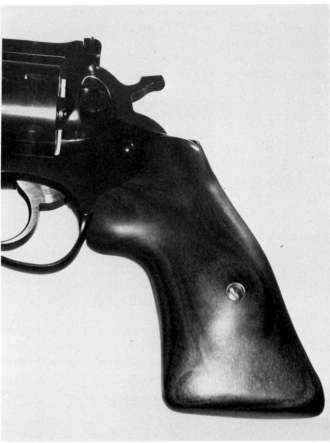

The Diamond profile grip by Guy Hogue has proved to be very adaptable for many different shooting hands. Simplicity and functional qualities meet a wide range of combat and field shooting needs.

pursued over a period of several months and culminated in what is called the "diamond profile" grip. This grip design maintains a full section at the recoil shoulder that is broad and contoured to the radius of the frame. It tapers out and downward to form gradual palm swells and then tapers back at the butt to make a thin, rounded section. Viewed from the back, the profile is roughly diamond shaped, but it is heavy in the upper section.

The left hand stock on diamond style grips is thinned and contoured down to the side plate just behind the cylinder swing-out position. This feature facilitates rapid ejection and smooth, precise recharging when using a multiple reloading device. Lack of an adequate loading slot in combat grips unduly delays reloading time. This grip design has worked quite well on square butt frames and offers outstanding combat grips on small frame revolvers and the round butt Model 19 S&W.

This diamond grip design was developed through Guy Hogue, a custom grip maker of outstanding talent and resourcefulness. Hogue is well qualified to produce exceptional grips. He was an LAPD firearms instructor for 10 years as well as an armored and DA exhibition shooter on the department team. He worked with the renowned handgun grip maker Fuzzy Farrant in getting his basic techniques and patterns developed while he was with LAPD. He has had years of hobby woodworking and cabinetmaking experience.

Hogue uses Brazilian hardwoods exclusively due to their great strength, beauty and workability. Pau ferro wood is standard for his line, with goncalo alves as an optional choice. Rosewood is offered at extra cost.

QUALITY CONSIDERATIONS

The buyer of a custom grip should be critical of what he gets. The finished set of stocks should conform to the basic criteria given above so far as fitting the hand and providing functional qualities. In addition, the stocks should be inletted accurately to the frame, lie flat without warping or gaps in the joint line, and the halves should mate without offset. Profile should match the frame closely when the backstrap is exposed. Checkering, if included, should be regular, without overruns and borders should be even.

Wood quality and finish are matters for individual choice. A number of exotic woods are offered by custom makers. Walnut is a standard, serviceable wood, but offers usually bland or plain figure except on high priced

grips. Rosewood has become quite popular in recent years; it has considerable variations in color and figure. Quality grips should have matched wood in both the right and left hand panels. Rosewood has become relatively scarce, and the best color and figure is available only at extra cost by many makers. Goncalo alves, another South American hardwood, is used in some S&W factory specialty grips. This wood has considerable variations in figure with a light toned, upbeat quality. Some shooters do not like it because it is so blonde. One of the best South American hardwoods for pistol grips is pau ferro. With a dense, close grain structure, it resembles walnut but with a more mellow, uniform brown color and varied, interesting figure. The wood inlets precisely, tends not to warp, and provides an attractive (but not garish), durable handgun grip.

Finishes on stocks should interest the handgunner. Applied finishes, such as lacquer or varnish, tend to chip and scratch with age. They are difficult to maintain and repair. If the grip shape is modified slightly, finish is

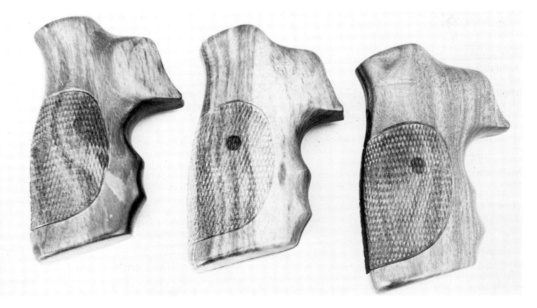

Three Latin American woods available in custom grips are (l. to r.) Brazilian rosewood, Goncalo Alves, and Pau Ferro. All offer variations in grain and color. Pau Ferro is one of the best, most consistently good stock woods still available at standard prices.

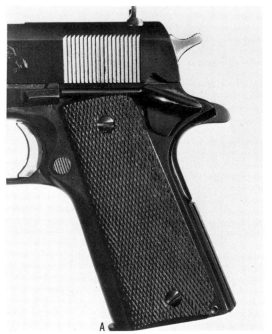

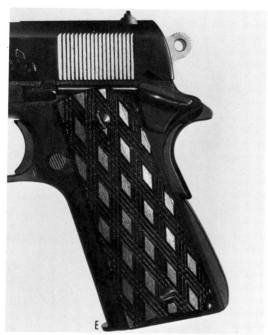

There is a limit as to what can be done for stocks on slab-side autopistols. The standard checkered GI grips (A) are still used by most autopistoleers. The older Diamond design (B) is available for those who want a touch of nostalgia. Guy Hogue's version of the GI (C) is simple, provides a bit more bulk on the sides. Herrett's (D) shapes the grip to fill into the curve of the back strap; this model is available 100 per cent checkered, also. Herrett's skip line GI style grip provides a lot of holding surface without skin irritation. Pachmayr's new Signature grip is molded rubber with a wrap-around front strap cover; very comfortable, very functional.

difficult to match. With penetrating and burnished finishes, maintenance and repair are much easier, requiring only polishing of the wood followed by application of hard wax or more penetrants.

More brittle or cross-grained woods, such as rosewood, may split if the gun is dropped. Repairs can be made with epoxy cements. Apply the glue with the stocks on the gun. Use wax parting agent on all gun parts adjacent to the repair to avoid cementing to the steel. A masking tape "bandage" will hold the chip in place overnight. After repeated firings, grip panels may loosen because the position pin hole elongates. This problem is easily remedied by epoxy resins in the pin hole, parting agent on the pin and frame. Let the gun stand overnight.

Grips are often damaged during their removal from the frame. Proper technique dictates loosening the grip screw halfway, then forcing on the screwhead to push the opposite panel away from the frame. The loose panel can then be removed, exposing the underside of the remaining panel, which is pressed off the frame. Never pry-off grip panels by wedging a knife blade, etc. into the center joint.

AUTOPISTOL GRIPS

Shooting autopistols is very demanding as regards uniformity and firmness of the handhold. Variations in hand-to-grip alignment can cause serious bullet impact changes with larger groups and lower scores. The web of the hand should be thrust into the handle yoke precisely to effect an extension of the forearm axis along the boreline. Fingers then close firmly to stabilize the hold. The handgun literally becomes integral with the hand and forearm.

In order to maintain a constant grip (especially on the .45 ACP), many combat shooters prefer checkered grips of standard GI configuration. The checkers bite into the palm side of the shooting hand. Checkering on flat autopistol stocks is not as irritating as it is on rounded and contoured revolver grips. Some shooters have the front strap and mainspring housing checkered or stippled as a further aid to gripping stability. Metal checkering is expensive and requires expert execution if the resale value of the gun is to be maintained or enhanced.

Recently Pachmayr Gun Works has offered a molded rubber grip set for the .45 ACP that has an integral front strap panel. The panel rolls around the front strap and provides a nonslip, checkered surface that is effective and comfortable in the hand. Herrett's makes adaptations of the GI panel grips for combat shooters. These Government Model stocks extend to cover the upper part of the frame back to the grip safety. This arrangement helps center the gun in the hand and provides some increased support against recoil. These stocks are made 100 percent checkered. This feature is a real aid to a firm hold, but some hands will be irritated by the checkering under the large thumb joint. The same grip is offered in a plain uncheckered style as well in fancier wood grain.

Herrett's also carries a skip-line checkered GI panel-type grip set. The large checks formed by the skip-lining anchor the hand well without the irritation of fine line checkering.

Colt's Government Model guns come with an arched mainspring housing. This feature was introduced back in the 1920's as an aid

While most .45 auto pistol shooters prefer the arched spring housing, the flat housing works well for some others. Switching off between the two types of housings can cause a vertical spread in bullet impacts. Choose one style and stick with it.

to more accurate shooting. The feeling among combat shooters is mixed regarding its effect. Most shooters use the arched housing, some prefer the flat housing. The main effect on shooting is the shimming of the arch that elevates the muzzle with any given handhold. That is to say, in point shooting, the forearm will not have to be elevated as much to strike the target with the arched housing. If the arched housing irritates the master hand, try the flat housing. There seems to be no discernable change in shooting scores with or without the arch. The main thing is to standardize according to your taste, since shifting off tends to change the vertical impact of bullet hits.

A good many points of view can be accomodated within the context of "good handgun grips." Many ideas put forth here are designed to aid the shooter to think critically and objectively about the design of stocks he uses on his handgun. Regardless of how the stocks are designed, they must fulfill a functional purpose. The interface between hand and handgun is critical to attaining success in combat shooting.

The following list of stockmakers will be helpful to combat pistoleers who want to obtain custom grips:

Custom Combat Grips
148 Sheperd Avenue
Brooklyn, New York 11208

J. M. Evans
5078 Harwood Road
San Jose, California 95124

Herrett's
Box 741
Twin Falls, Idaho 83301

Hogue Custom Grips
14540 Old Morro Road
Atascadero, California 93422

J-R Grips
1601 Wilt Road
Fallbrook, California 92028

Mustang Pistol Grips
13830 Highway 395
Edgemont, California 92508

John W. Womack
3006 Bibb Street
Shrevemont, LA 71108

CHAPTER VI

GRIPPING AND FIRE CONTROL

T HE ABILITY TO grasp the handgun and trigger-off rounds efficiently and without conscious effort is essential to success in combat shooting. So basic are these skills that shooters should work up routines for "dry" practice and analysis of the techniques. Even accomplished shooters can benefit from polishing and reinforcing skills.

The basic handhold establishes the human/mechanical link between shooter and the pistol. There are variations in individual hands but all grasping actions should accomplish the same fundamental purpose: to make the handgun an extension of the arm. The gun should function as part of body physiology.

Ideally, the axis of the bore should align with the center line of the master forearm as the shooter "shakes hands" with the grip handle. This detail is imperative for precision shooting with autopistols; it is not so critical with revolvers. Because the trigger reach on the revolver may be a bit long for a given individual's fingers, revolver shooters sometimes shift the handhold around toward the trigger slightly to make the DA trigger pull more controlled. A little use of this technique is not bad with the wheelgun if it is not overdone and is consistent. However, it is best to obtain custom stocks that will allow the "square" master handhold on the grip, since it is an aid to consistent scoring, control of recoil and rapidfire in the DA mode.

The handhold should be made high up on the back strap of the revolver to effectively lower the boreline relative to the hand and wrist. On the DA revolver, enough of the fore finger must engage the trigger to provide adequate grounds for the long, heavy pull. Ideally, the contact should be near the center of the tip so as not to interrupt articulation of the tip joint. The fingertip placement should be comfortable to the individual shooter within these functional guidelines.

Middle, third, and little fingers close on the grip taking a flexoral set against the front strap. This action should be strong enough to draw up the heel and palm of the hand against the backstrap in a vise-like motion. Little finger pressure should be substantial and coordinated with middle and third finger tension. If grip design has too large a girth at the bottom, custom grips should be obtained that allow the middle knuckles of these three fingers to align. Little finger strength is an important factor in recoil control and elimination of vertical stringing of shot groups.

THE BASIC HANDHOLD

The thumb should exert some side and downward pressure to give lateral stability to the handhold. In DA shooting, horizontal group dispersions can result from a passive thumb position. Thumb action can be overdone, however. Try holding the gun steadily between the thumb and forefinger with the other three fingers removed from the handle. Some opposition from the main joint of the forefinger helps to coordinate thumb pressure. Notice that this support also conforms the web between the thumb and forefinger to the recoil shoulder of the grip. This conformity is necessary to control recoil, stabilize the hand/pistol union, and prevent horizontal spread of the shot groups.

This basic grip hold should be practiced and criticized until a strong kinesthetic sense develops as to the correctness of the hold. In most combat shooting situations, there will

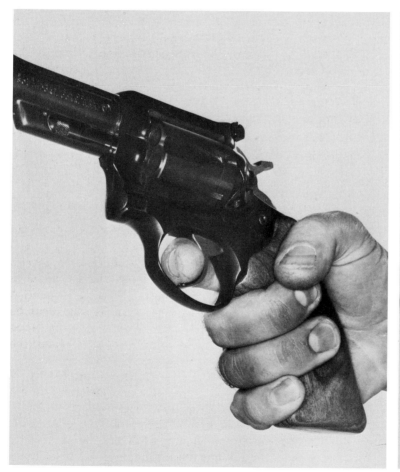

The master hand grip is essential to good shooting. It is critical because of the hand/pistol union. It is the basis of the two-hand hold, also. Poor master grips can nullify all other efforts for good shooting. The hand must ride high on the frame. Fingers align and clasp the grip, axis of the bore aligns with the forearm.

be no time to deliberately grasp the gun handle. The shooter needs some kinesthetic feedback to tell if the grip is properly taken. If the grip is not secure, cinching on a properly designed revolver grip will correct the situation. On an autopistol, the grip hold had best be taken correctly the first time, because cinching is not an effective technique on the slab sided handles of self-loaders. Proper master handholds are basic to effective shooting.

WRIST TENSION

An integral part of the master hand grip is the set of the wrist. Flexoral setting of the hand will make the wrist quite rigid, if the wrist is held in a straight position. Strong flexing of the hand aids the coordination of the wrist set. A number of ligaments stabilize the joint and tensioning of the fifteen tendons that go through the wrist can make this joint quite solid. Without a strong wrist set, it is difficult to control the handgun and consistently hit designated points of aim.

Shooting autopistols requires especially good wrist control for recoil recovery. Due to the shifts in the center of gravity of the pistol as it cycles, much of the recoil "effect" of autopistols derives from this dynamic shift as the slide smacks the frame. A strong wrist is needed to counteract this moment that tends to rotate the gun in the shooting hand. Wrist tension can be adjusted by setting the antagonistic extensor muscles (the muscles that open the hand) against the flexed fist. A balanced force must be adjusted or the arm will tend to tremor. Novice shooters think they are applying too much force when shaking starts. In reality, they may just have poor muscle tone or they are not coordinating muscle action, applying more antagonistic force on one side of the handhold than on the other. By developing a kinesthetic feel for equilibrium in the muscle sets, the shooter's gripping action becomes reflexive without needing conscious thought to achieve good form. Shooters should practice the basic master handhold with the regular shooting hand as well as the "weak" hand. The weak hand is used in many firing courses and developing ambidextrous capacity will aid in perfecting good standard form as well.

THE TWO HAND HOLD

Combat shooting brings both hands into play. While pistol shooting has been traditionally a one hand process, a little over a decade ago the two hand hold was introduced into competition shooting. The free-style nature of the sport encouraged developing new equipment and techniques. Jack Weaver, one of the all time great combat shooters, started using the weak hand to support the pistol during competitions in the late 1950's. His success was immediate and devastating and very nearly all other shooters began adapting the hold to their own shooting techniques. This handhold was later refined by Elden Carl to a form that adapts it more readily to average sized hands.

Taking the gun in the master hand, rotate the butt to the left. Place the heel of the weak hand between the finger tips and the heel of the master hand. Curl the weak hand fingers around the master hand. Curl the weak hand around the master hand fingers and extend the weak hand thumb parallel with the master thumb. This simple, basic arrangement is adaptable to almost any shooting position with any kind of handgun. This hold can be cinched tightly by curling fingers first, then closing the heel of the weak hand against the grip.

There are several adaptations of the two-hand hold. Many of these variations do not reflect the functional reasons why both hands are used to shoot the pistol. One version cups the weak hand to act as a cradle for the gun butt. While this technique gives a measure of steadiness and may be quite well adapted for very large hands, it tends to be passive, not providing the full benefit of active hand engagement. Another adaptation is where the weak hand grasps the master wrist. This hold further detracts from the kinesthetic union possible when hands clasp hands. Pressure on the master wrist distracts the shooter's concentration on master hand functions and interrupts circulation.

The weak hand thumb should not cross the web of the master hand. This will result in injury with a self-loader (when the slide intercepts the thumb) and reduces the back-pressure coordination of the weak hand.

Other variations use the thumb or thumb-forefinger web as a crutch support under the master wrist, etc. Analyse variations for passivity or distractions from master hand functions. The purpose for using the second hand is to complement and strengthen master hand coordination.

The basic principle of the two hand hold uses triangulation to achieve a stable plane of reference for gun alignment. With the arms

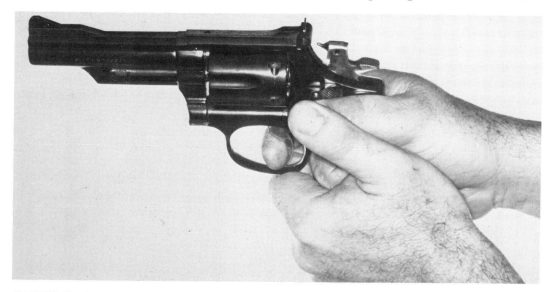

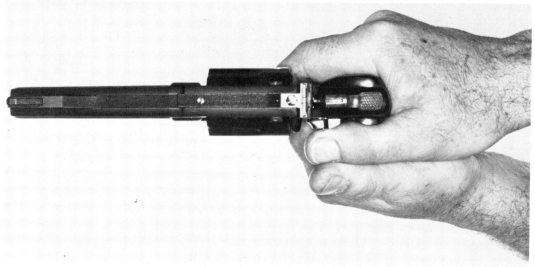

The two hand hold impresses the weak hand over the master hold, resting in the voids of the master grip. Maximum stability and kinesthetic control is provided by this grip hold.

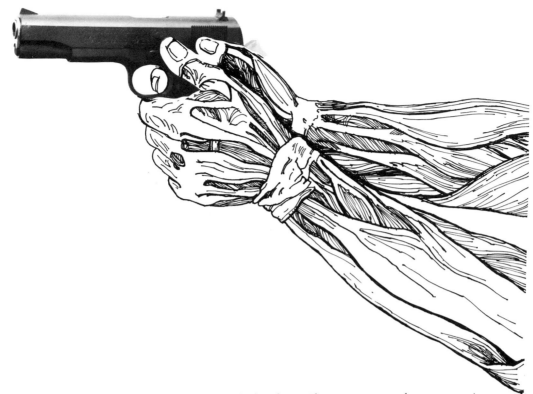

Forearm muscular sets cooperate to stabilize the handgun. This arrangement does not require a great deal of muscular exertion since coordinated actions reinforce the grip hold.

extended, the triangle of arms, shoulders, and hands gives the pistol a predictable, steady placement relative to the eye. Placement of the head on the upper arm further enhances the relationship. Slight rearward tension on the weak hand stabilizes the gun against recoil, tightens the master hand grip hold, helps stiffen the master wrist, and stabilizes the master arm. This handhold also brings the whole body into play, requiring the posture of back and legs with the foot placement that gives balance to the shooting position. This total body involvement enhances kinesthetics, focuses mind and emotions to the shooting task.

While two-hand shooting dominates combat marksmanship, mastery of one hand, point shooting techniques is also essential. Point shooting implies any stance where the gun sights are not used. "Hip" shooting is not an accurate description of the style; the hip connotation implies raising the muzzle to fire just as the gun clears leather. Little body mobility is required; kinesthesis and eye-hand references do not significantly play a part in execution of this movement. Consequently, while the hip shooting draw-and-fire time is fast, predictable hits do not register except at very close ranges.

MASTER HAND POINT SHOOTING

Point shooting has to involve total body functioning to be effective. Executed with finesse, point shooting time per hits is shorter than indiscriminate hip shooting. The basic body position for point shooting is very similar to that of a boxer; feet and toes pointing forward, left foot slightly ahead of the right, knees *slightly* bent, weight forward on the balls of the feet, torso bent slightly forward to place the body's center of gravity inside the

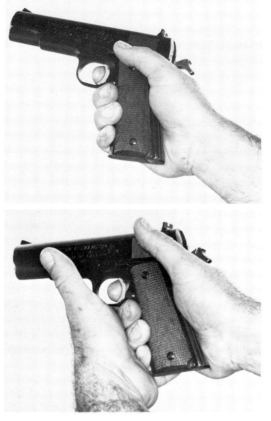

The two hand hold is acquired by first establishing the master grip (top). Next, the weak hand fingers are curled around the master fingers (bottom).

base made by foot placement. This stance focuses attention on the target, calling up a total mind-body response on cue.

Beginning point shooting should be done with the gun in the shooting hand. In the first stages of development, the fundamentals should not be complicated by the task of grasping the gun and drawing it from the holster. With the gun in the master hand, the gun butt can rest against the front of the thigh, muzzle pointing down and forward of the shooter. On signal, the shooter responds much like a boxer throwing a punch. The total body responds, not merely the arm and hand. The forearm is lifted off the thigh and the shoulder thrusts forward carrying the upper arm into exten-

sion. Torso muscles react, legs accommodate the slight shift in center-of-gravity. The gun in the "fist" is directed to the target by kinesthetic feel that results from eye-hand coordination.

A bit of practice at five yards on a silhouette target will reveal any deficiencies. The gun should be thrust far enough forward to enter the visual field. The more central the gun is to the visual field the more accurate hits will be. Raising the gun higher takes more time, so compromises must be made regarding reaction time and accuracy. At 3 to 7 yards the gun can be just barely in the visual field; at 7 to 15 yards the gun should be half-raised. Beyond 15 yards, the gun should be elevated up to the sighting plane and two hands should be used. To avoid confusion a single effective poise can be cultivated that suffices for all practical point shooting. At intermediate combat ranges (7-15 yards), two hands can be an option. The two hand hold enhances kinesthesis, results in more consistent scores, and adds little, if any, more time to the draw.

Shooters should determine for themselves the most effective position of the gun in the visual field rather than depend on some arbitrary instruction. This individual commitment helps "internalize" the learning process, shortening the overall time it takes to acquire point shooting skills, and raising the ultimate level of skill attained as compared to rote learning methods.

Position of the gun should be natural. Elbow placement should not be too far out, or too close in relative to the body. The "boxer throwing-a-punch" idea, if closely observed and refined in a full length mirror, will result in a well balanced, fluid motion. Exaggerated unnatural motions waste energy and are no more effective. Concentrate first on centering hits on the silhouette. Slow, regulated movements help develop the kinesthetic feel for the "groove." Once the shooter knows the center, adjustments in forearm set locks in elevation. Hits in the high center of the silhouette are most desirable. On paper targets this is the widest, biggest area for Vee scores, the "kill" zone for defensive combat. In defense shooting, the mid-chest is the area of vital organs and life processes.

Bullets hit the target in dispersed groupings. These groupings should have even distribution with no pronounced tendency to be horizontal or vertical. The tighter the group can be made, the narrower the cone of dispersion. A narrow cone of dispersion indicates good, consistent coordination and promises to influence favorably the shooter's ability to make longer range hits.

AIMED FIRE

Moving to a 15 yard silhouette target, timed firing exercises will build the capacity to acquire a sight picture and fire precise groups. Basic sight picture is standard with all patridge sights. The square front post is centered in the rear sight slot; the top of the post is set even with the top of the rear sight. The target is then placed on top of the post. Sight zeros will vary with different guns and loads. It is imperative that the windage setting on adjustable sights is centered for the particular gun and ammunition being shot. Most combat handguns are called on to fire anywhere from just a few feet range out to 50 or 60 yards. By setting sight elevation to strike a center hold at 50 yards most guns shoot 2 to 3 inches high at 25 yards.

This high-strike at 25 yards allows the hit area to be in full view over the sights. This is called "floating" the target and is useful in combination with pointing techniques where the gun is raised to the sighting plane but where a precise sight picture is not taken. The gun can be pointed quickly and quite precisely without actually taking a sight picture. In this technique, the gun is held just below the line of sight and the muzzle is pitched-up slightly to point to the impact area. Practice with this technique provides a very quick, surprisingly reliable hitting mode that can be used effectively out to 25 yards by shooters who have developed a narrow cone of dis-

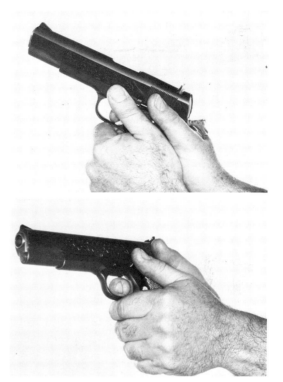

To complete the two hand grip, hold the weak hand so that the heel nestles in the void between the master fingertips and the heel of the master hand. This closing action will "cinch" the grip (top). The gun is ready to fire. The bottom picture shows a well-balanced, stable hand grip that will provide maximum control and stability under any shooting circumstances.

persion. When time permits or the situation demands more precise aiming, a small shift in the gun position brings the sights directly into play.

The critical factor in a good sight picture is front and rear sight alignment. Most shooters' eyes adjust best to focusing on the front blade. Depth of focus will keep the rear sight reasonably sharp to assure continuous alignment control. Minute misalignments in the sights creates enormous relative errors at the target, particularly past 25 yards. This is due to proportional geometry of the sights. Normally, the target will be blurred when eyes focus on the front blade, but errors due to lack of sharpness of the target will not be nearly as

In the raised position, the two-hand hold becomes the apex of a triangle of arms and shoulders. The gun is an extension of the master shooting arm, stabilized by the other two legs of the triangle. A slight back pressure on the weak hand locks the shooting position.

bad as misalignments between the front and rear sights.

During deliberate, slow firing from a supported position (prone) gun steadiness and ample time factors will allow the shooter to change focus from the front sight to the target, refining the alignments in both places before touching-off the trigger. This technique will maximize accuracy but is straining on the shooting eye. It is important to rest the eyes between shots by looking out to infinity for a few seconds. Due to accomodational changes, middle-age eyes will be especially strained and can be aided by the use of a small sighting aperture set in the corner of the shoot-ing glasses. The aperture will increase depth of focus of the eye lens, requiring less adjust-ment to maintain a sharp image between the front sight and the target. Wearing a small, one diopter lens attached to the lower inside corner of the shooting glasses will also aid focusing changes.

REINFORCING SKILLS

Practice dry firing to reinforce skills given above. A full length mirror gives a lot of feedback on stance and point technique. Small target silhouettes drawn to scale can reconstruct target size at 25 or 50 yards. These miniature targets can be very effective in reinforcing aimed fire and high point positions. Shooters are reminded never to have a tournament gun loaded except on the firing range. Also, the dry firing practice is no real substitute for actual live firing experience.

Trigger release is the real "moment of truth" in shooting. Handgunning demands quite exacting trigger release, since most factors of gun support and short sight radius work against the shooter. The marksman must develop the ability to synchronize sight picture refinement and trigger responses, anticipating the moment of optimum alignment, then releasing the trigger quickly and precisely. In combat shooting, most shot-strings are fired under time pressure, and most trigger let-offs involve some compromise with perfection. Various stages of standard courses create changing demands on trigger techniques. Adaptability is the watchword for successful combat shooting!

DA TRIGGER PULLS

Trigger techniques differ considerably for the autopistol and the DA revolver. Except for DA autopistols that will be discussed later self-loaders fire from a cocked hammer (single action) position. The DA revolver substitute manual cycling of the action for the self operating features of the autopistol. By work

For beginning point shooting, the gun should not be drawn from the holster. A steady position (left) is recommended until a novice has built confidence in point shooting skills. On signal, the arm is thrust forward in a "punching" fashion. Not so much knee-bending is necessary as shown here. It causes distraction from other body coordinations and serves to distract from consistent hits in the shortest time.

ing the long, heavy DA pull, the shooter manually retracts the hammer against the mainspring, rotates the cylinder to align a fresh cartridge with the barrel, and releases the hammer to fire the gun. All DA revolvers accomplish these functions with similar lockwork. However, designs differ enough that the characteristics of DA pulls vary considerably. Without going into a detailed design study of DA mechanisms, the characteristic trigger pull curves can be analyzed. Just how do DA pulls vary? What are the advantages or disadvantages of different designs? How can each type of pull be mastered?

First, a study was run to obtain data showing the relationship between the pull tension and arc movements of the hammers of several DA revolvers available on the market today. The data was correlated into the following composite charts. Firing characteristics for each of the revolvers were catalogued and verified from interviews with several combat revolver shooters. Data was taken with a Hooke's spring gauge and averaged for ten trials. The data are nominal since individual guns may vary significantly from empirical data shown.

Finger action during DA firing needs special attention. Two types of muscular action must be coordinated. Large muscles in the forearm flex the index (trigger) finger to start the pull. These big muscles continue to move the trigger through the action arc until the last few degrees. Then the refined coordination of the

small finger muscles causes the hammer to drop. Triggers that have a flat tension plateau at the highpoint of the pull make this DA finesse easier to execute than if there is a gain in spring tension toward the end of the pull.

When this gain in trigger tension begins, the large muscles in the forearm must come into play again to overcome spring resistance. While big muscles provide force, they are not easily controlled for precision movement. With end-gain trigger pulls, increasing spring tension must be overcome at the moment of hammer fall, while the large muscles are still contracting. This sudden release of spring resistance imbalances the grip and will cause the muzzle to jerk to the right (right handed shooter), resulting in a horizontal group dispersion. When time is not a factor the shooter can train the large muscles to anticipate the let-off, then damp big muscle contractions by

Some variations in point shooting are commonly used. The short or low point (A) is usable from three to seven yards. Some shooters feel that the short point is faster than the standard position (B) that is recommended for 7 to 15 yards. The standard position allows for more visual feedback and is only slightly slower than the short stance. Beyond 15 yards, the high point is used (C). This is an adaptable stance used for pointing or aiming with very high hit probabilities.

These two point stances are standardized by most veteran combat shooters. The standard point is used less often in competition as years go by. The high-point position is being used even at very close ranges for burst fire with devastating results. Time-delay for the high-point is almost negligible after practice compared to the standard position.

applying antagonistic force. The timing of this action is critical, however, and in rapid fire, it becomes even more difficult to control uniformly. Because of this, most competition combat shooters prefer DA guns that have a long flat tension plateau before hammer fall. All DA trigger tension problems can be improved by smoothing the action and adjusting spring tensions or leverages in the action. This process is described in Chapter 14.

A common fault in DA shooting is the over-activity of the large muscles, resulting in a jerking of the trigger. Properly pulled, a twenty-five cent piece can be balanced on the flat barrel rib just back of the front sight. When the trigger pull can be executed without disturbing the coin or having the sight picture move, the proper coordinations are being exhibited. Again, many shooters can DA pull perfectly in a deliberate cadence, but coordination goes awry during rapid fire or closely timed events. The best way to learn a smooth, efficient DA pull is to dry fire practice slowly to gain the kinesthetic feel, then translate this action into a reflexive response that works under stress. A properly regulated revolver is a *must* for achieving this state of the art.

THE SINGLE ACTION PULL

Single action (SA) shooting with a revolver requires a different physical set from the DA mode. The hammer is cocked with the weak hand thumb in the two hand hold by a simple motion up and over the master hand. With the mainspring compressed and the cylinder rotated, the only thing left is the disengagement of the sear to let the hammer fall. Only the small trigger finger muscles are involved with this type of let-off. The sensitive tip end of the forefinger engages the face of the trigger. The static pull tension is only one to two pounds and a portion of this pressure (enough to compress the fleshy part of the finger tip) should be applied just prior to let-off. SA combat shooting involves precision shots with

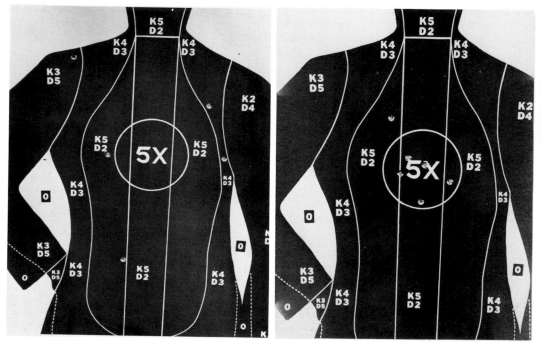

The proof of point shooting skills is in the dispersion of shot groups. Until definite patterns are established, no evidence of control is exhibited. The target on the left shows little if any control from seven yards. One bullet even missed the target completely. The right hand target is typical of a performance by a polished point shooter.

the utmost sight picture refinement for small group sizes, usually at long range with slow fire time.

The shooter's whole mental and physical set is different from rapid fire circumstances; body position is usually prone. Breath control is vital to regulating heartbeat and damping normal body oscillations. Deep breathing will slow a fast heart; taking a breath, letting half out and holding will give ten seconds for the sight picture refinement and let-off. Once the firing sequence is begun, delaying for more than ten to twelve seconds before let-off is self-defeating. Body processes lose efficiency and the capacity to deliver precise fire. If the shooter cannot get everything together

Just looking over the tops of the sights establishes accuracy out to 25 yards for most combat courses. Should the opportunity allow more time, sights can be aligned precisely without any shift in this basic stance.

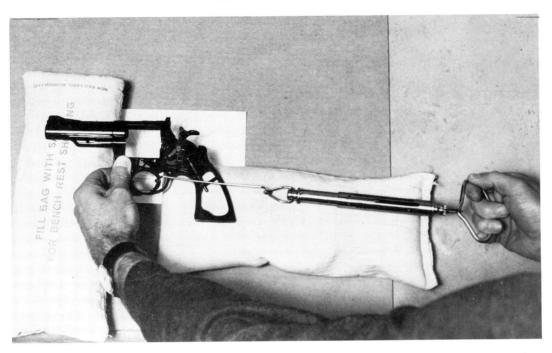

This simple Hooke's spring apparatus was used to gather trigger pull profile data. The average of ten trials gives nominally good data. Tension readings were taken for each five degrees of hammer arc.

in that time, it is best to ease off, rest and start again. For single action work, a trigger overtravel stop is useful. Overtravel of the trigger tends to imbalance the grip hold and increase horizontal group dispersions. If the SA let-off is well regulated, the effect of overtravel is minimized, but an overtravel stop is still useful in any case.

Autopistols will require similar techniques to SA revolver trigger control. In rapid fire work with the auto, a great deal of finesse is needed not to override the light trigger pressure and let-off the round before all other refinements are ready. Under such conditions using an automatic in the International Rapid Fire event, it is not at all unusual to see contestants firing between the targets because of over reaction to the sensitive SA pull. Likewise, there is a tendency to fire too soon in short duration draw and fire stages. Convenience of SA fire in the autopistol is counterbalanced by the increased control demanded of the shooter. In early training, autopistol

trigger control is an unconscious frustration to many novices. The chief problem seems to be big muscles overriding small finger muscle control. Eye and hand coordination is the problem, and it is a tough process to master kinesthetically due to the low threshold values associated with light trigger responses. If a shooter has difficulty hitting consistently with the autopistol, it is a problem almost certain to involve trigger control along with recoil stability and wrist set. An overtravel stop and lots of dry firing will help. A trigger adjustment to 4½ pounds pull is demanded for good .45 ACP performance. Dry practice should concentrate on gaining kinesthetic feel for trigger control; the sight picture should not be disturbed by the hammer fall.

Flinching, a reflexive tightening of muscles in anticipation of gun discharge, is also detrimental to shooting scores. Many good shots flinch occasionally, but their reaction is usually delayed until after the gun discharges. A good way to test for flinching is to have a

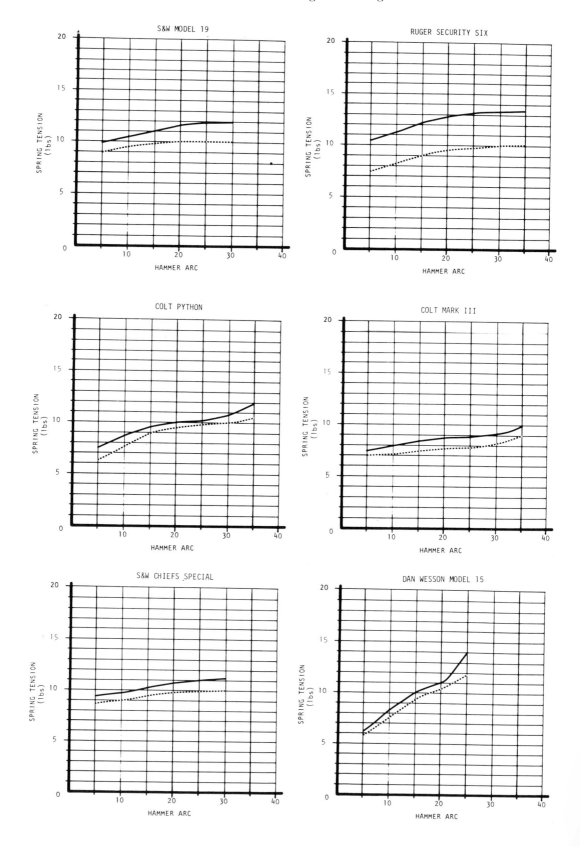

shooting partner load the gun with several dummy rounds mixed in with the live ammunition. With these rounds placed at random in the cylinder or the magazine of the gun, the shooter does not know which rounds will fire and which will not. The dummy rounds will reveal the presence and extent of the tendency to flinch. Flinching involves a psychic phenomenon that can be caused by bad shooting habits relating to coordination.

While gripping and fire control basics are being mastered, combat pistoleers can go on number of factors. Most shooters get over it or control their reaction by becoming conscious of what it is and how it adversely affects scores. The motivation to improve usually overcomes flinching, but each individual must discover the reaction for himself. Undetected or left alone, flinching can adversely affect shooting development, leading to frustrating experiences and ingraining of a number of to the study of basic combat shooting situations. While there are plateaus in development, many skills are reinforced concurrently.

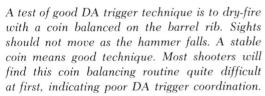

A test of good DA trigger technique is to dry-fire with a coin balanced on the barrel rib. Sights should not move as the hammer falls. A stable coin means good technique. Most shooters will find this coin balancing routine quite difficult at first, indicating poor DA trigger coordination.

The thumb of the weak hand provides a functional means of cocking revolver hammers for SA shooting. This technique does not disturb the master hand grip and is fast and efficient. Thumb movements are easy to coordinate without interrupting standard shooting routines.

These graphs show typical trigger pull profiles for representative combat revolvers available today. There will be considerable variation in trigger pulls from gun-to-gun, so these are not necessarily representative of individual guns. The relative characteristics of the tension gradients represent design factors, so this data is fairly valid regarding comparisons of the different gun designs. The solid line shows the out-of-the-box condition of the trigger pull. Dash lines represent changes after stoning and/or other modifications to smooth the action. In all cases, the best DA pulls are those that provide a tension plateau just before hammer let-off. This characteristic allows rapid DA manipulation with minimal sight movements. Triggers with tension gains at the end of the pull are more difficult to control during closely timed events. In practice, the maximum absolute tension level required to operate the lock is not as important as the changes in tension over the duration of the pull. The best trigger pulls tend to "roll-off" just before the hammer falls, providing no change in pull-tension for the last few degrees of hammer arc.

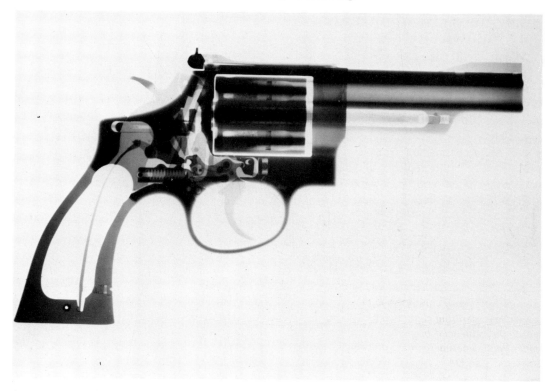

Trigger control for SA shooting requires great finesse. Big muscles tend to override trigger control, resulting in a jerk. It takes practice and concentration to perfect a good SA trigger technique, and it's easy to lapse concentration when time pressure is on. With a good technique, the hammer can fall without any sight disturbance.

Design features of various revolver locks may appear to be similar. This fact can be misleading, since the actual operating characteristics of different actions may be quite changeable to the shooter. So as not to be influenced by personal biases, the shooter must use each gun to see how changes in trigger pull affects shooting scores. An uncoordinated or inexperienced shooter may not be able to discern the differences in DA response; his scores may be poor with any gun.

The guns shown in these unusual photographs are the Model 19 S&W and the Mark III Colt. Both have identifiable similarities in lock design. Shooting experience will show decided differences in trigger pull and handling characteristics. Some shooters lament the fact that the best features of several designs cannot be combined into a single handgun.

These unusual pictures of the Colt Mark III and S&W Model 19 may appear to be X-ray views, but they are not. These see-through images are made by the Neutron Radiography (NR) technique. Neutrons from a radioactive source produce an entirely different view from that produced by X-rays. Dense material, such as lead, will stop X-rays. But neutrons pass through lead to cause exposure of the film (notice that the bullets are not completely clear in the print). Hydrogen saturated materials are more opaque to neutron radiation (see the lube oil shadow in the barrel threads of the Model 19).

Notice that the powder granules in the cartridge cases are defined, which would not register on a regular X-ray at all. NR photos are sensitive to small variations in thickness of similar substances. The cannelures are recorded on the bullets in the top and bottom chambers. The overlapping and inter-relationship of functional parts in the actions are clearly seen.

NR technology, a spin-off from the nuclear age, has become more advanced and capable of applications in many fields of mechanics, ordnance, medical and life sciences, as an entirely new way to see the unseen. These NR pictures were made at the TRIGA Research Facility of Gulf Energy and Environment Systems, La Jolla, California.

CHAPTER VII

BASIC COURSES OF FIRE

S INCE COMBAT SHOOTING draws its background from the martial arts, the purposes of the sport reflect practical or applied defensive tactics. As used in martial applications, the handgun primarily is intended for impromptu engagements. Its small size makes carrying a service handgun convenient, where it is easily accessible when defensive needs arise.

Since the majority of practical encounters involve little or no warning at close quarters, the appropriate response is a short range intense directed fire. Multiple shots are needed for any possible combination of targets. This could be a single fanatical attacker or multiple assailants. The options open for survival in a gun fight are varied; they demand recognition, adaptability, reflexive responses and a good measure of luck. The more prepared the pistoleer is to meet these challenges, the better the chances for survival.

COURSE DESIGNS

Emphasis in combat shooting is on designing courses of fire that will develop basic gun

handling skills and provide abstractions of real time shooting situations. The latter type of courses should demand a quickness of response, recognition and discrimination of targets, and challenges to inherent shooter weaknesses under adverse conditions.

The debate continues as to whether or not certain types of courses are, in fact, relevant to real-time circumstances. Is it best to emphasize only combat shooting basics and gun handling skills? Should the shooter's physical limits be taxed, emphasizing athletic ability in making shooting performance secondary? Is a course of fire valid in terms of developing skills to meet designated real time situations?

It is the author's contention that courses of fire should be graduated or "spiralled" so as to emphasize a continuity of skills carried to ever higher, more challenging levels of competence. Too often, courses are designed to be "cute," which only serves to confuse the shooter but does not teach anything new. Others are so bizarre that they have no continuity with existing courses and serve chiefly to frustrate all but the most competent shooters. Many courses are designed with unrealistic biases toward the pistol's purposes; overly emphatic military applications are sometimes wholly unrealistic in terms of usable, practical skills. For example, who is going to be firing his pistol at moving targets while swinging one handed on a rope from tree to tree? Such a course of fire is good if a specific training need or mission is called out, but the reality falls out of any general context for combat shooting sports. Military courses of fire should consider group tactical demands, not just swashbuckling individual performance. Most of these antics are figments of Hollywood imaginations, and some are thought up purposely to favor given individuals or types of equipment to be used in matches.

INDIVIDUAL PERFORMANCE AND EXPECTATIONS

Those courses of fire that are most successful reinforce basic skills and emphasize individual performance to given standards. Overemphasis of competition at the expense of individual skill development is going to "turn-off" a majority of sports shooters. Courses and programs that emphasize the peculiar skills of a few superlative shooters will tend to build an elite group surrounded by awe struck learners, who tend to drop out when they reach the ceiling of their capacity.

When match activities are dominated by small groups, courses of fire tend to become predictable and stagnant, so shooters with the time, skill and determination to win competitions specialize in the standard events. Soon, repetition means more than adaptability, as the veteran accumulates the basic savvy as to how to win the standard matches. Again, competition eclipses development as the major influence on behavior patterns.

Large, competitive regional matches are not the best places to cultivate individual development. The local club shoots and small personal group sessions aid the developmental aspects of shooting, so long as discipline and purpose can be maintained. Combinations of unexpected, unpredictable arrangements of standard shooting routines can be intermingled with structured "realistic" courses of fire. A basic core or repertoire of courses can be mastered. These courses should be run often enough to gain high levels of proficiency, particularly for beginning and intermediate shooters.

ELEMENTS OF PERFORMANCE

New course designs should reflect a purpose not covered by other standard matches. They can be general in nature, covering a wide range of shooting situations, or specific in purpose, embracing a variety of different approaches to a single group of skills. The elements or building blocks for events are diverse; a sampling of basic timed exercises is listed below:

1. Short range draw and fire; single targets, multiple targets, single or multiple shots.
2. Fire reload and fire again on multiple targets.

Basic shooting events must embody a mixture of developmental elements. Overemphasis upon specialized skills for beginning events can result in imbalanced rather than rounded development. The ability to deliver tight groups from 15 yards during short time intervals is one basic skill.

3. Fire then move forward, negotiating a barrier.
4. Firing from behind a barricade.
5. Positional shooting, deliberate and rapid fire.
6. Long range firing, beyond 30 yards out to 60 yards.
7. Firing on selected targets at mixed ranges.
8. Draw and fire and rapid fire at single and multiple targets at intermediate ranges.

Many of these basic events can be combined with different response cues. The most common cue is a whistle or voice command to begin and end the event. Gongs, bells, or alarms are optional audio cues. Occasionally, light stimuli are used. Target movement and recorded noises associated with target movement are seldom encountered as cues. However, they are excellent developmental devices.

BASIC EXERCISES

Beginning exercises should start with point shooting on targets 5 yards downrange. Slow, deliberate single shots will develop the kinesthetic groove for making the gun shoot where the marksman looks. Revolvers use DA mode, autopistols should be cocked and safety locked. Guns are unholstered and held at the ready, muzzles down and aimed in front of the shooters foot, butt resting on the thigh. As proficiency in vertical and horizontal bullet placement in the silhouette chest area grows, move targets to 7 yards and readjust impact patterns. Gradually, two then three shot strings are fired in cadence; no time factor should complicate fundamental gun handling objectives. Later, a test of dispersion control is to empty the gun into the target rapidly observing the amount of group expansion as firing proceeds.

Intermediate and high level pointing skills should then ensue at seven yards. With a

Firing on multiple targets requires considerable concentration to avoid clean misses. This 15 yard exercise should not be started until drawing and firing are smooth and predictable. Practice should be made on targets from left to right as well as right to left.

purpose of teaching precision gun handling, group sizes will close up noticeably. The two hand hold should be introduced at this time. Also, strong hand and weak hand point exercises will illustrate weak hand deficiencies and show what has to be improved. Multiple targets can be introduced firing singles, doubles, triples or mixed combinations.

Relocating targets at 12 yards and using two hand holds, aimed fire is introduced on the single target. The objectives here include mastery of the sight picture, precision trigger let-off for small group dispersions. Later, as gun mounting and aiming become smooth and natural, move targets to 15 yards and begin multiple silhouette firing. To increase objectivity, timed firing should be introduced at this time. Usually the shooter's confidence has developed to a point where time limits are a welcome challenge. Natural timing for shot strings can be taken and averaged. Early timing should be slightly slower than the beginner's natural cadence; timing should be shortened as skills develop further. Measured time can be applied in two ways. The usual timing method is to give a start and stop signal with a defined interval. The other method is to give a start signal then stop the watch when the final shot is fired thus measuring the open interval.

Closed interval timing helps create a mental measure of time and influences the pace within a given interval. Open ended timing is useful to test performance on standard or complex events; it gives time options and can be used as an integral part of scoring. Open end timing is often compared against par times for events. There is considerable controversy among shooters as to the effectivness of par timing. The split goes something like this: the top ten shooters in an event don't complain but everybody else is mad. Par time tends to be arbitrary, usually exaggerating the top scores while blitzing the slow time shooters. Score points are subtracted from hits when time averages go over par and this is negative

so far as accuracy performance is concerned. In most par time events, speed is emphasized over accuracy. One compromise is to tally the scores then divide by the time. This gives a quotient that equates hits directly and time inversely to performance. Shooter options are then left open as to the mix of hits versus time according to the individual's skills. For example, an event requires twelve shots scored five points per Vee and three points for any other hits. Timing is open ended; once the shooter starts, the clock runs until the last shot is fired. There is no par or designated time interval. If the shooter scores 52 points and completes the event in 28 seconds, the performance coefficient is:

In the beginning, timing of shooting events should challenge the shooter's ability without creating an impossible objective. Work up to prescribed time standards after fundamental skills are well established. Making times too short, too early discourages balanced shooter development.

$$\frac{52}{28} = 1.86$$

Another shooter scores 47 points in 22 seconds. His performance coefficient would be:

$$\frac{47}{22} = 2.14$$

The correlation between speed and scoring is obvious. This system is not well suited to all events, but it could be substituted, on notice to competitors, to upgrade the challenge of many courses of fire. The system makes any contest more objective where open end timing is used and allows for more performance options. Both speed and accuracy are important to the combat shooter!

DISTANCE SHOOTING

At 25 yards and beyond, a real test of combat marksmanship begins. Pointing and kinesthetic senses develop to assure hits at short to intermediate ranges. But, the shooter must marry fluid motions with the precision of aimed fire to meet competitive time intervals at 25 yards and beyond. Many events at this range are fired from unsupported positions. Development of an effective standing, two hand position is essential. Beginning DA work requires a sophisticated trigger technique at this range. The trigger should be pulled back to almost the let-off point, then held for an instant while the sight picture is refined. The last few degrees of hammer movement is taken up with finger tip movement, not unlike a single action let-off. Shooters will not do very well at this kind of activity without a well conditioned DA revolver.

Autopistol shooters discover at this 25 yard distance that every little imperfection in hold and trigger technique is magnified greatly. All basic techniques of the hold and squeeze must be further refined; this condition is not difficult to achieve, but it demands special attention. Some novice shooters start falling apart at 25 yards after they have done very well up thru the intermediate ranges. But

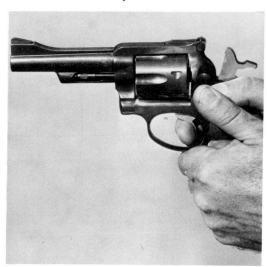

The DA revolver can be fired from the "step" with nearly the same accuracy and control as with single action shooting. This means using big muscles to raise the hammer and hold while sight picture is refined. The final few degrees of hammer arc are taken up with finger tip pressure. This kind of coordination takes practice and a well-conditioned revolver action.

The prone pistol position offers an excellent, stable base for precision long-range shooting. Few disturbances reach the hands or the gun while the shooter lies on the mat. This kind of position is nearly as stable as a machine rest for the experienced handgunner.

Kneeling position is not used often in combat shooting, but it affords a reliable option where cover is too high or where ground conditions preclude prone shooting. The low position (top) is braced and is preferable for longer range, deliberate shooting. The raised kneeling stance (bottom) is more flexible and quicker to enter and to leave. Notice how the basic hand, arms, and shoulder position is common to all other combat position shooting.

superior achievement at 25 yards is not all that illusive! New standards for perfection and attention to details must be observed.

At 50 yards, only a few shooters can qualify in the standing, unsupported position. For all but a very few shooters, some support is needed at this range in order to shoot consistently high Vee scores on silhouette targets. Occasionally, though, a surprise shoot will require or give a particular advantage to an effective unsupported or semi-braced shooting position at 50 yards. Also, under very dry conditions, rapid fire muzzle blasts and bullet impacts in the butts can kick up enough dust to obscure targets from a prone shooter. Many shooters have saved long-range scores by going into a kneeling or standing position where target visibility is above the dust cloud. Without having the option and skill to shoot passably well at long range in unsupported positions, the match could be totally lost. Without having the skill, the optional position would probably never occur to most shooters pressed by adverse conditions.

The problems of long-range pistol shooting demand a special set of techniques. The most common and probably the best position for the task is prone. A number of versions of the prone technique are used but one that combines comfort with bedrock steadiness is recommended. Prone positions that require lying out straight away from the target give a small profile. However, the head must be elevated much like a four legged animal and strain is placed on neck muscles and tendons as well as the small of the back. This is a hard position to maintain efficiently for any period of time.

By slightly rolling on one's right side (right handed shooter), and bending slightly banana shaped, low back stress is eliminated and body weight rests on the side and shoulder. This factor helps natural breathing and heartbeat. The right arm can be extended and the head rests on the upper arm without neck muscle strain. The shooting eye and master hand are aligned. The regular two hand hold is used which elevates the gun off the shooting mat and stabilizes the sight picture. The mat material should be of cotton waste or some composition other than sponge rubber or foams. Spongy materials allow the gun to bounce and this seriously affects steadiness for precision shooting. Since no muscle strain is used to support the body, this prone position is rather easy to adjust quickly to acquire a target. The basic aiming, trigger control, and breathing techniques described in Chapter 6 are employed. Guns used for long-range events should be zeroed for 50 yards center or six o'clock hold. A match grade gun with tailored hand loads is capable of delivering 2 to 4 inch groups consistently at 50 yards in the hands of a polished long-range shooter. This skill is not too common among combat shooters, but it is one mark of a polished hand-

gunner to be able to go clean regularly on 50 yard events.

Several courses of fire are well adapted to maiden efforts in combat pistol shooting. Among these are the Practical Pistol Course (PPC), PPC (modified), the LAPM qualification course, and the Advance Military Course. The order of courses given is significant regarding shooting ability. The PPC was originated for police training and standardized by the National Rifle Association as an official competition for law enforcement agencies. The PPC has been modified by the Southwest Pistol League (and other combat shooting groups) to increase the challenge and improve the value of this course of fire for combat shooting. Modifications include reducing the time intervals allowed for each of the stages. These two versions of the PPC provide a continuity for training shooters

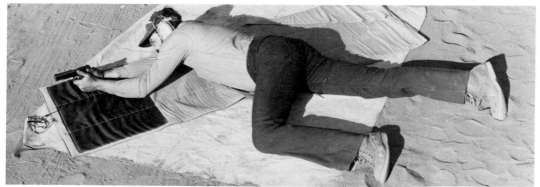

The combat pistol prone position is a free-style technique, unlike prescribed police prone positions. The idea is to achieve a solid, stable position free from stresses and limitations that distract from shooting performance. These two views show an ideal combat prone position.

without having the confusion of learning new firing routines as the level of difficulty rises. This arrangement has a disadvantage, too, since many trainees who do well on the PPC don't like to see their scores drop because of the shorter times demanded in the modified course. The LAPM course may be a better transition for beginning shooters to more competitive trials. After the LAPM, a return to the PPC (modified) may avoid the drop in morale mentioned above. The Advanced Military provides one of the best all-round training programs for basic combat gun handling, adaptable to both DA revolvers and the autopistol.

THE PRACTICAL PISTOL COURSE (PPC)

Originated by the FBI, this course has trained more peace officers than any other. Used for training and qualification shooting by many police departments, it is highly regarded by law enforcement officials. However, the course is not regarded as well rounded in development of gun handling skills in combat shooting circles. Skills are narrow and timing is quite long compared to those demanded in other competitions. But, this course of fire is excellent for introducing novice shooters to competitive drills. The long time periods allow for ample concentration on fundamentals. Shooters can "sort out" a lot of confusions about shooting basics while training for competitive disciplines.

The PPC is fired on T-8 silhouette targets, 50 rounds are fired at ranges of 7, 25, 50 and 60 yards. Shooting positions required are point-shoot crouch, prone, sitting, kneeling, and barricade positions. The procedures are as follows:

Stage I—7 yards—10 rounds—25 seconds. Load five rounds and holster. On cue, draw and fire five, reload and fire five more. The pistol is in the point shooting position, never rising above stomach height, sights are not used.

Stage II—40 rounds—5 minutes 45 seconds. *Phase one*—60 yards—load five rounds and holster. On cue, draw the pistol and drop to prone position, fire five rounds. Reload. Always keep the muzzle downrange when reloading. *Phase two*—advance to the 50 yard mark with the gun holstered and safe; fire five rounds sitting, reload, then fire five more rounds prone. *Phase three*—move to the 50 yard barricade and reload undercover. Using a two-hand braced position and keeping the body behind the barricade fire five rounds with the weak hand, reload and then fire five rounds with the master hand. Reload. *Phase four*—advance to the 25 yard mark and fire five rounds from the kneeling position. *Phase five*—move to the 25 yard barricade, re-

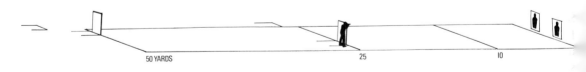

This same basic field layout serves three events: the PPC, PPC (modified), and the LAPM. The dimensions given here are for the PPC (modified), but the stages are fired in a similar manner for the regular PPC. Only the seven-yard range has been extended to ten yards, with shorter time intervals on each stage for the modified version. The LAPM has no firing beyond 25 yards. The three courses are related, but differ in the kind of emphasis structured into the event. The PPC is the easiest, good for novices. The PPC (modified) emphasizes movement and short firing times. The LAPM concentrates shooting stages on close-in rapid-fire situations and multiple target engagement. All three courses are very useful in developing combat marksmanship.

50 YARDS   25   10

Barricade shooting is an integral part of combat handgunning, especially in police shooting events. Using any available structure for support, the shooter can limit his exposure to return fire while attaining a stable, braced shooting stance that assures excellent fire control. Mastery of barricade techniques is basic for a full combat shooting development.

load undercover, fire five rounds with the master hand. Reload. Then fire five more rounds with the weak hand. Hits are scored according to the numbered zones on the T-8 target — 250 points are possible with 233 points or better rating Expert, 215 points or better rating Sharpshooter, 188 points classifies for Marksman. Each procedural violation or overtime shot will cost the shooter five points.

THE PRACTICAL PISTOL COURSE (MODIFIED)

This is the PPC modified for use by the Southwest Pistol League. Firing modes are free-style and times have been cut considerably to put more pressure on contestants. In stage one, the firing range has been increased from 7 to 10 yards and the firing sequence is with the master hand then the weak hand unsupported. Barricade firing stages require movement from a starting point in to the barricade as part of the overall time for the event. Barricades have a 2 by 3 foot firing area that the shooter must stay inside during all firing behind the barricade.

Stage I — 10 yards — 12 rounds — 15 seconds. Load six and holster. On cue, draw and fire six at one of two targets spaced three feet apart (edge to edge). Reload. Fire six more rounds at the other target with the weak hand unsupported.

Stage II — 18 rounds — 40 seconds.
Phase one — stand at the thirty yard mark, five yards left of the 25 yard barricade. Load six and holster. On cue, draw and fire six, three at each of two targets.
Phase two — reload on the move to the 25 yard barricade, fire six rounds from the right hand side of the barricade. Reload. Then fire six more rounds from the left side of the barricade at the second target.

Stage III — 18 rounds — 55 seconds.
Phase one — stand ready at the 60 yard mark, five yards to the left of the 50 yard barricade. Load six and holster. On cue, draw and fire six, three at each of two targets.
Phase two — reload on the move to the 50 yard barricade, fire six from the right hand side. Reload. Then fire six more from the left side of the barricade.

The shooter is left the option of what position to take for the most effective fire. Starting positions are always from standing and require the gun to be drawn from the holster. The time needed to assume any position is included in the overall time for the event, placing a premium on fluid body motion as well as shooting skill.

Hits for this course of fire are scored from the number zones of the T-8 targets. Two hundred and forty points are possible. Expert (93%), Sharpshooter (86%), or Marksman (75%) scores are not used in League shoots, but may be applied by individual groups or clubs who keep track of these classifications. Procedural violations or overtime rounds cost five points each.

THE LOS ALAMITOS PISTOL MATCH

This match emphasizes short range firing situations, the type usually encountered in

Reloading phases can cost a lot of time if bungled or confused. The biggest problem to overcome is fear of reloading against a tight time requirement. Big muscles tend to override small muscle finesse, producing clumsy gun and ammunition handling. In revolver reloading, especially, coordinations must be polished and consistent. Ambidextrous manipulation requires a little practice to perfect.

law enforcement work. It was developed by the Los Alamitos Police Department and adapted to League shoots. Combined with the PPC (modified) and the Advanced Military, this makes a very good repertoire of contests for beginning and intermediate shooters. Too often, the novice enters graduated competition too soon and falters. But this need not be condescending to the basic shooting matches. These contests are so designed that it takes a skilled, alert shooter to keep from stubbing his toe. It is a challenge to consistently go clean in these contests.

Stage I—7 yards—6 rounds—2.5 seconds for each of three strings. Load six and holster. On cue, draw and fire two rounds at the center target of three T-8 silhouettes set one foot apart edge to edge. Reholster. On cue, draw and fire two more rounds at the righthand silhouette. Reholster. On cue, draw and fire the remaining rounds at the left hand silhouette.

Stage II—7 yards—6 rounds—5 seconds. Load six and holster. On cue, draw and fire two rounds at each of three targets.

Stage III—7 yards—6 rounds—6 seconds. Load six and holster. On cue, draw and fire two rounds at each of the three targets with the master hand only.

Stage IV—10 yards—12 rounds—18 seconds. Load six and holster. On cue, draw and fire two

An effective weak hand barricade technique is needed for shooting such courses as the PPC, PPC (modified), and the LAPM. At 25 yards or beyond, the ability to deliver accurate, controlled fire is essential to good scores. Switching hands is not as difficult as it may seem. The two-hand hold "educates" the weak hand to many master hand functions. A bit of practice and concentration on kinesthetics soon reinforces this skill so that left hand barricade shooting is nearly as accurate as master hand techniques.

rounds at each of three targets, reload, and again fire two rounds at each target using the weak hand only.

Stage V—25 yards—12 rounds—10 seconds for each of two strings. Load six and holster. Stand in the 2 by 3 foot firing area behind the 25 yard barricade. Remain covered behind the barricade until the signal to commence firing. On cue, fire two rounds at each of the three silhouettes from the right hand side of the barricade. Reload and reholster. On cue, draw and repeat the sequence from the left hand side of the barricade.

Possible score is 210-42X. Deduct five points for each violation or round fired overtime.

THE ADVANCED MILITARY COURSE

This contest embodies a well balanced set of basic combat handgunning skills at a level that challenges novices as well as skilled pistoleers. Developed by the USMC, this course of fire has been perennially scheduled for League competitions throughout the years. Mastery of the Advanced Military should be considered a prime goal of the beginning shooter. Going clean on it regularly is a challenge even to master pistoleers. It is an excellent event to keep basic skills ·conditioned and polished.

Stage I—50 yards—5 rounds—reasonable time. Load five and holster. On cue, fire five rounds at the NRA 50 yard pistol target. Most shooters assume the *prone* position. Hits in the black (8 ring or better) count 10 points. Hits in the white count 5; anything outside the 5 ring scores zip. No target spotting is allowed.

Stage II—50 yards—5 rounds—15 seconds. Load and holster. On cue, draw and fire five rounds at a league silhouette target. Any hit counts ten points. Strikes in the center 10 inch circle are Vee's.

Stage III—25 yards—10 rounds—2.5 seconds per round. Load and holster. On cue, draw and fire one round at the League silhouette. Reholster and repeat this procedure on cue for a total of 10 rounds.

Stage IV—10 yards—10 rounds—14 seconds. Load five and holster. On cue, draw and fire five rounds at the league silhouette, reload and fire five more rounds at the same target.

Stage V—10 yards—12 rounds—4 seconds each for two strings. Load six and holster. The shooter faces 90 degrees away from the center of three targets placed three yards apart (edge to edge) with the holster turned away from the targets. On cue, draw and fire two rounds at each target. Reload and reholster. Repeat the procedure on cue.

Stage VI—10 yards—8 rounds—1.5 seconds per shot. Load and holster. On cue, draw and

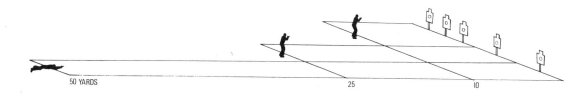

50 YARDS   25   10

This composite field layout for the Advanced Military shows positioning for shooters in all stages. Stages I and II are fired from the 50-yard line. Stage III is shot from 25 yards, while Stages IV, V, and VI are fired from 10-yards. In reality, the shooting field is not laid out as shown here. All stages are shot over the same ground, normally. Each stage must be set up after the others have been fired. The Advanced Military is one of the best all-around shooting courses for developing handgun skills.

Drawing and firing single rounds within short, prescribed times is a valuable handgunning skill. Shooters have 2.5 seconds to draw, refine a sight picture, and fire a single round at 25-yard silhouettes. This stage of the Advanced Military illustrates the fine developmental aspects of this important course of fire. It demands consistent coordination and concentration to avoid missing a target completely. Even veteran shooters can mess-up on this event if concentration lapses.

fire one round at the league silhouette. Re-holster. Repeat the procedure for a total of eight rounds.

A possible score for this event is 500 points. Ten points are subtracted for each procedural error or each overtime round.

While these courses of fire may appear simple and not overly complex, acquiring the skills for reliable performance will take time and a further description of these skills is needed.

A test of agility and fire control is provided in this stage of the Advanced Military. The shooter faces 90° away from the targets, then draws, turns, and fires on multiple silhouettes at 10 yards. Without a firm grasp of combat shooting fundamentals, the pistoleer can fall apart at this seemingly easy event. Overall performance on the Advanced Military is a good test of a shooter's development.

CHAPTER VIII

STANCES AND MOVEMENTS

COMBAT SHOOTING IS a dynamic sport, requiring complete body coordination even in what appears to be static postures. But while all body parts are involved in a combat shooting stance, economy of movement, balance, and coordination are paramount.

Achieving a steady shooting stance that allows for quick, fluid changes in position is a challenge to bodily mobility. The approach to this goal in combat shooting must be done in a free-style manner, since each individual will adapt his movements differently from others. Short, wiry statures will have freedom of movement not practical for tall, thin body structures. An attitude of awareness toward the basic problem of mobility greatly benefits development.

Regardless of individual needs, however, some basic postures will serve all shooters. One only needs to play or observe a number of sports where body mobility is a decisive factor in success. Tennis, handball, or boxing are common examples that can teach stance and movement. Tennis players need to move

rapidly on the court, then assume a return stance quickly and precisely to assure control of the swing and placement of the ball into the opponent's court. The boxer has to maintain rhythmical, coordinated lower body movements that synchronize with the upper body at split instances to deliver the punch. This upper/lower body coordination has to be cultivated for effective combat shooting mobility; it is not difficult to learn, but requires attention to detail.

ANALYSING STANCE

Quite a number of pet shooting positions are presented in the literature. All too often, these are exaggerated or stilted adaptations from static rifle position shooting. Most all positions have some merit and are recommended by shooters of recognized ability. However, few of them are free from anatomical faults or limitations that seriously hamper mobility, waste time, or interrupt the kind of free-style, common-systems approach necessary for efficient, adaptable combat shooting.

The point shooting crouch is one such position. Many handgunners gain a positive sense of body involvement from bending the knees during the draw and fire; and to this end, a slight bending of the knees is recommended. However, the deep crouch has been taught as a means of lowering the shooter's profile; a kind of defensive posture. Since point shooting is usually done at very close range, time is essential. A deep crouch takes energy and concentration that increases average time per hit. When time is a critical

Flexibility of the Weaver stance is shown in these three basic variations. B shows a top quartering view of the basic stance. Traversing the gun position from the waist (A) does not change foot placement. Pivoting by displacing one foot (C) causes a shift in target engagement with no upper body change. Combinations of these variations makes the upright Weaver stance the most versatile single shooting position in combat handgunning.

factor, the stable, boxer-stance is recommended with human focus on the motor response of drawing and firing. Any complication of this pure, straight forward posture tends to detract from the prime objective, which is to deliver a disabling first round in defensive combat.

Another example of superfluous action is the folding of the "weak" arm over the chest. This action takes concentration away from the primary goal of delivering fast, accurate rounds into the target. This measure is supposed to guard the heart in case of a hit from the adversary gun. Indeed, if the shooter is slowed down by raising the arm, the hit is more likely to occur. Also, with modern ammunition, the arm provides little if any protection. In fact, initial contact with the arm can cause early bullet expansion, making the passage through the torso all the more devastating. Again, the primary goal of short range draw and fire techniques is speed, accuracy, and reliability. Any secondary actions that distract from these objectives should be discarded. The individual shooter must become the best judge of the technique. Any specified stance, gun hold, or movement should be "tried on for size," analyzed, modified or rejected. Following rote advice dispensed by "experts" is not the way to develop combat handgunning skills.

WEAVER STANCE

Most combat handgunning is done standing up. The Weaver Stance gives the individual shooter a basic, adaptable shooting position. This stance is well balanced, promotes total body coordination, and lends itself to easy,

The standard "S" shaped police stance (top) shows how strained a position this can be; body poise is static with poor coordination of the musculoskeletal systems. Merely by moving the left foot forward and slightly shifting the center of gravity, body pose changes into the Weaver stance (bottom). Physical dynamics change completely from the former position.

fluid movements. Positioning the feet boxer-style with one foot ahead of the other makes pivoting to the right or left to engage various targets a natural, controlled movement. Pivoting on one foot while moving the other forward or rearward aligns the body without dislocating upper body readiness to shoot. Poise is not interrupted by small vector changes needed to traverse for moving targets or to engage assorted single targets. These movements are accomplished by rotating the waist, again without disturbing the two hand hold and upper body set. Combinations of waist and foot movements provide many variations that are quickly adaptable to irregular or unpredictable shooting conditions. This body mobility enhances control and shooter confidence without interruption of a consistent eye/hand relationship.

Other off-hand positions that emphasize static body placement have several disadvantages. It takes time to acquire, and additional time to leave these positions and shift into a dynamic mode. A classic example is the straddle-legged two handed hold where

Kneeling position in combat shooting demands lower body adaptation, while upper body poise remains the basic stance. Position shooting with the handgun is used mainly to adapt the body to various types of cover or gun supports. The low kneeling position shown here allows the shooter to take advantage of low cover.

the shooter faces square to the target. The back is usually crooked like an "S" in a distortion that neutralizes the main back muscles and puts a strain on the low back. Abdominal muscles are strained trying to stabilize the torso and support the cantilever of the arms. The diaphragm muscles are constricted as is rib cage expansion, so breathing is limited. This position is changed completely by shifting the left leg forward, bringing back muscles into coordination. Rotating the left shoulder forward allows the left elbow to drop, giving bridged support to the cantilevered shooting arm. Body center of gravity has a stable base. The modified position allows rapid shifts in position, reduces strain, conserves energy; it is a much more dynamic, effective offhand position.

POSITIONAL HANDGUN SHOOTING

Sitting and kneeling positions are often confused in the shooter's mind. Unlike static formal rifle target shooting which emphasizes conformity, combat handgunning is an adaptational sport. A shooting position is not taken arbitrarily, it is a means of adapting to a given firing condition. From the basic Weaver standing position, other positions are adapted to conform to the need to take advantage of available gun supports or cover. Under most conditions a shallow knee bend or a high kneeling position can adapt the lower body to accomodate low down cover and supports, while still retaining standard upper body sets. The right handed shooter will fall to the right knee, the left leg bent with the foot on the ground. The back, shoulders, and head position is the same as with the standing stance. The bridged left leg provides mobility to rise quickly and move or to shift position slightly to engage different targets.

Some pistol kneeling positions call for contact between the knee and the upper arm, with the buttocks contacting the heel. While steadiness is improved, mobility is limited to

The braced sitting position is quite steady, good for long range, deliberate shooting. Entering and leaving this position is slow, and it is not well adapted to most combat situations.

The high kneeling position is used here to fire from behind a moderately high embankment. Many courses designed for police and military programs require using available cover with appropriate position shooting.

The standard two-hand hold is used supported by the knees in the braced sitting position. This whole arrangement is quite steady for precision shooting, particularly with SA triggering.

engaging targets within a narrow vector. While this kind of position is adaptable to single-action slow fire, the prone position is better suited for that purpose. Some shooters have difficulty conforming to this particular kneeling position.

A sitting position that has received wide publicity is a kind of "Creedmoor" variation. The shooter reclines, supporting the torso with the weak hand and arm stretched out behind him. The right knee is raised to support under the gun butt. While this is fairly adaptable to single action fire in the field, it denies the advantage of body involvement and control of the two hand hold. Because it is alien to the basic upper body set it requires a new adaptation that more than likely will distract the shooter under pressure.

Low cover and support may call for sitting positions. Where the back can be supported against a wall or tree, etc., the knees can be drawn up and clamped around the hands to form a rock solid braced condition.. Where back support is not available this sitting position becomes strained and is not recommended. The upright torso and two hand control of the standing position can be maintained simply by sitting flat, folding the left leg under the right, and having the right leg bridged. Mobility out of this position is facilitated by placing the weak hand on the ground,

A good sitting position for combat shooters can be used with low cover. The right leg is bridged to allow mobility up and out of this position. Sitting flat on the ground allows upper body poise to be unaltered from the basic standing stance. Center and bottom photos show the rising technique. This position is just as easy to enter by reversing the movements shown here.

rolling the body to the left and lifting body weight on the right foot. Otherwise, sitting positions are awkward from a mobility standpoint. For the amount of support they offer they take too much time to enter and leave. Their singular recommendation is filling the few occasions when a position between prone and kneeling is required. It is seldom required but should be practiced for those few occasions when it can be indispensible.

PISTOL PRONE SHOOTING

When really precise pistol shooting is required, the prone position in several variations is the best solution. It can be said that a combat pistoleer will spend 85 percent of the time on his feet and 10 percent on his belly. A perfected prone position and knowledge of some variations is a basic requirement of a combat shooter.

The mainstay prone position is covered in detail in Chapter 6. But to recap the main features, it involves lying on the shooter's right side rather than flat on his stomach. This position facilitates normal breathing and heartbeat and eliminates back and neck strain. Bending slightly banana shaped and slightly raising the left knee relieves stress in the low back. The shooting arm is extended with the head lying on the upper arm in line with the sights. The weak hand clasps the pistol in the classic two hand hold. Even in the prone position, the same handhold is possible to maintain the continuity that assures positive uniform gun handling without mental concentration. The base provided by the two hand grip gives rock solid support to the gun with flexible positioning options. It is easy to engage targets across a wide vector from this prone position.

Another prone variation is called the "fetal" position (psychoanalysts will have a field day with this one!). By lying on his side, the shooter sandwiches the gun between the knees. Properly executed, this position is as solid as a machine rest. The orientation lays the gun on its side, so sighting compensation is necessary. In a normal upright position, the handgun sights are elevated to compensate for gravitational pull on the bullet. Normally, sights are set to center the bullet impact as regards windage. But when the gun is 90 degrees on its side, windage relates to elevation corrections, so there is no gravitational correction. Elevation settings then affect a horizontal bullet strike. It is not practical to reset sights for a temporary position. By applying hold-off and hold-over techniques to the sight picture, the necessary corrections can be made to adjust the center strike on the target. Lying on one's right side, with a gun zeroed for 50 yards, most combat loads will print about 9 inches low and 9 inches to the right of the sighting point at 50 yards. By holding on the left shoulder of a silhouette target, bullets should strike the center of the chest area. If the shooter is on his left side, hold on the right shoulder. Dimensions vary on different targets as do loads and the shooter's hold; some experimenting is called for to determine the exact amount of hold-over needed.

BARRICADE SHOOTING

Barricade shooting techniques must be mastered. Not only are these vertical structures encountered regularly in shooting matches, but the basic techniques can be applied to almost any impromptu support. Quite a variation of supported stances are touted in the literature. The barricade itself provides a paradox, since the thing must be fired *around*, it means a shift in the normal, natural balance of the standing stance. But the barricade also provides a stabilizing means for precise shot placements. Any frustrations experienced at first are soon overcome as the shooter learns to appreciate the braced positions made possible by a stable, vertical surface.

There is probably more advice given to novice shooters on how to negotiate the barricade than on any other aspect of combat

No combat shooter can be called polished until he masters the prone position. While this technique has limited applications in combat shooting, when it is used it is indispensable. The top picture shows the recommended posture; rolling on the side eliminates breathing and heart strain, neck muscle tension. A bent back and raised knee eliminates low back strain. (Lower left) the head rests on the deltoid muscle of the upper arm in line with the sights. (Center) the standard two hand hold is employed to stabilize the gun. (Lower right) the master arm and hand create a rock-solid floor; the gun shoots like it was in a machine rest. The 10-X mat provides comfort without bouncing the gun during recoil.

match shooting. Nearly everybody has a pet technique that they pass on. The fundamentals should not be forgotten here, however. Most of the favorite supports involve laying the nonshooting hand flat on the barricade only to project the thumb or fingers out to engage the wrist of the shooting hand. This technique violates the integrity of the two hand hold, so necessary to maintain continuity in *all* combat firing positions. The hands-meet-hands continuity is essential to kinesthetic feedback that is vital to precise handgun control. By violating this premise, the shooter invites a number of coordinational ills that spell lower scores when the pressure is on. Because of the inordinately long time intervals for the various stages, the PPC has been a breeding ground for many inadequate gun handling techniques. The long time factors do not sufficiently tax shooter coordination and concentration so that the inadequacies of techniques do not become apparent to individual shooters.

But how can the handgun be gripped with two hands and still find support on the vertical barricade? Simply use the thumb and bent forefinger of the supporting weak hand to press against the barricade. It just takes a bit of practice to develop the proper "feel," but the end results are rewarding. Cushioned surfaces provide adequate grounds for support of the regular two hand hold without modification. This technique rounds out a complete set of adaptations for the uniform two hand hold. For the trained pistoleer, this hold becomes completely reflexive and requires no concious effort when time pressures tax capacities.

Foot placement at the barricade requires attention. In order to brace the shooting position when firing from the right side of the barricade, the right foot is placed against the limit line and to the rear of the firing box. This action shifts the body center of gravity forward. The left leg adjusts to place enough of the body weight forward on the hands to stabilize the hold. The proper feel comes when the

position is secure, balanced, and no strain is felt on any one part of the body. Just reverse directions for shooting from the left side of the barricade. The shooter who has developed a kinesthetic awareness will find the "grove" in just a few minutes of experimenting and firing.

This same bracing technique works well for the kneeling barricade position, also. Not too many courses of fire require low level barricade shooting and this is a deficiency that needs correction in planning and designing for shooting events. For long range barricade shooting, the "fetal" position is adaptable, but requires considerable agility to squeeze into the 2 by 3 foot firing box and still meet the time requirements.

Combat shooters should conduct a warmup routine before each stage of competition in matches or in practice. Natural tension tends to tighten muscles and inhibit coordination of movement. Physical agility and mental adaptability tend to change unfavorably during long waits between stages at big matches. These seemingly small considerations can cost quite a lot of points when the competitive pressure is on. A warmup exercise works off tension, improves circulation, builds positive and competitive mental attitudes that prime the shooter for the event. Proper attention to relaxation, elimination, water intake, and nourishment are also important as a long competitive day wears down the resolve of the shooter.

Mastery of basic stances and positions builds a family of skills that will bolster confidence for unrehearsed surprise events as well as actual defensive combat. It is best always to avoid tricky, cute, or specialized solutions to shooting problems and to favor basic, uniform, adaptable techniques. Always analyze a new position in terms of the movements associated with entering and leaving the posture. Streamline and economize on movements; simple direct solutions build strength and confidence. Minimize the amount of distractions; this allows the shooter

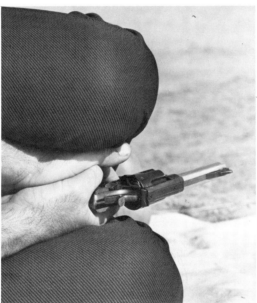
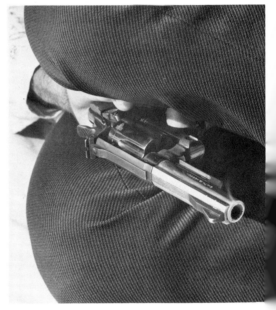

Elden Carl, one of the great all-time Combat Masters, demonstrates the "fetal" position, which h[...]
originated. On the preceding pages, the top picture shows Carl falling to the mat with his eyes alway[...]
on the target. Each succeeding step shows the sequence of changes into the final position.

The top picture on this page shows the details of this shooting position that provides the most stead[...]
gun hold of any combat posture. The fetal position can be used in close quarters where prone woul[...]
not be feasible. Lower left and right pictures show details of the knee-braced sandwich arrangemen[...]
The shooter has to allow for sight changes when the gun is on its side. Also, revolver cylinder blas[...]
can char trousers if the gun is nestled too far back between the knees.

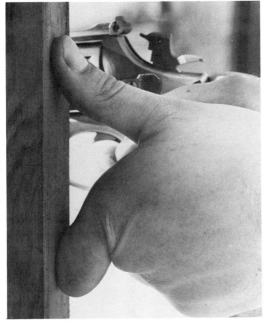

The standard two-hand hold can be maintained even when bracing the gun on a barricade. Basic grip holds should not be altered for barricade shooting, since it interrupts kinesthesis. Thumb and forefinger can be adapted to conform to the barricade surface. The gun becomes quite steady when the shooter leans into the barricade, bracing the whole position.

to concentrate on fewer variables. Applied over a period of time, such a program will pay dividends in mastery of gun handling and formidable competitive ability.

Where barricade surfaces will not irritate the backs of fingers and knuckles, the regular two-hand hold can be used by bracing the weak hand against the supporting surface.

Al Nichols, five times Southwest Pistol League Champion, demonstrates effective barricade techniques. Weight distribution and bracing are critical to achieving best results. Shooters are often "up-tight" during these stages and strain to counter imbalanced posture. Foot placement is the key to control. Left-hand barricade shooting can be done without using the weak hand as demonstrated above. This option is useful for quick transition from right hand to left side shooting. Switching to the weak hand takes considerable time on a short clock.

The standard point shooting stance provides a great deal of directional mobility; it can be acquired from nearly any upright bodily position with only minimal adaptation. Mastery of gun-handling and movements results in formidable competitive ability.

CHAPTER IX

RELOADING TECHNIQUES

COMBAT SHOOTING PLACES certain premiums on fire power, the capacity to deliver a volume of hits within a given time period. For most handguns, this means reloading the piece during the course of shooting events.

A good part of the controversy between autopistol and DA revolver proponents is the factor of reloading time. Since the autopistol can be reloaded easier and faster than a DA revolver most wheel gun boosters shut up on the subject. This is a pity. On the other hand, autopistol wags tend to be most aggressive in pressing their point and will not 'eave well enough alone. Curiously, autopistoleers nearly always compare the self-loader with its spare loaded magazines to the revolver shooter, fishing the new rounds out of his jeans. Such comparisons are ridiculous.

LOOSE ROUNDS

But to carry this whole affair to an even more outlandish score, a test was run to see how fast an autopistol could be reloaded *with loose rounds*. The proposition involved the autopistol shooting clean, followed by drop-ping the magazine into the weak hand, parking the open pistol in the waist band, removing loose rounds from a hip pocket, loading the rounds into the magazine, inserting the magazine, and then charging the gun. This process was roughly akin to employing the revolver, reloading the cylinders by hand, and closing the crane. The comparisons of time are shown below for the two methods using a Model 19 S&W revolver and a .45 ACP Government Model.

Revolver		Autopistol	
Trials	Time	Trials	Time
1	12 sec.	1	16 sec.
2	12.5	2	12.5
3	12	3	15.8
Total	36.5	Total	44.3
Mean	12.2	Mean	14.8

Trials were run with loose rounds in hip pocket. Autopistol was tucked into waistband during magazine loading. Box magazine reloading time was much more erratic, less predictable than revolver technique.

It is no more ridiculous to assume the reloading of loose rounds in an autopistol than to state the same conditions for the revolver. In more recent years the appearance of multiple loading devices has made the reloading of cylinder guns easy and quick. This ease of loading places the wheel gun on a par for practical purposes with the autoloader. The techniques vary considerably for the two guns, with the revolver requiring more manipulations and more time than the best designed self-loaders.

SPEED LOADING DA REVOLVERS

The sequence for reloading a DA revolver needs considerable practice and coordination. Starting with the gun in firing position with the two hand hold, after the last shot is fired the gun is brought to waist level. During this transition the cylinder latch is opened with the right thumb and the cylinder is swung out to the side of the frame by the middle and third fingers of the left hand as they pass through the cylinder opening in the frame. When the

crane stops open, the left thumb punches the extractor rod down as the gun muzzle tilts up; gravity helps spill the empty shells out of the chamber. At the same time, the left middle finger rotates the cylinder a few degrees to spin empties off of contact with the wood grip panel, a place where cases tend to hang-up on ejection.

Meanwhile, with the gun supported and controlled by the left hand, the right hand picks up a multi-loader from the belt pouch. The loader is raised between the thumb and the middle fingers with the forefinger lightly touching the center-rear of the loader. This technique aids kinesthesis for control in aligning the chamber openings with the bullet noses for gang reloading.

After the cylinders have been emptied, the revolver should be pointed down by the left hand so the cylinder openings are facing up. The hands guide the cylinder rotation and manipulate the loader so that a single chamber and bullet point align. Light, precise coordination is needed to deftly mate the cylinder

A

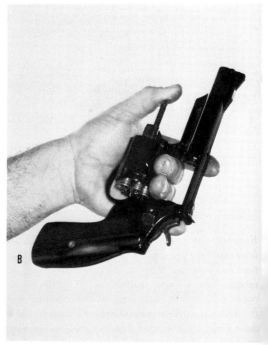

B

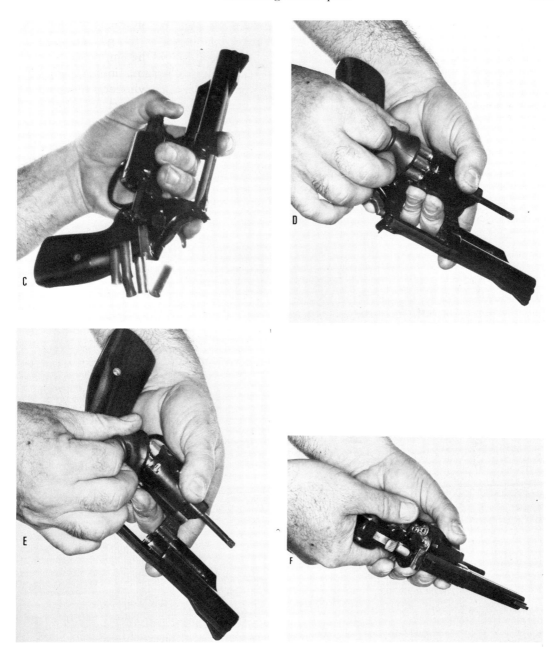

Revolver reloading procedures call for a great deal of practice and concentration. In (A) the cylinder latch is thrown with the right thumb while the crane is opened with the middle and third fingers of the weak hand. The gun is then transferred to the weak hand (B) while the thumb pushes on the ejector rod. A smart downstroke (C) dumps empty cases positively. A weak ejector stroke can leave cases partially in chambers. While ejecting is going on, the right hand retrieves a full speed loader from the gun belt and inserts it (D) into the cylinders. The loader is peeled back (E) to free the case rims. The master hand regrasps the handle, while the weak hand closes the cylinder. This process can be accomplished in about 3 to 4 seconds by a practiced shooter.

openings to the bullet noses. Once positive contact is made, the loader is pushed home with the forefinger and then thumb and forefinger peel the loader away from the shell rims when using the Kel-Lite® Multi-Loader. The right hand clasps the gun handle, the left hand closes the crane, and the gun is raised for firing.

This operation can be done perfectly in about 3 seconds by an accomplished shooter. Average times will run between 4 to 6 seconds. The biggest time waster is panic during the fitting of the new rounds into the cylinder. Anxiety over the time factor results in the big arm muscles overriding small finger muscles. The result is loss of precision finesse replaced by "Armstrong," ham-handed technique as

Bullet nose shapes can affect reloading time. From left to right are represented the poorest to the best nose shapes for reloading. Wad cutters are the most difficult to speed load. Semi-wad cutters must get all the sharp shoulders past the cylinder openings. Note that the Super Vel International Police Round shown here has the shoulders radiused slightly to ease insertion. Hollow point bullets with exposed lead tips can hang-up on cylinder openings, particularly if the cylinder edges have not been deburred. The standard round nose service bullet is reliable, but the spirepoint design on the right is the slickest of them all. Note that solid crimping folds the case mouths in so that they do not catch on chamber openings.

the shooter tries to jam the cases into the cylinder openings. This is strictly an operation for a cool head and a light touch. Practice it that way with dummy rounds and think through, analysing each step. Chamber openings have sharp corners, usually with burred edges. A very light relief of these shoulders will eliminate hang-ups of soft lead bullet noses. Round nose or preferably spire point bullet noses will load most easily. Semi-wadcutter or other blunt nosed projectiles take more control to start into the chamber openings.

TWO PRINCIPAL LOADER DESIGNS

There are two main multiple loading devices on the market for revolvers. The original Hunt Multi-Loader® is now distributed by Kel-Lite and Dade Screw Machine Products offers a molded plastic unit. The two units differ considerably in construction and operation. The Kel-Lite unit is a one piece affair molded from flexible neoprene. Cartridges are held by the rim in recessed molded lips. Rims must be fitted into recesses which are stretched to ride over and around the rim as the cartridge is rotated. Once in the recess, turning the cartridge slightly assures positive placement. The last case to enter the holder may not align with the rest. But, if the unit is placed between the hands and rolled several times, the cartridges align properly.

Upon inserting the cases in the cylinder, the Kel-Lite unit is "peeled" off the rims. This action must be accomplished with a minimum of upward movement, since there is a tendency to pull cartridges out of the chambers. A little graphite in the rim recesses will lubricate the whole process, easing both insertion and stripping of cartridges. Without lube, cartridge rims will stick badly if stored over time.

The Dade loader is molded from plastic and is a rigid, five piece assembled unit. Cartridges are held in the loader by a radial coil spring that engages case rims. Loading is

One of the first successful speed loaders was the Hunt Multi-Loader (now distributed by Kel-Lite). Molded of pliable neoprene, these loaders have many advantages over the more rigid plastic type devices. These loaders are not completely carefree, however, requiring maintenance and proper techniques to assure reliable service.

The Dade loader is quite popular for its ease of operation and reliability. Operation of this speed loader is simpler to learn than that of the neoprene device. Made with simple, rugged construction, these Dade loaders will give years of satisfactory service.

easy and direct, requiring only pressure on the bullet point to engage the rim on the retaining spring. Once the bullet noses are guided into the empty chambers, pressure on the ejector piece in the base of the loader pushes all rounds free of the retaining spring; gravity carries the fresh cartridges into the chambers. The loader then falls away as the crane is closed.

Both of these loaders do the job with some minor differences. The Kel-Lite unit provides positive seating pressure in case of a malformed reload, tight or dirty chamber. The Dade loader applies direct pressure for only a bit over half of the insertion distance, depending on gravity for the final cartridge seating. An occasional sticky round may require individual thumb pressure for full

chambering. For competition shooting, it is good to check the night before a match to see if all reloads will drop freely into the chambers.

Clearance must be provided on the left hand wood grip panel for insertion of the multiloader. If adequate clearance is not provided, binding of the device against the grip will occur. Under these conditions, a recess should be hollowed out of the grip panel that allows clearance for the loader. But the recess should not reduce the recoil shoulder width and its support of the web of the hand. This same recess serves to thin down the grip panel relative to the side plate to facilitate ejection of empty cases. Cases from inboard chambers tend to hang-up on the wood ledge, so the cylinder must be spun slightly during ejection to dislodge the cartridges.

Ejector action should be positive and accomplished in one swift stroke with the cylinders pointing down. A half-hearted push on the rod with the chambers relatively horizontal can cause an empty case to ride over the ejector star. The case rim will then be under the ejector. In this condition the ejector cannot reseat and there is no ready means of removing the stuck case, especially if it has a tight fit in the chamber. The cylinder

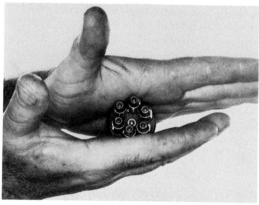

Fresh rounds are fitted into the Multi-Loader by stretching the molded rim receptacles as shown above. After the last round is inserted, all rounds are aligned by rolling the loader between the palms of the hands. While the one-piece neoprene loaders are more complicated to charge and release rounds, their pliability is an aid in manipulation during the loading process. Use of the Multi-Loader or the rigid Dade design is a matter of personal choice.

can not be reloaded until the ejector seats, so the gun is out of action. This is one of the most serious stoppages that can happen to a revolver during reloading. It can be completely eliminated with good ejector techniques.

CHAMBER DIMENSIONS

Modern manufacturing methods being what they are, cylinder diameters on revolvers are sometimes too large to allow reliable ejection of reloaded brass cases. As chambering reamers wear, the chamber opening gets smaller in diameter. So, one economy in tooling expense can be realized by making the reamer cut on the large side of chamber dimension tolerances. Such a large reamer will cut many more chambers before it has to be discarded for being too small in diameter. As a practical matter, Smith & Wesson revolvers are most likely to have large chamber openings, but that doesn't mean that other makes will never have large chambers.

The Smith & Wesson policy has been to maintain chamber tolerances that will eject factory fresh cases. The first firing of brass has considerable springback, so as the case walls are forced out by chamber pressure, they shrink back enough to clear the chamber and eject properly. However, after resizing and firing again as a reload, the brass is not so resilient and tends to form to chamber walls if it expands beyond its elastic limit. This situation plays hob with the reliable ejection of reloads. On full-sized .38 caliber revolvers, the ejection rod throw is sufficient to retract .38 Special cases fully from the chamber. However, an insufficient ejector rod stroke may leave cases stranded in the chambers. But the problem becomes especially acute on snubnosed revolvers where the ejection rod action is not as long as the cartridge case.

One way around this problem is to check the diameter of chambers with a small-hole gage. The largest diameter chamber (.38 Special/.357 Magnum) that has consistently ejected reloaded empties in the author's ex-

 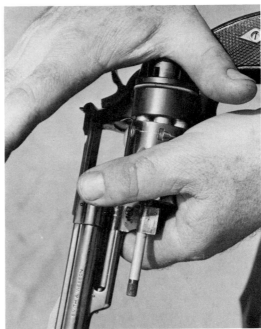

Stripping of the Multi-Loader is tricky. Dry powdered graphite lube in the rim recesses is an aid to reliable operation. Peeling action must be made across the cylinder face to avoid pulling rounds out of the chambers. The direct injection of rounds from the Dade loader (right) is quick and easy. Rigid loaders do not have the "feel" of pliable units, but they do have other virtues.

perience has been .3830-inch (front of chamber) and .3852-inch (chamber opening). Anything larger than this dimension has tended to fail to reliably eject fired cases. The chamber diameter determines the amount of cold working of the brass not only in the chamber expansion but during resizing in the loading press. Big chambers are hard on brass, shortening service life. Moderate chamber diameters of .3834-inch have worked well in another S&W revolver, providing consistent, reliable ejection and with no unsightly bulges near the base. Heavy .357 Magnum loads especially need tight chambers for good case life and ejection. The following specimen dimensions will serve for comparison. Remember that chamber diameter is all a matter of how big the reamer was at the time the chamber was finished. These dimensions vary throughout the production process and their limits are dependent on the

This case rim stuck under the ejector star is the most serious reloading problem with the revolver; it puts the gun out of operation. Vigorous ejection techniques will eliminate this happening which is easier to prevent than cure.

design and QC specifications of the particular manufacturer.

| | Random Chamber Diameters | |
Front	Make	Rear
.3823-inch	Model 66 S&W	.3840-inch
.3830	Model 19 S&W	.3852
.3817	Model 19 S&W	.3834
.3798	Colt Python	.3823
.3796	Detective Special	.3822
.3806	Ruger Security Six	.3827
.3794	Dan Wesson M15	.3810
.3802	High Standard MK III	.3816

Other types of multi-loaders organize the cartridges in strips for ease of handling and proper orientation of the bullets. The Bianchi Speed Strip® is well known and provides a simple, inexpensive device that is compatible with a good many standard belt cartridge boxes. Strip reloaders are much less bulky than the round multi-loader. Reloading time

The Bianchi Speed Strip is not as fast as other cylindrical speed loaders, but it has a good many virtues of its own. It organizes fresh rounds in a compact package for easy carrying. Two-at-a-time loading techniques take only a few seconds longer than the more rapid speed loaders.

is not as fast for the strip configuration, but with practice, chambers can be loaded two at a time on most revolvers. The strippers are about twice as fast as loading loose rounds by hand, and take about double the recharging time of multi-loaders. While they are not recommended for competitive shooting, the strip-type loaders are most useful for home defense, in the field, and for off-duty police where ammunition needs to be carried conveniently as a single unit organized for quick reloading.

AUTOPISTOL ROUTINES

Efficient reloading of the autopistol demands a set of coordinations wholly different from recharging a revolver. We will assume the use of the Colt Government Model or its many variations and imitations. These guns have a particular design of magazine release and grip configuration that facilitates easy reloading. Autopistols having the butt-type magazine catch require both hands to release and extract the empty magazine, eliminating the whole advantage of Government Model speed and convenience.

In combat shooting, strings of six rounds are the usual maximum. The .45 ACP shooter loads seven rounds and never shoots clean; that is, he always leaves one round in the chamber while reloading. Notice that for speed, this procedure differs from the military practice where the slide stop holds the action open after the last round is fired. By shifting the master hand around so the thumb presses the magazine catch, the empty magazine can be dropped to the ground by gravity. The magazine catch engagement on each magazine should be adjusted so there is about 1/32-inch of vertical free play when the magazine is locked in place. A tight fitting magazine has no advantage and it could fail to seat properly. Never file the magazine catch itself, only polish its contact surfaces if burrs or tool marks are present. The upper ledge of the magazine catch slot on the leading edge of the maga-

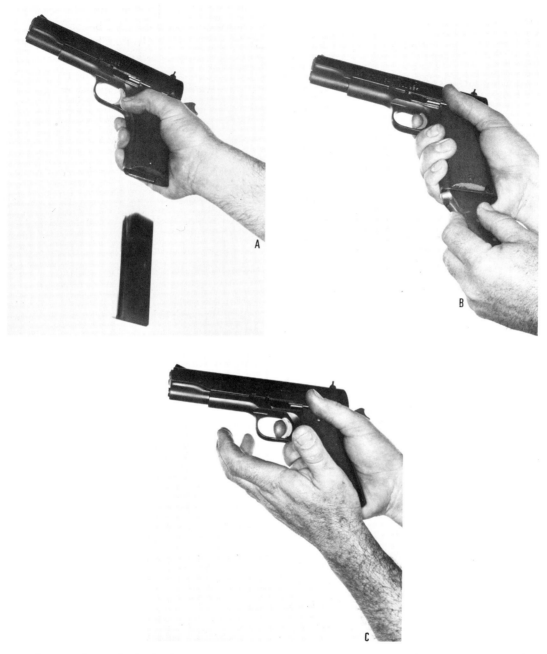

Simplicity and speed of reloading recommend the Colt Government Model as a premier combat handgun. The push-button magazine release is operated by the master hand (A), allowing the weak hand to retrieve a spare loaded magazine from the belt pouch. Insertion of the new magazine is done by placing it spine first (B) into the chamfered magazine well, then straightening it out before running home. This technique avoids disturbing the top round in the feed lips. Fingers part and the heel of the weak hand drives the magazine home (C), assuring that it engages the catch. This whole operation can be accomplished in one second by a trained shooter.

zine can be dressed with a fine cut warding file to adjust the height of engagement. A little filing goes a long way. If the magazines are allowed to hang down too far, it can cause feeding problems (short rounds) as bullet noses strike too low on the feed ramp.

While the released empty magazine is dropping, the weak hand is reaching for the loaded spare in the belt pouch. The master hand rotates 45° to the right to expose the opening in the butt. Magazines should be arranged in the belt pouch so bullets face forward as the left hand grasps the box. Magazines should not be jammed deep into the pouch pocket so the hand can grasp them approximately half way up from the floor plate; the nearer the finger tips are to the feed lips of the magazine, the easier and more accurately the box can be guided into the magazine well. Practice grasping the magazine with the little and third fingers so the forefinger and thumb are near

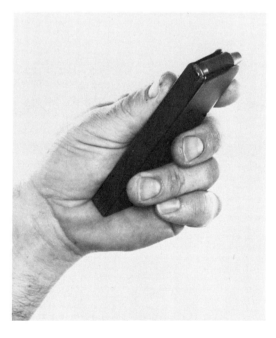

The weak hand must grasp the magazine with third and little fingers, the floorplate against the palm. This arrangement will place the thumb and forefinger close to the feed lips for accurate insertion into the magazine well.

the top of the magazine as it is withdrawn.

The kinesthesis of autopistol reloading is natural. Hands-find-hands easily, especially after shooting experience with the two-hand hold. The magazine is introduced into the butt and with a single fluid motion, fingers part while the heel of the hand slams the magazine home. Chamfering the inside edges of the magazine well opening makes for reliable insertion.

The master hand wrist rotates the gun upright, the weak hand clasps in the two-hand-hold, and the autopistol is ready to continue firing. This whole sequence can be accomplished in one second by a polished pistoleer. Loading the revolver on the same basis takes about 3 seconds. While this is a significant time difference, it tends to be magnified by autopistol boosters as a decisive edge. In reality, the time differences in a close gun fight are not likely to be decisive; if a shooter has not dispatched his adversary in an open fight within the first six rounds he is in trouble regardless of what handgun he has. To reload behind adequate cover within 3 seconds is acceptable for safety in a continuing gun battle.

The real weakness to revolver reloading is in the many separate steps and critical coordinations needed to negotiate the routine. Because autopistol loading routines are so simple, trained shooters tend to be consistent in *average* reloading times. In those very rare instances where a host of adversaries are presented, the real advantage would go to large capacity autopistols, whose magazines hold up to 15 rounds (Browning Hi-Power, Model 59 S&W, MAB, etc.) that would require no magazine change. But again, unless the shooter can gain adequate cover, it is dubious if the extra rounds will do him any good. Also, large capacity means the shooter can lose track of how many rounds are left in the gun. It could be mighty embarrasing to be firing exposed in the middle of what is thought to be a four round string and have the slide stop engage after the second shot.

People who try to rationalize clear cut advantages for given handguns on the basis of reloadability and fire power alone will have to erect straw men to make the case stick!

MAGAZINE PROBLEMS

Little is said about the vulnerability of the autopistol to damaged or malfunctioning magazines. Dropping a magazine in the dark or on a hard surface or into loose, sandy soil can put the autoloader out of business. Magazines that are jettisoned into loose, sandy soil during the reloading phase should be thoroughly cleaned in solvent to cleanse them of grit that can contaminate ammunition, cause feeding stoppages, or find its way into the gun mecanism. Feed lips should be inspected frequently for cracks, burrs, or indentations that will cause feeding stoppages. Faulty magazines should be discarded or relegated to practice use. A set of tested magazines should be set aside for tournament firing. These magazines should have impeccable performance records and should be reserved for use where maximum reliability is needed. Having these magazines chrome plated will facilitate maintenance and aid reliable feeding.

For best results, loading one round less than maximum into a magazine (six rounds maximum into .45 ACP magazines and seven or eight into 9mm magazines) is recommended. The overloaded magazine compresses the spring and can lead to the weakening of this vital element over time. Also, the first round out of a tightly loaded magazine can tip up on the feed ramp and stem into the chamber roof. When extra magazine space is needed (the first magazine for a standard ACP string needs 7 rounds) pick a magazine that has proved to be reliable with the full capacity. Never take magazines for granted. Most all common feeding ills in autopistols are traceable to this most sensitive element of the system.

CHAPTER X

DRAWING AND FIRING

P ROBABLY NO OTHER activity distinguishes combat handgunning from formal target shooting more than drawing and firing from the holster. The defensive role of the handgun and its compact size dictates that it will be (1) carried on the person, and (2) that it must be carried in a way so as to be easily accessible for use.

Holsters and other related equipment have undergone a lot of development just in the past few decades, with many of the most effective ideas now standardized into commercial products. While much emphasis is placed on individual designs, there are some basic principles that have influenced the broad use of particular holster rigs. We find these most effective ideas recurring in cycles throughout the years, as designers rethink older equipment, improving on it with new technology.

The gun leather business has boomed in the past decade with the expanded interest in handgun shooting. A variety of product lines are available. One of the best known companies is Bianchi Leather Products. Bi-

anchi has been a leader in designing, manufacturing and marketing a broad variety of quality holsters. Bianchi's impact on the industry has opened many competitive lines and this has improved the variety and utility of holsters and shooting rigs.

In the past, drawing and firing was associated chiefly with western gun duels, and the exhibition antics of Tom Mix, Hopalong Cassidy, and the like. Serious police work came to public notice in the 1930's with practical emphasis of shooting courses designed to train FBI agents. The U.S. Border Patrol also placed premiums on the fast draw as an integral part of handgun training. The purpose is to place the gun in the shooting hand quickly and securely, not merely to out-draw an opponent in "High Noon" style.

Sport shooting of fast draw handguns saw equipment designs such as those of Berns-Martin (currently owned by Bianchi) and Chick Gaylord that incorporated ideas gained from applied experience. Holsters patterned after standardized equipment for law enforcement agencies appeared; the FBI tilted scabbard, the Jordan River holster and belt rigs are examples. John Bianchi later applied pistol packing technology to a host of designs for nearly every conceivable application. Not all of these specialty holsters are applicable for tournament use in combat shooting, however.

GUN LEATHER

A holster design must incorporate certain compromises between function, safety, and applied use. For combat tournament shooting, functional principles and safety considerations resulted in distinct configurations with several variations. Characteristics of the usual combat rigs include forward rake angle on the holster. While a rake can be a garden implement or a person of dissolute character, in the holster business it refers to the angle of the center line relative to vertical when the holster is strapped on the shooter. Rakes can be forward, where the bottom of the holster points forward, or it can have a back rake where the muzzle tilts to the rear. Both configurations have functional reasons for their design.

Back rake design was made famous by the first FBI holsters. By carrying the gun close to the body and high on the hip for concealment, the gun muzzle had to be tilted rearward to allow for a quick draw. A vertical holster mounted high on a pants belt would cause an exaggerated, time wasting movement to draw even a moderately long 3 to 4 inch barrel gun. The back rake holster requires that the wrist be cocked off-center in order to grasp the gun handle. Before the gun fires, the wrist has to be straightened, complicating the movement and giving rise to poor kinesthetic wrist "feel." This distortion reduces wrist and hand strength and affects the accuracy or

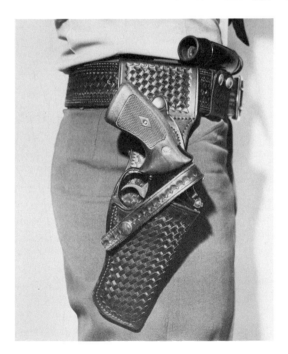 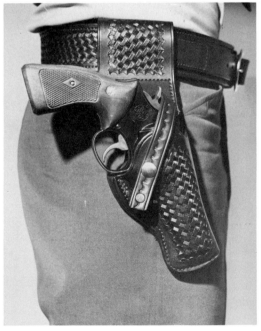

The back rake holster (left) has several disadvantages as a duty or combat shooting rig. It requires wrist distortion to grasp the gun handle and the muzzle crosses the body plane during the draw. Forward rake designs (right) are required in combat competition and provide advantages in safety and ease of training for new shooters.

speed of the first shot for the average shooter. This is probably not too big a price to pay for a concealed holster when it is needed; however, it is not optimal in a duty or match holster rig.

POLICE DUTY RIGS

The high ride, close fitting feature for holsters has been popular in recent years with police departments. To carry the handgun high and vertically without exaggerating the drawing movement, the front opening configuration has appeared. Adapted by Bianchi from older Berns-Martin and Hoyt original designs, this holster has many favorable applications for the duty officer. It still requires some wrist distortion to draw the gun and the muzzle will cross the body plane on its way out of the holster. The covered trigger guard will also slow the critical hand-to-gun union for the most effective speed and/or accuracy of the first shot. Safety considerations dominate design of a police rig. About 1 in 5 officers who are shot are done-in with their own guns grabbed by an assailant. The Break-Front® design is one of the safest rigs from this standpoint even though it is not optional for drawing and firing, nor is it acceptable for combat match shooting as a serviceable holster.

Carrying the gun vertically requires the conventional holster to extend downward below belt level in order to allow easy arm movement during the draw. For the duty officer, this means an uncomfortable rig when riding in a radio car or jockeying a desk. The swivel device was designed to overcome this feature, allowing the holster to conform to the seat. This swivel holster surely illustrates the fact that popularity is a poor measure of efficiency. With the almost universal acceptance of this design over the past decades, the patrolman who wears it runs several risks. Without the holster snapped down, there is no consistent reference to where the gun handle will be when it has to be drawn. Also, by unsnapping the safety

strap and not resnapping the swivel, getting out of a radio car can dump the service revolver in the street. The holster is flipped by the armrest bolster, seat, door edge, or steering wheel. Again, the front opening holster design has overcome these bad features of the swivel rig.

Bianchi has recently introduced another front opening design (Model 2800) called "The Judge.®" Improved from a 1931 Hoyt design, this holster has no closed bottom as is usual on most other front opening configurations. Instead, a special spring design keeps the two halves of the holster closed "clamlike." The revolver is stabilized in the holster by Bianchi patented cylinder recesses. A thumb snap safety strap is provided for speed. Initial spring tension and the slight back rake of the holster tend to reduce overall speed and convenience of the draw for combat work. However, this rig is especially well designed for police duty use or field carrying.

FORWARD RAKE RIGS

Back in the early 1950's, live bullet western quick draw competition became quite popular, especially on the west coast. Many rigs of that day were adaptations of Buscadero outfits made famous in western movies. Stylized western costumes were part of the pagentry of fast draw events also.

Lowering the gun handle to improve the fast draw was first done by western gunfighters when they wore pistol belts diagonally across the pelvis. Other gunfighters attached holsters to long belt loop extensions to allow the gun to dangle down near the knee. A tiedown leather thong stabilized the holster against the leg. These same kinds of rigs were used by quick draw competitors in the early 1950's. Just as a few drunken or over anxious cowboys fired 250 grain .45 Colt slugs into their legs or feet, so did the latter day fast draw pistoleros. The self-inflicted wound syndrome started to have an ill effect on the reputation of the sport. A few holster makers

and prudent contestants decided the answer to the hazard was to cant the holster forward. Some of these first rigs placed the muzzle 30 to 40 degrees forward of vertical. This design eliminated the almost certain possibility of self-inflicted wounds. Even the best shooters will occasionally go spastic, shooting out a holster bottom during a maximum effort against the clock.

A special bonus accrued to the users of this new "safety" holster; they started winning all the quick draw events. The change over was rapid, and forward rake configurations have become a permanent feature of standard combat rigs. The advantage in speed and accuracy from the forward rake is due to the wrist set. The hand closes naturally around the gun handle with little bending of the wrist. Gun handle placement is such that the normal withdrawal action leaves the muzzle pointed

Bianchi's new Model 2800 ("The Judge") is a front-opening design ideally suited to police duty. The gun is carried high for seated comfort and easy grasp. The gun cannot be commandeered easily by a suspect. A flick of the thumb release and the curling of grasping fingers (center) carry the gun forward out of the spring-loaded front opening. Final clearance releases the gun to be elevated for shooting. While not as fast as forward rake holsters for combat shooting, this rig is a "natural" police duty holster.

Triple-K's forward rake duty holster offers safety and simplicity for the draw and fire. A fine rig for combat shooters, it has many design features originated by Combat Master Elden Carl and tested by other combat shooters. This is one of the few forward rake combat rigs currently available as production items.

forward toward the target as the gun clears leather. For safety, the muzzle never crosses the plane of the body during the draw and, while in the holster, the gun points at the ground several inches in front of the toes. The draw is natural, easy to learn; it is accomplished in one fluid motion and requires a minimum of body adaptation in the process.

Combat holsters do not use the exaggerated 30 degree rake of the quick-draw rigs. The standard 15 degree rake that is used in most of todays holsters makes it suitable as a service rig. Indeed, Triple K Manufacturing Company makes a forward rake holster that serves well for combat shooting. The holster was designed by Elden Carl, a San Diego County peace officer, who won the Senior Combat Quickdraw (Leatherslap) at Big Bear, California three years in a row (1960, 1961, 1962) with this duty holster design.

Two San Diego County Sheriff's Deputies warm up before testing the speed of forward rake holsters. At the time, Deputies Walker (left) and Sanders were in the Police Academy undergoing small arms training.

EFFICIENCY OF FORWARD RAKE

Further proof of the effectiveness of forward rake holsters was demonstrated in a test conducted with four Sheriff's Academy cadets. These relatively inexperienced shooters had no previous quickdraw schooling. They were given wax ammunition and a few minutes to practice drawing techniques before trial times were taken. The deputies were using their issue back rake swivel holsters as the control item, while a Triple K forward rake rig was used for comparison. Both holsters were used unstrapped so as to test configuration effectiveness only. A Fasdraw® electromechanical timer was set up with the control box not less than 4 inches away from the gun handle. The shooter places his hand on the switch; when the hand leaves the switch the clock starts. The gun is drawn and fired and the report excites a microphone that stops the clock. Each revolution of the sweep second hand on the clock takes one second and there are 100 intervals on the dial. The clock is accurate to plus or minus .01-second.

Each shooter was timed on three trials; the times were totaled and the grand total for all four shooters was averaged to determine the composite performance for both kinds of holsters.

Deputy Bird recorded the fastest time during the test of forward rake holsters. Shown here is a .24-second draw out of the holster. Bird is a strong, well-coordinated shooter with many natural gun handling skills.

HOLSTER TRIALS

DEPUTY	FORWARD RAKE				BACK RAKE			
	1	2	3	Total	1	2	3	Total
A	.33	.27	.24	.84	.66	.54	.41	1.61
B	.43	.47	.39	1.29	.53	.53	.50	1.56
C	.62	.49	.41	1.52	.55	.68	.55	1.78
D	.67	.48	.54	1.69	.71	.48	.65	1.84
	Totals			5.34				6.79
	Average			.45°				.57

°21% time improvement for the forward rake holster.

The results speak for themselves. A 21 percent increase in time performance illustrates the effectiveness of forward rake design. All this comes with the added safety feature inherent with the forward rake. Many police departments forego draw and fire training because of the danger of injury. By issuing forward rake holsters this danger virtually is eliminated. Combat league shooting requires the forward rake design.

DESIGN QUALITY

Quality combat holsters have metal shanks and/or liners used in their construction. Sheet metal shanks conform the holster to position the gun consistently on the belt without a tie-down thong. The master hand finds the gun handle kinesthetically. The shanks are bent to conform to the hip line, eliminating the press and bulk against the body. This also positions the gun handle away from clothing and eliminates the need for a tie-down thong

Combat rigs require certain design features to assure reliable, fast, and safe operation. Forward rake design (left) tilts the gun muzzle forward, setting the gun handle at a natural angle for the grasping hand and wrists. No leather is placed behind the handle to intercept with curling fingers. The welt of the holster and proper wet fitting cambers the handle away from the body (center). A steel shank conforms the holster to the hip, eliminating the need for a tie-down and tilts the gun away from the waist (right).

to keep the holster from riding up when the gun is drawn, although some shooters use the thong as a precaution anyway. Good holsters use leather wedges to camber the handle away from the body. Shape of the holster should fit the gun snugly. But the gun should release at the time of the draw without any drag. A bit of graphite dusted on the touch-spots inside the holster smooths the release.

An all leather holster can be made to conform to individual guns by soaking the leather in water until soft, then forming it around the gun. When dried, the exact shape of the gun will be impressed on the holster interior. Be sure to spray the gun with preservative oil (WD-40®) and wrap a thin plastic bag around the gun before fitting it into the wet holster. The gun stays in the holster until the leather is dry. Do not force-dry the holster as this process can remove oils that eventually makes the leather crack. A quality leather dressing will renew the luster and finish. Do not use oil base dressings since they will tend to soften the leather.

There should be no holster leather behind the gun handle for the fingers to contact dur-

ing the draw. Safety straps, if used, should be of the removable type or thumb release de-

Soaking a holster in cold water makes it pliable. The gun is sprayed with WD-40 and placed in a heavy duty plastic bag. Inserting the gun in the holster, then form fitting with finger pressure produces an excellent fit. Air dry the rig. Single-ply holsters work best with this technique. This Triple-K Model 149 makes an excellent small frame holster.

One of the finest leather rigs available is this Andy Anderson "Corso" set, which is named after the League shooter who first ordered this high-ride combination. The gun handle is at a natural position for the fast draw. The low-cut holster front aids in clearing the leather. The rig is fully serviceable for field use.

For duty rigs, the thumb snap strap produces a safe carrying rig that releases as part of the natural motion of drawing the gun. Virtually all combat rigs come with removable straps; most combat matches are fired with holsters unstrapped.

sign. Most combat rigs use removable straps so the gun can be carried securely strapped in the field, but left free for drawing during matches. Police duty holsters using a variation of the thumb snap release are fast and secure. This safety strap can be released with the natural movement of the thumb as it grasps the gun for the draw. All straps will slow down the speed of the draw, but the thumb snap design requires the simplest, least distracting technique.

COMBAT RIGS

A number of specialty rigs are available for the combat shooter. Andy Anderson is considered by many combat pistoleers as the Dean of holster makers. Andy was one of the first makers to standardize the forward rake design. His uncompromising quality in design

and fabrication are hallmarks of his work and standards for excellence in the trade. He has adapted the forward rake to the high belt position that can be used in the field or for combat shooting. This version is called the Corso rig, after the League shooter, Tom Corso, who first ordered it. The low front of the holster allows early clearance of the leather without an exaggerated arm movement. At the same time, the rig is fully serviceable, not being a hybrid specialty like the open front combat rigs. This high belt, front rake configuration has possibilities for use as a duty rig for police, combining the advantages of forward rake design with close in, unobtrusive image. Both Bianchi and Triple-K offer commercial off-the-shelf rigs that are quite adequate for combat shooting. Custom leather may take up to a year for delivery and cost nearly $100. For half that price, Bianchi offers the Model 47 "Pistolero" rig that provides a first-class holster, belt, and magazine pouch for the .45 ACP. Triple K's Forward Rake rigs are less expensive and offer quite a good value. They are made for both the revolver and the autopistol. A number of detail options are available for shooters who want individual features or combinations.

OPEN FRONT HOLSTERS

The open front holster has been a standard specialty rig for nearly a decade in the combat shooting circuits. These rigs should not be confused with front opening type duty holsters mentioned earlier. Considerable contro-

versy exists within shooting circles regarding open front desirability. Designed essentially to produce speed, the rig is not serviceable, being little more than a channel to support the gun. Normal body movements will drop the gun to the ground unless it is strapped securely. Most makers offer an optional snap-on front panel to enclose the gun. The advantage for open front design during quick draw events is obvious. Since no retracting motion is required to put the handgun into action, the shooter merely grasps the gun handle and raises the piece to fire. It is difficult to beat this design for quickdraw competition (i.e. the Leatherslap), so contestants tend to buy this rig and use it for all events. So many competitors have open front holsters, that it is hard to get a rule change adopted that would outlaw its use in league competitions. Most all shooters agree that its use is unrealistic, however.

CROSS DRAW DESIGNS

The 15 degree forward rake high-belt holsters are adaptable to cross draw, also.

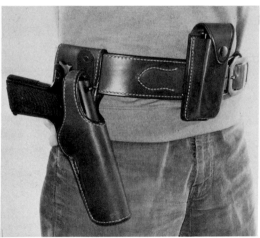

These two leather rigs are available off the shelf for combat shooters. Triple K offers the Model 5 Forward Rake Revolver Rig shown here. Bianchi has the Model 46 "Pistolero" set. These are both serviceable rigs, capable of fulfilling the needs of most combat shooters.

This open-front Anderson rig has seen many seasons of competition. This style of holster is seen universally in League shooting due to its great speed advantage in the Leather-slap. These rigs are highly specialized and are not generally serviceable off of the combat shooting field.

This feature makes an attractive option for field carrying of a hand gun as well as for use in certain competitive events. Where competition requires a great deal of body movement, particularly pivoting movements, the cross-draw is quite desirable. The running crouch position used in the military for advancing under fire also favors the cross draw motion. The Mexican defense course requires a 180 degree turn at the time of the draw. By wheeling to the left the gun is picked up on the way around and is in shooting position pointing

Triple-K makes a standard belt sheath for both autopistols (shown here) and revolvers and has a 15° forward rake. The holsters are convertible in that they may be worn for a regular draw or as a cross draw. This configuration is very good for use in the Mexican Defense, where cross draw holsters have some distinct advantages. These holsters are completely serviceable in the field, also.

downrange. The 15 degree rake places the handle at a natural angle to the hand and wrist. Cross draw holsters that hold the gun vertically will require wrist distortion during the draw. Triple K Manufacturing Company makes a unique convertible holster configuration. Mounted at 15° forward rake, these holsters can be worn in a high-hold standard position or as a cross draw combat rig. Variations are made for autopistols or revolvers. These items position naturally on the gun belt and offer fully effective holsters for combat or field use.

Many police departments shun cross draw holsters for duty officers, because of the danger of the service revolver being grabbed by a suspect in a close confrontation. For plain clothes officers, the cross draw offers the advantage of concealment without having to displace the suit coat to reach the gun. Bianchi offers a complete line of cross draw holsters for all sizes and types of handguns. Triple K has a sheath (Model 149) for short barrel revolvers that can be used convertible as a highbelt forward rake or a crossdraw, or it is available as a back rake FBI type belt holster. Good cross draw holsters do not require safety straps for small to medium sized guns. Bianchi's cross draws feature a spring loaded edge opening while Triple K's Model 149 is molded to conform the unlined sheath to the revolvers recoil shields.

SHOULDER HOLSTERS

Shoulder holsters provide a means of carrying a variety of sizes and types of handguns in a convenient, concealable manner. The close-in position of the gun is useful for field applications, also where the gun is not left open to snag on underbrush or to interrupt body movements. Plain clothes police officers have long favored shoulder holsters for their convenience and unobtrusive gun placement under clothing. Quite a large gun can be concealed in a good shoulder holster without creating a telltale bulge.

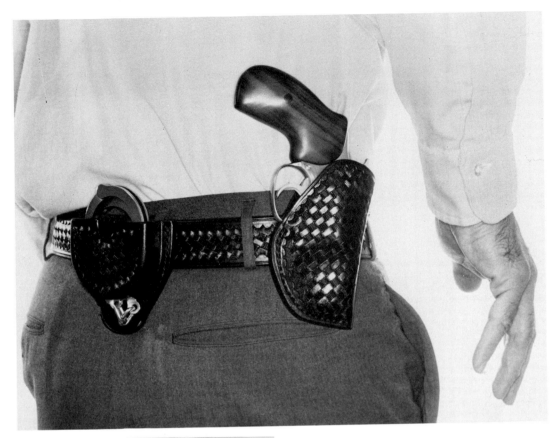

But the use of shoulder rigs for combat matches is not recommended. DA revolvers or DA autopistols have a built-in safety factor that makes them better candidates for the shoulder holster rig. One well known combat pistoleer and .45 ACP proponent very nearly shot himself through the left *gluteus maximus* during a match, while drawing Old Slab Sides cocked and locked from a shoulder holster.

For small to medium sized handguns, the "upside down" or armpit shoulder holster has become very popular. The upside down placement put the gun handle at an awkward angle so wrist position is unnatural at the

Short barrel guns need special leather. Triple-K's Model 149 sheath is especially well-adapted for small frame guns or short K-frame revolvers. The Bianchi Cross Draw is a classic, one of the trimmest holsters made for small frame guns.

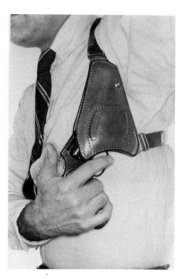

Bianchi has one of the biggest selections of shoulder holsters, many of original design that have been copied throughout the industry. The X-15 (left) is one of the most versatile, being made for just about every handgun. The new, improved 9R is a unique blend of features, one of the most efficient shoulder rigs made. It has an unsurpassed release action.

time of the draw. It is usual with this configuration to have the gun held in the holster by spring or elastic tension, with the trigger guard hooked over a ledge at the mouth of the holster. This feature has tended to limit the use of this holster design to revolvers and has limited the size or use of grips with filler blocks that will not allow the guard to seat under the retaining ledge. Recently, Bianchi has improved their 9R model. The new 9R eliminates the trigger guard ledge and offers a more accessible handle angle. The gun is securely held by cylinder recesses and a positive spring on the opening side of the holster. The design combines handgun accessibility with safety; it is virtually impossible for the gun to fall out of the holster without deliberately pulling it out. This new rig can be removed from the shoulder harness and used as a belt holster; it is slotted for left hand or right hand belt use. Small ears on the spring opening shroud the hammer spur, protecting clothing. This is easily the most functional revolver shoulder holster available.

TECHNIQUES FOR DRAW AND FIRE

Reaction times must be carefully tailored for effective draw and fire techniques. While getting out of the holster quickly is important, it is equally important to have a uniform and secure grip on the handgun, and to hit the target. Here, the shooter applies SOR (stimilus-organism-response) theory. Having to discriminate a cue from among conflicting stimuli is not as simple as it sounds. An overly anxious shooter can jump the start signal; the overly careful shooter can take too long to recognize the cue. One difficulty with some shooting drills is that the same stimulus is used all the time (usually a whistle). Changes in stimulus or multiple stimuli and variable time lags after the warning signal make a good matrix for teaching shooters to identify and discriminate from among different kinds of cues.

Audio signals are used most often in combat matches and tend to gain the quickest responses from contestants. In realistic combat scenes, however, movement tends to be as important a cue as noise. Training courses that incorporate audio recordings of sound stimuli can be coupled with target movement to sharpen sensory discrimination.

Good physical tone and proper health habits (diet, sleep, exercise) will optimize the organism's capacity to transmit and assimilate sensory and motor information. Motor responses themselves improve with conditioning and reinforcement of simple, direct movements. The most economical movements tend to be those that can be repeated without error, overexertion, or conscious effort.

The shooter can train to trigger reactions so they closely coincide with stimulus reaction. The shooter will minimize elapsed time by concentrating the mental set on the response. By thinking about the response while listening for the start cue, the shooter can mobilize body reactions much quicker. The concentration necessary for this technique can be conditioned to follow the ready signal. It should blot out all other conscious thought and preferably modulate subconscious involvement for the brief instant. Focusing on the reaction phase of SOR comes after stimulus recognition techniques are mastered. In summary, then, the shooter must put together the following set of prerequisites in order to master the draw and fire:

1. Acquire and condition an adequate leather rig (preferably forward rake type).

2. Master the hand grip on the initial grasp.
3. Gain the ability to discriminate stimuli without conscious or intellectual effort.
4. Learn to "think response" and concentrate on motion economy.
5. Master pointing and aiming techniques and a flawless trigger control.

Training for the quick draw can be conducted using wax bullets and primer loads. Using a timer to measure the draw is a great help in creating incentives for improvement. Techniques of shooting style and practice will improve the shooter's effectiveness, and a timer shows this improvement objectively. Avoid overemphasis on competitiveness between novice shooters, since the timer tends to inhibit many marksmen who do not do well at first. Other beginners may strain for short clock times rather than to learn the fundamentals that will improve performance naturally. A plywood silhouette target with an impact microphone on the back will stop the clock when the wax bullets strike. This arrangement makes hitting an integral part of the draw and fire, since the clock will not stop until a hit is registered. The learner then has to adapt to the eternal compromise between speed and accuracy.

Once the shooter is skilled in the fundamentals there are more advanced challenges to combat shooting. Advanced courses of fire will lead toward mastery of combat handgunning.

Combat Pistol Champion Leonard Knight demonstrates the high point position from the holster. This is a quick, positive technique, quite accurate out to 25 yards. Gun-to-target alignment is possible without taking a critical sight picture. Most competitors are now using this high point position routinely; it is only slightly slower than the standard single hand point.

A well-coordinated draw and fire technique is an essential skill for combat shooting. Compromises must be made by individual shooters between speed and accuracy. Hitting consistently well builds confidence and poise, provides a behavioral base for further development.

CHAPTER XI

ADVANCED COURSES OF FIRE

ADVANCED SHOOTING COURSES can be misleading by name. As in all sports, the advanced stages are built on the mastery of fundamentals. The ability to function flawlessly in terms of gun handling and movement means that attention can be given to increasing scores and shortening performance times. What separates more difficult courses of fire from basic courses is the number of distractions and the level of applied skills that are involved.

Among the most important skills in combat handgunning are the abilities to (1) deliver fast, accurate fire; (2) to move during the time of firing, still maintaining accuracy and control; and (3) to respond quickly and effectively to random stimuli. There are three standard courses of fire that provide one or more of these challenges to the shooter. The International Rapid Fire, the Mexican Defense, and the FBI Duel provide a trio of events tailored to polish advanced combat shooting skills.

THE INTERNATIONAL RAPID-FIRE COURSE

This is an adaptation of the regular Olympic course of fire that bears the same name. It consists of five international rapid-fire targets placed one target width apart at 25 meters from the shooter. The course requires a measured firing cadence, traversing from one target to the next. Each target is acquired, sight picture is refined, and one round is fired before moving on to the next target. A slow, then moderate, then rapid cadence is designated for the three successive stages. A great deal of control with consistent sighting and triggering is required. This is a course of fire that looks easier than it is to perform. Combat handgun course modifications call for the use of a full-powered service handgun rather than the .22 short self-loading pistols used in the Olympic version. The half-course (30 rounds) is fired in combat matches. While no foot movements are required, the gun must

25 METERS

The International Rapid Fire course has a very simple layout. Targets are spread one target width apart at 25 meters down range. All stages can be fired in place, making the IRF one of the easiest matches to administer.

be traversed to acquire each separate target, providing a considerable challenge.

Stage One—25 meters—10 rounds—8 seconds for each of two phases. Load and holster, on cue draw and fire one shot at each of five targets in 8 seconds. Reload and reholster. On second cue, draw and repeat the phase.

Stage Two—25 meters—10 rounds—6 seconds for each of two phases. Load and holster. On cue draw and fire one round as each of five targets in 6 seconds. Reload and reholster. Repeat the same phase on cue.

Stage Three—25 meters—10 rounds—4 seconds for each of two phases. Load and holster. On cue, draw and fire one shot at each of five targets in 4 seconds. Reload and reholster. Repeat the phase on cue.

A ten point penalty is charged for each premature start or round fired overtime. Score according to numbered rings on the targets. 300 points are possible for the course.

The International Rapid-Fire is deceptively simple. It is a very efficient match to administer, since all three stages can be fired in place, eliminating the changeover of targets, firing lines, etc., necessary in other more varied events. Common errors committed in this match relate to time pressures. Stage one times are really quite long, so deliberate sight pictures can be drawn. A possible 100 points for this stage is not difficult to achieve with the right mental set and shooting technique. Traversing moves can be distinct, halting at

each target in succession, allowing for a refined sight picture with a crisp let-off for each round. The difficulty comes when the second stage arrives. With two seconds less time the shooter must mentally shift gears to fire faster, making intuitive compromises between speed and accuracy. Unfortunately, this time change tends to be on the shooter's mind during stage one, so the first stage is usually shot too hurriedly. There is tendency to hurry shots and not to adapt techniques appropriately to the time allotted. Then, when the third stage arrives, the contestant tends to "sweep-shoot," that is, to move the gun across each target, picking the trigger as the sights cross the edge of the target image. This practice invariably results in firing many bullets between targets for clean misses. Target number five nearly always looks good, however, since the gun stops there at the end of the string.

During stage two and stage three, recoil control and recovery are especially needed. The ability to stabilize the gun quickly will give more time for sight refinement. Unlike shooting the .22 short autoloaders of Olympic marksmen, the full-caliber combat handgun calls for compromises, especially in stage three. The center of the ten ring is rather well indicated by the rows of manila colored numerals designating the scoring rings. By traversing across the targets with the horizontal numerals guiding elevation, and then stopping under the vertical numerals to fire, a compensating technique is available to help

This view makes the IRF appear to be a deceptively simple match. Successive stages shorten time from eight, to six, to four seconds for the five shot string. Firing full-bore combat guns out of the leather makes mounting, sight alignment, and traversing between targets quite difficult. A score of 230 to 250 out of 300 possible for this course is quite respectable.

deficiencies in sight picture refinement on stage three. Criticism has been laid on the use of international rapid-fire targets for this reason, but similar, although coarser, techniques are used to refer the center on plain combat silhouettes, too. The need for concentration cannot be overemphasized in this intense, rapid-fire event. Superlative basic shooting technique is taken for granted. Without it the novice is lost; there is no time to think through stance, grip, trigger pull. All these elements have to be down pat or the scores will be abysmal, the whole event frustrating. Mastery of the International Rapid-Fire should be considered a basic credential for a polished combat handgunner.

THE MEXICAN DEFENSE COURSE

This course has been borrowed and modified slightly for combat league shooting from our Latin American neighbors. This is a popular standard course of fire in Mexico and other Central and South American

Concentration is one of the main factors for success in the IRF. Contestants have to develop a precise "internal clock" in order to take full time advantage without shooting past the time interval. Al Nichols, shown here, holds the current League record of 268 for the IRF. Nichols has won this match every time it has been scheduled in League competition.

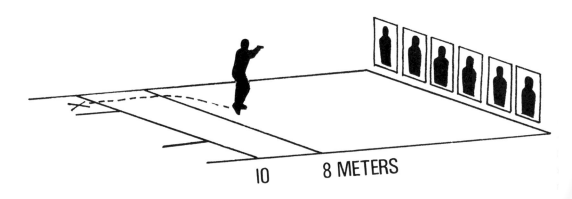

The Mexican Defense layout does not require a great deal of area. The Mex is a short coupled shoot that places premiums on body mobility. Times average one second for each shot regardless of the movements involved. This is one of the most challenging and prestigious events in combat shooting.

countries. It demands a broad selection of shooting skills, including single targets, multiple target traversing, as well as diagonal and horizontal body movement while shooting at single and multiple targets. Many shooters denounce the "Mex" as a "dancing contest," mainly due to the rather detailed procedures for foot placement and movement. This aspect of the event is judged closely and foot faults can cost 5 points each. In spite of all the grousing, this is considered to be one of the most prestigious standard events in the combat shooting repertoire.

The basic field layout and shooting procedures are the same for all stages of the event. The field has six silhouette targets (T-8 or equivalent) spaced equally on frames along a 22' 6" line. Two firing lines run parallel to the targets; one is at 8 meters, the other at 10 meters. The left-hand boundary of the shooting field is defined on the edge of the left-hand target. Perpendicular to the 10 meter firing line, a lateral line is drawn 2'11" inside the left boundary. Another lateral is drawn 16'8" farther to the right of the first lateral.

The contestant loads and holsters facing downrange in front of the 8 meter line. Then, he turns his back to the targets and waits for the command to "walk." On cue he walks forward toward the ten meter line until his foot crosses that line. He must not touch the pistol after crossing the ten meter line until the command to fire. On cue, the handgun is drawn, the shooter pivots 180 degrees while bringing his other foot inside the 10 meter line so he is standing completely in the shooting box formed by the 10 meter line, the boundary on the left, and the first lateral line on the right. This standard procedure effects the start for all stages of the shoot. All stages require six shots to be delivered in five seconds. Variations from the six separate stages are given below:

> Stage One—On cue, draw, turn, and fire all six rounds at target one while standing fast in the firing box.

> Stage Two—On cue, draw, turn, and fire one round at each of the six targets while standing fast in the firing box.

> Stage Three—On cue, draw, turn, and fire one round at target one. The second round must not be fired before the foot is inside the 10 meter line. Continue firing at target one while advancing, never stopping to shoot. The last round must be fired inside the 8 meter line.

> Stage Four—Follow the procedures for stage three, but fire one shot at each target. This will call for a diagonal movement across the shooting field as each target is engaged.

> Stage Five—On cue, draw, turn, and fire one round at target one. Then, step to the right across the first lateral line before firing the second round at target one. Continue walking laterally across the field but outside the ten meter line, firing all but the sixth round at target one. Before the five second time limit, the shooter must have crossed the second lateral line. The sixth round must be delivered on target one after crossing the second lateral line, but before the five second limit.

> Stage Six—Repeat the procedure for stage five, but fire one round at each target.

> Each overtime round, foot fault, or procedural error costs five points.

This is a fascinating, challenging event. It demands a great deal of control and stability to shoot it well. Shooting techniques are subject to breakdown when the marksman is required to move the lower body during firing. Irregular ground surfaces further complicate the problem. The tendency for most shooters is to fire too fast and to hurry movements. Shooters who have a good "internal clock," and excellent intuitive measure of time intervals, tend to do well in this event. By using all the time available, but not firing overtime rounds, a cool, collected technique can be developed. Stages one, two, and three do not pose exceptional problems. Stage four requires footwork that pivots the shooter straight on each new target with every other

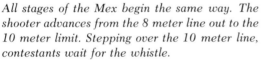

All stages of the Mex begin the same way. The shooter advances from the 8 meter line out to the 10 meter limit. Stepping over the 10 meter line, contestants wait for the whistle.

On cue, the shooter pivots and brings both feet across the 10 meter line. Movement occurs after the first shot in the last four stages of the event.

stride. The interim strides must be straight forward toward the target and the gun is discharged during that particular interval. Otherwise, sweep shooting is the only other alternative, which results in erratic scores. Awareness and judgement are hard to apply at first in this event, since so much happens so quickly. To do well consistently at the Mexican Defense is a measure of combat shooting maturity.

Stages five and six are the most difficult. The lateral walk, parallel to the targets, is difficult to coordinate with upper body poise. The alien nature of this movement tends to create tensions that override arm and hand

coordinations. Triggers tend to be jerked, eyesight is out of phase with gun sights, and hand muscles tend to alter the grip hold from normal sets. This last factor commonly results in "heeling" the gun handle; that is, exaggerating master heel pressure on the back strap. This tends to make the gun shot high and accentuates recoil effect with auto-pistols. The tendency to sweepshot shows up in bullet placements predominately to the right of center on targets.

Practice will overcome these difficulties, but the shooter will have to analyse each phase of each stage to thoroughly understand both what is required and what is being done

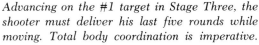

Advancing on the #1 target in Stage Three, the shooter must deliver his last five rounds while moving. Total body coordination is imperative.

The lateral walk of Stages V and VI are the most difficult of the Match. It is very awkward to walk parallel to the targets at 10 meters and deliver fire while on the move.

incorrectly. Mastery of this course of fire will build confidences that carry over into other shooting events.

THE FBI DUEL

The FBI Duel provides extensive application of the draw and fire technique practiced at variable closing ranges. The organization of the event makes it a man-against-man competition on an elimination basis. It is one of the most realistic combat courses, since the usual circumstances of encountering most felons in police work are recreated in the FBI Duel. The shooter must convert the changing, vari-

able circumstances into judgments as to what specific firing techniques will be used. The shoot starts at the 36 yard line with both contestants loaded and holstered. There are no separate stages, and the best two out of three hits wins the elimination.

On signal, the two shooters advance on the targets. Targets can be silhouettes or balloons on a balance beam. The task is to ascertain which shooter records the first hit. This can become quite difficult if many shots are required to register the first hit. Also, in the final stages of the event, shooters are closely matched as to ability. Electronic timing devices are ideal, but for casual shoots, a balance

Ray Chapman, Combat Master and three-time League Champion, advances in Stage Four of the Mex. Ray holds the current record of 180/22X for this event. Here, he demonstrates the impeccable style that has won him this match more times than any other League shooter.

beam can be used. This is a horizontal stick 36 inches long mounted on a center pin attached to an upright post. At each end of the stick an inflated balloon is attached that has a wound wire weight around its neck. The first balloon hit jettisons its weight, causing the losing balloon to descend. Hits so close as not to be decisive are ties. Electronic timing that can not ·discriminate more than five hundredths of a second are judged ties. As the shooters advance at a walk from the 35 yard line, the first call to fire must be made by the director before the shooters reach the 25 yard line. After firing, the shooters reload, the most forward contestant backs up even with his competitor and both pistoleers wait for the walk signal.

The next call ordinarily comes inside the 25 yard line but outside the 10 yard line. The third call comes between 10 and 5 yards. One point is given to the shooter for registering the first hit. One point is deducted for each procedural error, so if the heat is not decided by the third call, the contestants return to the 25 yard mark to continue until scores are decisive. Ordinarily, the best two out of three calls wins. There are no time limits or required shooting positions for this event.

The proximity of competitors makes the FBI Duel an intense kind of contest. With no time limit, the shooters have to go all out to score rapidly, since they cannot know how quickly the opponent will hit. Many an experienced pistoleer has been eliminated by

This view of the lateral stages of the Mex demonstrates the difficulty of this particular phase of the match. Care must be taken to avoid "sweep" shooting and to concentrate on sight alignment while walking 90° to the direction of fire.

an unknown marksman who goes for broke figuring he's got nothing to lose. This shoot requires very polished gun handling skills with quick judgements and adaptable stances.

PROGRAM VARIATIONS

A well rounded shooting program will include a number of events that can be designed according to the resources and imagination of clubs or small groups. Moving target events are quite valuable, providing adaptation of training skills to a single target on the move. A single speed range setup offers only a limited challenge, since the aiming lead becomes a set judgement for given loads at given ranges. Stations can be arranged to offer varying oblique shots; intermittent barricades can be planned along the target's path to interrupt target exposure.

Target motion need not be limited to linear tracks. Oval or "S" shaped tracks can be constructed. Pop-up or turning targets provide a motion (visual) firing cue that introduces more realism into shooting events. Limited time exposure can put additional pressure on shooters to acquire targets and deliver effective fire before losing the opportunity to score when the target drops out of sight.

NIGHT SHOOTS

Night shoots are rather difficult to stage, requiring adequate ranges away from civilized

The confusion of the Mex often causes shooters to "heel" the gun handle, causing shots to hit high. The top photo shows a normal grip hold, while below the thrusting of the heel of the hand against the backstrap results in elevation of the muzzle. The action is exaggerated here to illustrate the point.

areas. Some mode of lighting has to be available for general illumination and target changing. Many night shoots use lights for the cues to commence firing. Illumination on the first and last targets in a row graduates and limits light intensity on targets in between. Sound signals can be used as cues for contestants to turn on handheld flashlights to illuminate the targets. Beam illumination played on areas adjacent to the target also produces a kind of twilight condition. Probably the best kind of night shooting facility is a large tent or structure where rheostat controls can produce whatever level of illumination is needed to simulate realistic conditions. Such a facility could be used during the daylight hours, too, and would be especially useful in police training programs. In better than 90 percent of law enforcement shooting encounters, light conditions are too dim for the use of sights.

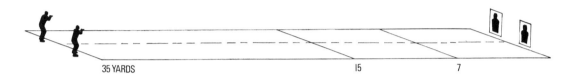

The FBI Duel is nearly 40 years old, being one of the earliest training courses for FBI agents. The shoot combines forward walking motion with stopping to draw and shoot. The best two out of three hits wins the elimination. This is one of the few combat events where shooters compete man-against-man.

Whatever technique works best for individual shooters is what is used. The first hit wins, so contestants must decide what accuracy/speed compromises are to be made.

At close ranges, the FBI Duel requires the fastest effective shooting position. Most shooters train with the standard master hand point position, seen above. At 25-35 yards distance during the Duel, perfecting a high point position may get more hits during a given time interval. Experienced contestants must always beware of the "go for broke" novice shooter who goes all out for speed and "lucks-out" with the first hit. Many a master has lost sets to talented novices in this demanding course of fire.

Night shooting matches are difficult to stage and no adequate facilities are generally available for indoor shooting. This is a sorely neglected area of combat shooting for sport as well as for police and military training. The vast majority of actual shoot-outs for police take place at close range under very dim illumination.

This aspect of combat shooting has been sorely neglected in formal police training and many military marksmanship programs.

SURPRISE SHOOTS

Surprise shoots are good tests of applied marksmanship. From a competitive standpoint, though, they have certain drawbacks. The surprise shoot tends to favor the most superlative shooters by a wide margin over even quite competent pistoleers. In order to get "top-name" shooters to attend, there is always a possibility of "hints" being given so the "surprise" aspect falls most heavily on the uninformed contestant. Also, after a few people have been through the course, there is the posibility that a "plant" early in the lineup will communicate the course layout to friends and cohorts. The sponsoring committee can also design the course to favor certain candidates as to location, range conditions, amount and kind of athletic prowess needed, etc.

For these reasons, the semi-surprise type of shoot gives developmental potential to the majority of pistoleers. These events should emphasize open-end combinations of basic skill shooting situations. By cataloging a broad set of such skills, course designers are aided in the design of events and contestants are aware of what could be expected. Shooting events should always be designed anticipating the size of the crowd. Small groups can be accomodated on a single facility, multi-phase shoot. Where changeover time is required between stages, large groups should be accomodated where the various stages can be set up on separate ranges. The most efficiently run matches are those where all stages are

Where shooters have to wait an inordinate time between stages and return four or five times to the shooting line, motivations decline rapidly. Anticipating this possibility, the shooter should gear his emotions and activity program for the ensuing boredom. Efficiently run matches are most appreciated by contestants and they contribute to high morale and a good return rate for succeeding matches.

The key elements emphasized in advanced courses of fire are judgement, adaptability, and decision making capacity. Basic skills should be taxed, but mastery at this level is considered prerequisite to success in advanced matches. There is no effective limit to the challenges that can be made in the advanced shooting sector. This area is pregnant with possibilities for the development of procedures, equipment, and facilities to carry forward the sophistication of the sport. Law enforcement and military agencies can ill afford to be without R&D in this field.

Surprise and semi-surprise shoots provide challenges for continual development of combat shooting skills. Formalized courses of fire sometimes lose the spontaneity that should characterize combat shooting. The design of these free-style courses of fire is limited only by imagination, course terrain, and financial resources.

CHAPTER XII

SHOOTING LIGHT FRAME HANDGUNS

THE LIGHT FRAME handgun is usually not included in a discussion of combat shooting. Many cartridges used in these guns fall below arbitrary power levels deemed adequate for defensive work. Some combat shooting *aficionados* refuse to consider small handguns seriously. But, the many thousands of these pistols used for home defense and by off-duty police calls for their consideration. While they are not recommended as a first choice for combat use, there are techniques that can overcome most of the disadvantages to enhance the effectiveness of the small handgun. The challenge of shooting these small guns surely calls for greater recognition in sports shooting.

The chief problem arises when full-bore combat loads are fired in lightweight guns. These include .38 Special small frame revolvers and aluminum framed autopistols. Firing stability and recoil recovery are greatly magnified with lightweight guns. One might say that recoil would be the same shooting the same loads, and to a degree this is correct, but we must define what is meant by recoil.

The bullet is pushed forward by a given force on the projectile base. That same force is applied to the mass of the gun. Newton's third law explains that for every action there is an equal and opposite reaction. In terms of force magnitude and duration, the amounts of energy will be identical for a given load in a light gun as in the heavier one with the same barrel length. If the gun and bullet weighed the same, they would both accelerate at the same rate. The shooter would get slammed with the same kinetic force as the target. This is due to the fact that momentum transfer to the gun would be at the same rate as transfer to the bullet if both objects weighed the same. Total momentum (mass times velocity) is always the same for both the gun and the bullet. This condition would be disastrous except that the gun weighs much more than the bullet. This is fortunate, since the expansion forces accelerate the bullet at a much faster rate than the gun. The bullet attains a high velocity and kinetic energy, while the weight of the gun "absorbs" energy, accelerating its comparatively heavier mass more slowly, so it attains a much lower velocity and kinetic energy. Understand that the momentum factors are the same for both the gun and the bullet, but kinetic energy values are quite a different thing.

FACTORS OF RECOIL

There are two important things to observe: (1) the velocity attained by the gun is the most important single factor related to "recoil," and (2) all other things being equal, the heavier the bullet relative to the weight of the gun, the greater the recoil of the gun. Take two practical examples to illustrate these points. First, a standard .38 Special service load is fired in a Model 19 S&W 4 inch barrel revolver (35 ounces) and in a Model 36 Chiefs Special 2 inch barrel (19 ounces). Recoil in gun systems is caused by a combination of factors. The reaction to driving the bullet up the barrel creates the major component of recoil. Recoil also derives from acceleration of the propellant gases generated from the burning powder charge. (Handgun powder charges are rather small compared to bullet weight and this recoil factor is not too significant.) The third recoil component comes from release of propellant gases that creates a "jet" effect at the muzzle. Since the mass of gases is also small in a handgun, and pressure is relatively low, molecular accelerations are relatively slow making this factor small. The combination of charge weight and gas thrust

Recoil on a small frame gun can affect its use in combat shooting. Through selective loading practices, serviceable combat ammunition can be assembled to minimize recoil effects without sacrifice of kinetic energy from regular service loads.

Standard weight combat guns, such as the Model 66 S&W Combat Magnum, moderate free recoil of heavy bullet loads. Firing the same loads in small frame guns, e.g. the S&W Model 60 shown above, creates significant control and recovery problems that are solvable with special handloads.

amounts to less than 10 percent of recoil in most combat loads. However, since the thrust of escaping gases depends on their velocity at release time, short barreled guns (usually found on lightweight handguns) will produce more relative recoil from gas thrust than will longer barreled guns shooting the same load.

For simple comparisons, only the recoil reaction generated from bullet acceleration is usually considered. For this calculation use the formula from Hatcher;

$$V = \frac{wv}{W \times 7000}$$

Where V equals the velocity of the gun, w is the weight of the bullet in grains, v is the muzzle velocity of the bullet in feet per second, and W is the weight of the gun in pounds.

Further refinement is possible for more accurate calculations of recoil that include powder charge weight and an arbitrary factor for gas velocites. The formula:

$$V = \frac{w + (1.5 \times cw)v}{700 \times w}$$

where cw is the propellant charge weight in grains gives a recoil velocity figure that considers both gas pressure and propellant weight.

The V value is then converted to kinetic energy by the following:

$$KE = \frac{MV^2}{2}$$

Where M is the mass of the gun, V is the velocity of the gun. This last conversion gives a significant measure of foot pounds of free recoil which is what is felt in the shooting hand.

Recoil energy and momentum are two different things. The momentum (mass times velocity) of the gun (MV) is equal to the momentum of the bullet (mv) where (MV=mv). The mass of the handgun is so large, its attained velocity is quite low. The mass of the bullet is so relatively small, its velocity is quite high, giving it considerably more kinetic energy than the gun.

EFFECTS OF VELOCITY AND BULLET WEIGHT

To show these relationships and how they apply to shooting, we will take a standard .38 Special minimum combat load. This round is assembled with a 158 grain bullet on top of 3.6 grains of Bullseye powder. The load delivers 860 feet per second at the muzzle of a 4-inch barrel and generates 259 foot pounds of kinetic energy. Fired in a Model 19 Combat

Magnum revolver and a Model 36 Chief's Special, the results follow:

Model 19

$$V = \frac{158 + (1.5 \text{x} 3.6) \text{x} 860}{7000 \text{ x } 2.19} = 9.17 \text{fps}$$

Model 36

$$V = \frac{158 + (1.5 \text{x} 3.6) \text{x} 757}{7000 \text{ x } 1.19} = 14.85 \text{fps}$$

Converting:

Model 19

$$KE = \frac{\frac{2.19}{32.16} \text{ x } 9.17^2}{2} = 2.86 \text{fp.}$$

Model 36

$$KE = \frac{\frac{1.19}{32.16} \text{ x } 14.85^2}{2} = 4.08 \text{fp.}$$

The results speak for themselves. The lighter frame revolver has 143 percent of the recoil energy of the service handgun firing the given load. The only difference is the barrel length and weight of the two guns. With its narrow frame at the recoil shoulder, the Model 36 can bruise the web of the hand painfully and the gun is significantly more difficult to control in recoil. The differences get more dramatic as the power of loads increases or when gun weight decreases.

To further illustrate this relationship, a set of data was calculated based on the .38 Special combat load. Sets of gun weights were chosen to match available models with 2 and 4-inch barrel lengths.

The longer barrels produce higher bullet velocities, therefore greater recoil energy in a given weight of handgun. While the two inch barrels produce inferior ballistic performance, they also generate heavier free recoil, especially with heavier bullet loads. There is a way to increase ballistic efficiency and reduce the level of recoil in small frame guns, however.

TABLE XII – I

COMPARATIVE RECOIL DATA

Two Inch Barrels

Gun Weight	Gun Velocity (fps)	Free Recoil (fp)	Recoil Index°
14 oz.	20.08	5.52	1.93
19	14.85	4.08	1.43
23	12.27	3.37	1.18
28	9.40	2.58	.90
33	8.58	2.36	.83
39	7.24	1.99	.70

Four Inch Barrels

Gun Weight	Gun Velocity (fps)	Free Recoil (fp)	Recoil Index°
23 oz.	13.94	4.35	1.52
30	10.68	3.33	1.17
35	9.17	2.86	1.00
42	7.63	2.38	.83

°Based on firing the standard .38 Special load in a 35 ounce, 4 inch barrel revolver.

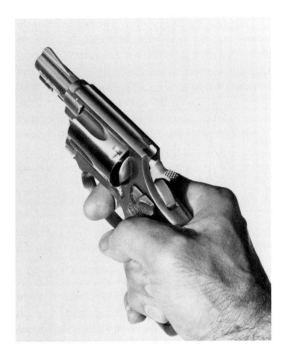

Narrow frames of small combat revolvers concentrate recoil energy in sensitive parts of the hand, adding to recoil distractions. Special grips are needed to overcome these difficulties.

RELATIONSHIP OF BULLET TO GUN MASS

The second part of recoil analysis has to do with the mass of the bullet relative to the mass of the gun. As gun mass drops, recoil rises with a given bullet weight, so what effect would lowering bullet mass have on ballistic performance? Recently, Remington Arms introduced a commercial .38 Special round to take advantage of this mass ratio relationship. The Remington cartridge uses a 95 grain bullet loaded to a velocity that duplicates standard service load (158 grain bullet) kinetic energy. Remember kinetic energy varies directly with bullet mass, but as to the *square* of velocity.

The standard .38 Special combat load delivers 201 foot pounds of energy out the two inch tube. A comparable energy level with a 95 grain bullet is reached with a velocity of 975 feet per second. Energy of the standard load for a four inch barrel is 259 foot pounds and the equivalent KE can be produced with 1110 feet per second with a 95 grain bullet. Both loadings are attainable from the 2 inch barrel. Running out the data we get the results shown in table 12-II.

Load A produces the same kinetic energy as the standard service load shot from the 2 inch barrel. The 95 grain bullet generates only 2.90 fp free recoil compared to 4.08 fp for the 158 grain bullet in Table 12-I. But, the recoil equivalent is that of a 4-inch barrel 35 ounce gun shooting the standard service load. This circumstance illustrates one point regarding recoil and bullet weight. *Effective free recoil can be reduced in a light gun by using lighter bullets loaded to equivalent kinetic energies of the heavier bullet loads.* But notice too, that with the light bullet we can duplicate 4-inch barrel kinetic energy with load B and still generate slightly less than the free recoil produced in the short gun with

TABLE XII-II

LIGHT BULLET LOADS°
(95 grain bullets)

Loads	Gun Velocity (fps)	Free Recoil (fp)	Recoil Index°°
A 975 fps/200 fp	12.52	2.90	1.01
B 1110 fps/259 fp	14.66	3.98	1.39

°.38 Special cases fired in 2 inch Chiefs Special.
°°Standard .38 Special combat load fired from 4 inch barreled 35 ounce gun.

the standard load (3.98 versus 4.08 foot pounds. See table 12-I). A careful choice of bullet weights is one means of overcoming the recoil problem of full bore loads in lightweight guns.

The problem of recoil is a relative one. Design of handgun stocks, operating mechanisms, mass distribution and location of c.g. all can moderate "felt" recoil. Not all shooters are as affected by recoil as others. There is a personality dimension, also. Many people convince themselves that no amount of recoil disturbs their ability to shoot. We can see the effect, though, on scores after 50 to 60 critical rounds are fired in a match. Mental control is one thing during practice, but what happens during an emergency or after long, wearing strings on the firing line when concentration lapses. Will the fatigued or surprised light frame shooter flinch when he cannot consciously control his aversion to heavy recoil? What happens in defensive situations when fear or anxiety overcome rational control? These are questions only the shooter can answer from experience. It is best to experiment with various load levels in light handguns and observe the relative change in scores as recoil energy builds up. Don't adopt a light load for practice and then slip in an uncontrollable screamer for defense. Try to shoot regularly with the maximum load you would intend to shoot in combat; something compatible with adequate stopping power, then learn to place the hits with certainty.

RELATED SENSORY PROBLEMS

Recoil is not the only distraction associated with short, lightweight handguns. Muzzle blast and flash both can be frightful, depending on the loads. Muzzle flash is the greatest with heavy charges of slow burning propellants used in "belly-buster" loads. Night shooting shows up the orange plume of flame that is produced by excess hydrogen in the propellant gases. The flash is distracting but not blinding as is sometimes told. The duration is short, but the effect will temporarily obscure the target. The flash, mentally associated with recoil and jolt of a hot load, serves to distract the shooter's attention and gives away his tactical position. Keeping the gun down low in point position, with the shooter looking over the flash, the illumination can give stop-action night time glimpses of the target in a fairly bright, reflective environment; but, it also lets the adversary see the gunner.

Muzzle blast from high-pressure loads can be punishing, especially with short barrels. Within just a few rounds, especially in an enclosed area, concussion can make even an experienced shooter weary to the point of distraction. Loads should be selected with a power-to-blast buy-off. And, like recoil, this decision is an individual matter. The shooter should be critical of the effects (costs) of using heavy loads in light framed guns. Prudent load selection can make or break the effectiveness of these guns.

GRIP SELECTION

A good deal of recoil control can be managed by proper grip selections. On small frame revolvers, an enclosed backstrap grip is recommended so as to increase the girth and recoil shoulder area. A well fitted grip, one that allows the hand to ride high on the backstrap, will effectively distribute recoil energy in the hand and lower the bore line. Hand gripping techniques will also contribute toward effective control of small frame guns.

Light guns are easy to carry for plain clothes and off-duty police. They provide compact fire power when frame size and width of revolver cylinders reduce bulk. Handle designs are usually short and rounded for maximum concealment. Some compromise must be made here, since the most concealable handguns may cause the greatest recoil control problems. Regarding grip choices, some concealment virtues can be sacrificed for control. Herrett's Shooting Ace Grips work well. Grip maker Guy Hogue does an excellent job on small frame stocks, providing open strap models for concealment and closed strap

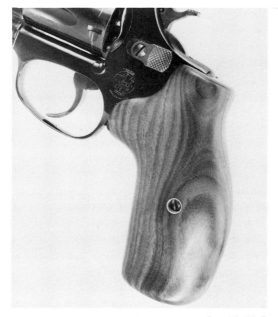

This small frame combat grip on the S&W J-frame is ideal for shooting full-bore loads. Notice the full body of the palm swell and high-hold, broad recoil shoulder.

JR Grips' hybrid design permits unrestricted handhold high on the recoil shoulder. This effectively lowers the line of the bore relative to the hand and wrist. Shrouded hammer aids smooth drawing from under a coat.

Hogue's Diamond Profile small frame grip meets the compromise requirements between concealment and good combat control.

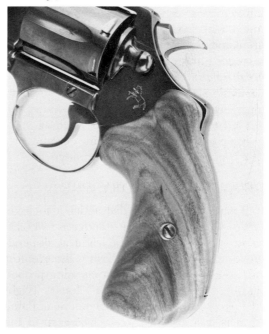

For maximum concealment, this open-back design by Hogue still gives good combat control, but not without some compromise.

versions for combat. The combat shooter does not have to sacrifice a great deal of concealment for control, provided the grip is designed well. Hogue's combat style small frame grip is one of the very best for maximum control, comfort, and taming of the lightweight revolver. JR Grips has a hybrid design that is made for the Chief's Special and is especially effective on current Colt D frame guns (Detective Special, Diamondback, etc.). This design allows very high, unrestricted hand placement on the recoil shoulder, and gives uncanny improvement to shooting scores with full-bore loads. It has to be tried to be appreciated.

SHORTENED AND LIGHTENED AUTOPISTOLS

Growing popularity of "chopped and channeled" autopistols has brought forth design variations on the Colt Government Model, the S&W Model 39 and the Browning Hi-Power. These variations cut back barrel, slide, and shorten handle length to produce a pocket auto in full-caliber. Weight and size reductions create recoil and recovery problems for full-load combat guns. The two hand hold helps stabilize these guns, but still, there will be considerable hop because of their light weight, and low inertia. The ability to recover and get back on target is the chief consideration

for the shooter. Gun weights as low as 26 ounces (equal to the aluminum frame Commander) can be achieved in .45 caliber. The S&W Model 39 starts at 26 ounces with its aluminum frame and weights as low as 18 to 19 ounces can be achieved in bobtailed versions. Using loads that will produce minimum combat match ballistics out of the short barrels, these conversions generate considerable free recoil.

Another factor involved with shooting autopistols is the delayed recoil moment caused by the movement of the slide. The slide is lighter than the whole gun, so it accelerates faster, generating more free recoil than the whole piece. While it reciprocates, the handgun's center of gravity is shifted rearward. When the slide slams against its stop abutment, its momentum transfers to the frame. This delayed transfer factor coincides with the slide mass being to the rear of the frame. This situation accentuates the rotation of the wrist, contributing to what shooters think is excessive recoil. In reality this jostling is just an inherent fire control problem with self-loading pistols. Wrist strength is the basic means of handgun control and recovery. With heavy loads in light, abbreviated self-loaders, the problem can become even more magnified. Individual guns and shooters will vary in the interpreted effects of "felt" recoil, however.

TABLE XII-III

GUN WEIGHT-RECOIL

Caliber	Gun Weight	Gun Velocity (fps)	Free Recoil (fp)	Recoil Index[*]
.45 ACP	39 oz.	9.86	3.69	1.29
(200 grain bullet at 800+ fps)	26 oz.	14.65	5.44	1.90
9x19mm	39 oz.	8.46	2.71	.95
(115 grain bullet	32 oz.	10.32	3.31	1.16
1165+ fps)	26 oz.	12.66	4.06	1.42
	19 oz.	17.34	5.56	1.95

[*]Based on recoil developed by standard .38 Special Service load in a 35 ounce 4 inch barrel gun.

POCKET AUTOPISTOLS

Pocket autopistols fire a lower powered ammunition and do not present the control problems associated with bobtailed guns mentioned above. None of these cartridges (.22 LR, 25 ACP, .32 ACP, .380 ACP) for handguns of this class have sufficient power to meet requirements of combat match shooting. The .380 ACP is regarded generally as the minimum caliber for personal defense work. In recent years, the .380 has become the leading cartridge for full-size pocket autos.

The generic term "Pocket automatic" takes in three frame sizes of guns. The small frame characterizes guns in the .22LR or more likely, the .25 ACP caliber; these include such guns as the Baby Browning and the S&W M61 (both since discontinued). These were considered women's purse guns and were used a great deal as hideout guns for law enforcement personnel. Poor hand grip size and low magazine capacity, especially in the ineffective .25 ACP cartridge, makes these "panic" guns. They are better than nothing in an emergency and their diminuitive size requires at least a little practice for effective shooting. In an emergency, these guns are used against a single assailant by merely emptying the magazine as quickly as possible into the vitals.

Middle-sized pocket autos are just big enough for a comfortable grip by all fingers of an average sized hand. Most of these guns are chambered for .32 ACP with a few models in .25 ACP. The Model 1910 Mauser in .25 caliber is a good example of this handy sized pocket auto. Not too many of this type of gun survived from the pocket auto heyday of the early century. Full sized pocket autos such as the Walther PP or Mauser HSc are most numerous today and are offered principally in .22LR, .32 ACP and .380 ACP. Magazine capacities and grip size make these full-frame pocket autos usable for regular combat shooting events. With their standard ammunition, they present no real recoil or recovery control problems and are quite pleasant to shoot.

MAXIMIZING BALLISTIC EFFECTIVENESS

Without going into ballistic comparisons, it is noted that pocket auto ammunition is deficient in power for defense purposes. This concern does not eliminate the pocket auto from consideration for defensive use; however, they are not recommended if more powerful handguns are available. Pocket autos in .32 ACP caliber have been standard issue to European police since the early part of the century, although more recent issues have favored .380 or the newer 9x18mm Markarov cartridge. Low-power is not a disadvantage in home defense where penetration through walls and across property lines is a consideration. Firing techniques should be developed so three or more shots are triggered in fast cadence. This "burst" effect, if it can be held within an 8-inch circle in the mid-chest area of a silhouette, can be most effective in defense. Hit in the vitals with three fast shots, an assailant is bound to be slowed down and seriously distracted even if he does not go down for the count.

If the first string does not do the trick, the shooter has time enough to trigger off another. With seven or eight shot capacity in full sized pocket autos, a single assailant can be dispatched. Multiple, rapid hits provide a buckshot effect. Each round from a .32 ACP is about like a single 00 buckshot, and 2 or 3 pieces of .33-inch smooth bore round shot has a most deadly terminal effect. Low power bullets of low sectional density transfer the major part of their kinetic energy to the target at the terminal end. What may be lacking ballistically in a single round is made up by the collective impact of several rounds hitting in a small area within a short time interval. Before the assailant can recover from the shock of a single hit, he receives 2 or 3 impacts. Recoil recovery and rapid, precise trigger techniques have to be practiced. With a quality pocket pistol, most shooters can acquire an adequate technique after 50 to 100 rounds of practice, if they understand what has to be

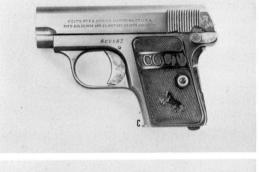

A number of small-frame autopistols are available. They vary in quality and useability for defensive or combat sport shooting. The Mauser HSc (A) features clean lines and adequate size to be used for serious defensive work. Walther's PPK-S (B) and the related family of guns are the standard of excellence for pocket autos. Like the HSc, these guns provide the DA first-shot feature. The PPK-S has push-button magazine release that gives a significant edge during reloading. Small frame pocket autos like this old Colt .25 ACP (C) make ideal hideout guns, but have very limited defensive applications. Concealability is obtained at the cost of fire control and marginal ballistics. S&W's Escort (D) in .22 LR holds five rounds, is better than nothing for defense. Used in close on a single assailant, with specialized trigger control, these little guns are serviceable for "panic" emergencies. The Mauser 1910 New Model in .25 ACP is one of the most useable guns in this small caliber. However, these models are rare and collector value precludes their use for regular shooting.

Although short on ballistic performance, any of these cartridges can provide secondary defensive protection if used effectively. (l. to r.) .22 Long Rifle, .25 ACP, .32 ACP, .380 ACP. Hollow point bullets in .22 LR will enhance terminal ballistics. The hotter loads in .380 ACP have enough energy to expand hollowpoint projectiles effectively. The Super Vel load shown here gives excellent performance. Cast lead bullets are somewhat more efficient ballistically than factory FMJ bullets in .25 ACP and .32 ACP.

Diminuitive pocket autopistol calibers, such as this .25 ACP, are not recommended for combat use, but still can be lethal. These guns require special handling techniques to be used effectively in "panic" defensive situations.

This photo was taken with a sub-microsecond flash unit that stops bullet action in flight and clearly defines the muzzle flash; notice the inertia delayed slide has started to retract, under impetus of chamber gases pushing on the spent cartridge casing. At this moment, slide movement was very short compared to bullet movement.

Burst control is the secret of effective pocket pistol use. Combat shooting has ignored the potentials of pocket auto courses of fire. Women shooters can use these light guns as a vehicle into shooting sports, as well as for learning home defense skills.

accomplished. Used properly, these little guns are formidable for limited defensive applications. Too little emphasis has been placed on the use of these guns in combat match shooting. Special courses of fire are necessary.

With more attention given to combat matches especially designed for the small frame guns, the development of handling techniques for these little guns would advance. With so many home defense guns numbering among small frame pieces, there is a great opportunity for the local clubs to bring more people into sport shooting. Instructional situations would decrease potential accidents and increase effective defensive use of handguns by citizens. In particular, women shooters would be encouraged to participate

in combat shooting. Women's interest in recreational shooting will have a powerful, if not decisive, influence on the future of private arms ownership. Promotion of rational public images for shooting sports will deter rash legislative moves. The appearance of women participants at recreational shooting events serves to modulate many emotional and irrational feelings directed against firearms. Women's increasing influence in politics can be beneficial to shooting sports if more feminine constituents are numbered on the firing line. Self-defense skills are included in the assertiveness aspects of the feminist movement. Combat shooting can not afford to overlook these possibilities.

CHAPTER XIII

DOUBLE ACTION AUTOPISTOLS

S AFETY PROBLEMS IN handling autopistols are well known. Among other things, the cocked hammer and loaded chamber of these guns is sensitive to relatively light, short trigger movement. An inexperienced person or poorly coordinated shooter can trigger-off a round without realizing it.

This factor has favored the DA revolver in some quarters with its long, rather heavy 10 to 12 pound maximum pull. The DA trigger requires deliberate manipulation to discharge the gun. A little over forty years ago, the Walther PP was introduced that featured a double action trigger mechanism. This design was unique in that it allowed the autopistol to be carried safely with the hammer down and a round in the chamber. The first shot was fired with the long DA pull. As the gun cycled, the trigger bar was disconnected, allowing the hammer to set on single action cock. Each succeeding round was then triggered-off in the usual autopistol SA mode. The firing pin was engaged by the safety lever; on applying the safety, the firing pin was cammed out of engagement with the hammer and the sear was tripped releasing the hammer to fall

harmlessly. This movement locked the trigger out of sear engagement. The basic Walther mechanism appeared again in the well known P-38 German Army side arm. More recently, the S&W Model 39 and Model 59 have been available in the U. S. These guns feature a DA draw bar trigger that differs in its action from the Walther unit.

It would seem that a DA mechanism solves the autopistol's safety problems. To a degree it does, but it creates some problems of its own for the shooter.

INHERENT DISADVANTAGES

The dual trigger mode of the DA autopistol has characteristics that hamper consistent fire control. DA pulls are manipulated with entirely different coordinations from those required in the usual SA mode. Because of this, a disparity arises in the control of the gun, especially between the first and second shots.

The large muscles contract to fire the DA first shot, coordinating to a point just short of let-off. The small finger muscles take over to give the last short arc movement needed to

S&W's Model 39/59 and Walther's P38 are the only combat sized DA autos available. Aluminum frames of the current production models of these guns makes them undesirable for use in combat league shooting. Also, rules and courses of fire favor SA autos. Little interest in these guns has been shown by combat shooters.

drop the hammer without disturbing the sights. Normally, the DA recovery is as long as the pull, so retraction of the large muscles follows an expected pattern established during the initial pull. But, in the DA auto there is no DA recovery; releasing the trigger shifts the gun to the SA mode after the first shot is fired. This change over causes considerable disorientation to the average shooter's mental and physical set.

One mechanical change can benefit the SA recovery from the DA pull. An over-travel stop can be applied to the trigger and adjusted to function on both the DA and SA pull. While this feature is no panacea for transition problems, it will minimize one source of disequilibrium in the system. A small truncated pyramid of steel can be silver soldered on the back of the trigger about half way to the tip end. This is then filed lightly to adjust the stop engagement with the frame behind the trigger. For shooters who want to have an adjustable overtravel feature, the trigger can be drilled through the stop and tightly threaded for an Allenhead nyloc set screw. After installation, first check the DA pull and then adjust SA functioning before firing. On some guns the set screw can be threaded in the

Dual-mode trigger design creates second shot control problems in rapid fire situations. A long DA coordination for the first shot is followed by the short, light coordination demanded by SA triggering. This DA/SA shift can produce some safety problems in duty handguns.

frame in back of the trigger. This technique eliminates the hole in the trigger face.

Autopistol SA triggering requires action of the small finger muscles for best results. Just the tip-end of the forefinger should engage the trigger face. Coordination recovery is distinct for SA and DA and psychomotor responses function best when they are geared to one trigger mode or the other. Many shooters require resetting of the hand hold to perform exceptionally well in one mode or the other, so when both modes are met in the same shot string, shooting capacities in terms of both speed and accuracy is impaired.

For this reason, among others, few DA autos are used by combat shooters. This may be a shame, for since these guns are with us, the best possible techniques should be developed to overcome the disadvantages; this is best done in match competition. Without rule changes favoring the DA auto, though, this situation is unlikely to happen. Since the two full-size DA autos available (P-38, Model 39/59) have aluminum frames, combat shooting leagues probably will not give them serious consideration. Aluminum is not considered desireable for extended use in combat match shooting. Durability and weight factors (recoil) are not favorable to the demands of match shooting, where several hundred rounds are fired each weekend in preparation for competition.

COMPARISON TESTS

From evaluations fired by several knowledgeable combat competitors, the consensus was that the first shot with a DA auto was not as quick and/or as accurate as the first round with a DA revolver (Model 39 versus Model 19). The primary reason being that the slab sided autopistol handle was more difficult to grip. The same conclusion was drawn regarding a three shot string. Speed and/or accuracy of the DA auto was inferior to the revolver. The first shot was slower, as mentioned above. The second shot recovery

was significantly slower if control was established for accurate delivery. The pistoleer had to "shift gears" from DA to SA mode. The second shot tended to be inaccurate if it was fired for speed. After some practice, the third shot tended to be on target with arm and hand coordinations under control.

The DA/SA kinesthetic confusion, in-

Comparison shooting of DA autos against DA revolvers showed advantages for the DA revolver. Dual-mode of triggering in a handgun action serves to confuse smooth, precise coordination and fire control.

herent in dual-mode triggering, causes un-disciplined shooters to spray a lot of lead wildly at the target, if they do not make an effective grip transition. This is particularly true if there is a press of time on the shooter. Shooters who lack the training or capacity to focus attention on the trigger mode changes can become quite inaccurate. Because so much time is available on such elementary courses as the PPC, deficiencies in trigger technique do not show up. The PPC is a rather poor test situation for realistic trials. With ample time to resurrect the hand grip and shift the trigger finger, second and third shots can be delivered accurately without much disturbance. However, where time is a factor as in real defensive or combat match situations, the DA/SA distraction becomes apparent and scores suffer.

EFFECTIVE DA/SA TRANSITION

There are two tacks in solving the problem: (1) develop a psychomotor pattern that can operate effectively under stress, or (2) train for the SA mode and "throw away" the first shot, using it primarily as a means of getting the hammer cocked. The principle DA autos in use for combat shooting today are the P-38 and the S&W Model 39/59. The P-38 is more nearly a military curiosity, not seen often, if at all, at combat matches. The butt location of its magazine catch precludes its use for fast reloading time. The S&W Model 39/59 is most often encountered through police organizations today; it is not readily available currently to the civilian market because of heavy police demand.

So far as the first solution is concerned, the S&W 39/59 is blessed with a very fine handle shape and DA pull. This pull is usually quite even and relatively free from hangups even in out-of-the-box condition. Some light stoning, deburring, and lubrication helps modulate top-end resistance, so the hammer can fall without disturbing the sights. It is useful to study the kinesthetic

messages relating to muscular sets for the DA phase at the moment of hammer fall. This is the condition from which the shooter must recover to undertake SA fire for the second and subsequent shots. The forefinger tip is usually too far into the trigger to give sensitive SA control. Sliding the finger tip slightly out to the halfway position (assuming average hand size) is part of the SA recovery that can be done without much distraction. Medium-sized hands (and some big ones, too) usually slide around on the handle so the DA can be reached and controlled effectively. While this technique does not bother a revolver handhold, it is definitely unstabilizing for autopistol shooting. The DA grip can be shifted slightly as the forefinger is moved on the trigger, by relaxing the master hand and pressing the heel of the weak hand into the left grip panel. This action squares the forearm and grip hold on the axis of the bore. Master hand tension is reestablished after the shift. If this technique is practiced, a shooter can become quite adept at the transition. This DA/SA switch is a distraction from regular, uniform practices, however. It takes concentration with no guarantee of results when time pressure is on. Also, it is not quite as fast as a DA revolver on the first two or three shot strings.

The second solution is to grasp the handgun squarely like any SA automatic. The forefinger will not position well for an optimum DA pull with average sized hands. The first round will be fired with no particular DA finesse; it can be jerked through hurriedly. The muzzle may very well shake, and the first round may not center, but the hand and finger set are ready for the second and subsequent rounds without making any further shift. This technique is not as fast as a cocked and locked autopistol and not as accurate as a revolver for the first round, but possibly it may be the most effective compromise, especially for police work. Again, no combat shooter will bother with this

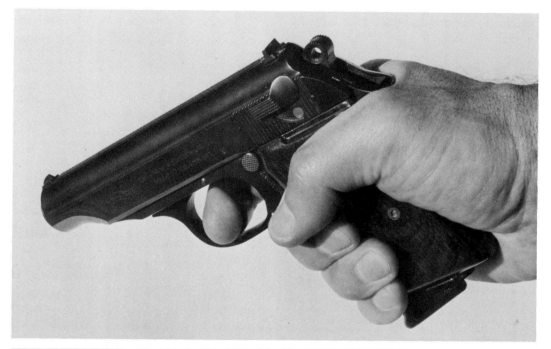

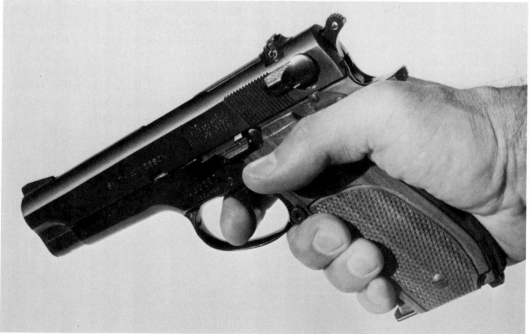

Small frame DA autos (top) have slightly more favorable trigger reach, smaller frame girth. Better finger leverage helps overcome DA/SA transition problems as compared to standard frame guns. Even under the best conditions, DA autos do not deliver consistent fire control given by either purely DA or SA systems.

handgun configuration without a rule change to subsidize the shift. Test work indicates that if shooters do not work on the DA/SA transition, they tend to shoot wild in emergencies. Performance on the PPC or similar slow courses is not a good indication of what will happen in real time defensive situations.

SAFETY AFTER THE FIRST SHOT

Also, the safety feature of the DA auto holds true only for the first round fired. After that, a lightweight, short SA trigger trip is the rule of operation. Having set big muscles in action for the DA pull, the shooter is liable to overcontrol the SA trigger in an emergency, even if he has had specific training for this problem. That is to say, quoting Murphy's law, "If something can happen it will happen."* Most all of the safety ills associated with SA automatics are present after the first round is fired in a DA auto, and training programs must take this fact into account. Many more hours of instruc-

tion and practice rounds will be required to teach safety alone, much less tactical effectiveness with DA autos.

It would seem that the virtues of self-loading and DA could be combined into a gun for combat by specifying a DA only trigger. Dual-mode triggers *do not* solve all the problems attendant with either safety or fire control, especially on full sized self-loaders. Fewer transitional problems are presented in the pocket auto sized guns. The Walther PP and PPK-S after trigger smoothing and regulating work, do a respectable job in terms of the DA/SA transition. The smaller frame size gives the trigger finger and the hand hold more favorable control in DA. The trigger finger shift is all that is necessary in the transition. A compromise position, if carefully chosen, serves both modes effectively on the small guns. However, one never achieves with the dual-mode trigger system the overall finesse and control possible with a consistent DA revolver or SA auto.

---

*This law was attributed to the legendary Edsel Murphy who formulated it after being informed of his imminent parenthood by his bride to be.

CHAPTER XIV

CONDITIONING HANDGUNS
FOR OPTIMUM SERVICE

A S IN NEARLY EVERY sport that uses mechanical equipment, shooting demands
attention to maintenance of the handgun.
Most shooters take a great deal of interest in
maintaining and modifying their match guns
to assure reliability and effective operation.

Not all shooters wish to work on their guns,
but a number of modifications are needed or
are desirable to improve functional characteristics of combat handguns. No handguns are
altogether ready for match competition as
they come from the factory. To pay a gunsmith
to do all necessary conditioning can be quite
expensive. Shooters with moderate to good
manual skills can learn to do routine or even
complex servicing and modifications. Most all
of the jobs basically involve common sense
with attention to procedure and details.

However, if a handgunner has any doubts
about his ability to handle a job, he should
consult a competent pistolsmith. These pro-
fessionals usually rejoice at the publication of
home gunsmithing information, because a
good many of these projects end up on their
benches for correction. The cost then may
exceed the tariff for the original work, de-

pending on the amount of damage. All
shooters need to have knowledge of what has
to be done to their guns, even if they do not
do the work themselves. The ability to specify
what is desired and to expertly evaluate gunsmithing work will improve the relationship
with one's gunsmith and assure top-flight
work.

BASIC TOOL KIT

A basic tool kit should be assembled and
organized in a pocketed tool roll. This equipment can be used on the bench or in the field
to make necessary repairs or modifications.
These items should include #600 and #400-
grit emery; a few pieces of crocus cloth; half
round, round, and flat, fine cut Swiss files; a
fine cut flat, safe edge warding file; a pair of
medium sized, high quality diagonal cutters;
a pair of small, round-jawed pliers; a small
Visegrip® plier; pin vise; toothbrush and small
metal fibre brush; two or three assorted dental
picks; light bronze hammer; rawhide mallet;
brass or nylon drift; 1/32 and 1/16-inch pin
punches; a small, fine grain carborundum

A few selected tools will perform nearly all servicing jobs done on handguns. A tool roll organizes the kit that can be valuable in the field or at matches to tune-up and maintain guns.

stone; hard, Arkansas stones or small triangular, round, and square or rectangular sections. In addition, a deluxe kit should include a set of assorted gunsmiths screwdrivers with ground tips; a high-grade 6-inch vernier caliper and/or 1-inch micrometer; a small machinist's square; a set of leaf thickness gauges; and a 5 or 10 power jeweler's loupe. These tools can be organized in a leather or fabric tool roll and kept in a shooting kit. Most any repair problem can be tackled in the field or at the workbench with this assortment. A few special tools are convenient, such as a Swiv-O-Ling® vise and an electric Moto-Tool® with a complete set of cutting burrs, grinding wheels, and polishing tips. If a lot of guns are to be modified or maintained, these specialized tools are quite handy.

SERVICING ROUTINES

Cleaning and servicing of handguns is necessary for reliable operation. Initially, a new gun should be broken down after firing about a hundred rounds. All parts of the gun should be cleaned in a solvent (do not use gasoline or other highly flammable or toxic fluids — it's too dangerous when other effective solvents such as paint thinner or Stoddard's solvent are available). All parts of the gun should be inspected under magnification. Parts such as plungers, guide rails, and slots where surfaces articulate should be given special attention. Using a hard stone, smooth down projections that are scoring (evidenced by shiny metal burnishing). Remove burrs on sharp edges of frame parts. Dress down tool marks where they interfere with smooth operation. Clean parts once again to remove metal and stoning residues. Apply a molybdenum grease sparingly and reassemble the gun. This initial preparation for internal parts will last quite a long time. Lock work once conditioned does not require lubrication or cleaning each time the gun is fired. During barrel cleaning, however, the shooter should take care to keep solvents out of the lock work so as not to dilute grease or other lubricants. Lock work should be cleaned anytime water, dirt or abrasive materials enter the gun. Otherwise, only periodic cleaning needs to be given to the lock parts.

Chamber and barrel surfaces should be treated with Rice's lubricants, especially if lead bullets are fired. Rice's X-10® solvent applied with the special compression swabs, flushes all dirt and oil from the microscopic pores on the bore surface. Application of Rice's liquid or spray lubricant fills these pores and guards against the collection of metal and powder fouling on the bore. If a bore has already been leaded, Rice's solvent applied with the special swabs followed by a vigorous bronze brushing will remove the lead scale as a fine dust. Continued application will check even the worst kind of lead fouling. Later application of Rice's X-15® or X-20® bore lubricant will virtually eliminate leading problems with even the hottest loads.

Heat and friction on the bore surface treated with Rice's lubricants evidently cre-

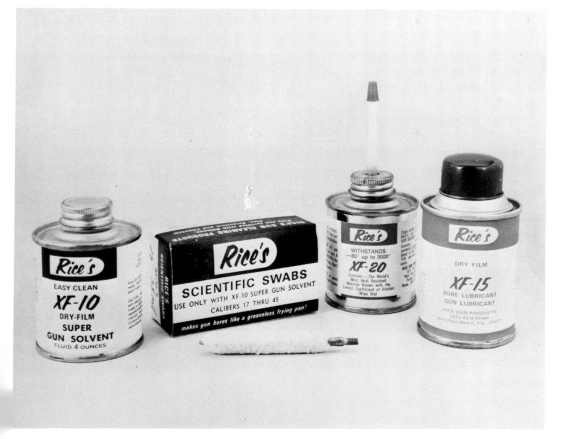

Rice's cleaning preparations work wonders with bore maintenance and accuracy. Used as directed, they will virtually eliminate bore leading and fouling problems with nearly any kind of ammunition.

ates a hard, durable layer that is so slick, metal fouling simply doesn't build up. Periodic dry swabbing to remove residues and light re-application of the lube is all that is needed for bore maintenance. This technique also works in .357 Magnum chambers where .38 Special cases are fired. Normally, there is a crusting on the chamber walls where the short .38 Special case mouth lies. Such a ring can interfere with .357 Magnum extraction when the longer cases are fired. Removal of the crusting and subsequent Rice's lubrication applications keeps the chamber free of residue buildup. After a few initial, thorough applications, bore maintenance becomes casual. Rice's products tend to "sweeten" a new barrel faster than normal, bringing the bore into a smooth, glassy finish after just a few hundred rounds.

Observe any buildup of lead or powder residues on the cylinder face and barrel stub. Regular wiping with nitro solvent removes residue sufficiently well. A closer than usual cylinder-to-barrel union (less than .003-inch) can cause the cylinder to drag from metal fouling. Maintenance of a .005 to .006-inch gap is about optimum for reliability. Metal fouling can come from molten lead eroded

The cylinder bearing tube on the crane should be cleaned and lubricated periodically to maintain a free-turning cylinder. This practice eliminates one possible source of drag during DA trigger pulls.

from bullet bases or fine slivers of gilding metal stripped off jacketed projectiles as they enter the forcing cone of the barrel. Extraordinary amounts of metal might indicate too hot reloads and/or a misaligned cylinder. Either situation needs correction.

Periodically, the yoke should be removed from a revolver to clean the cylinder bearing tube. Residues and small metal flakes enter the bearing in the vicinity of the gas ring on the center hole of the cylinder. Over time, these residues put a drag on cylinder rotation. Similarly, a tooth brushing of the cylinder ratchet removes fouling or dirt that can interfere with proper indexing and timing.

Autopistol feedways need to be cleaned regularly. Locking lug recesses should be kept free of residues and foreign matter. Build up of dirt in slide guideways, grit in the magazine channel can spell malfunctions or stoppages if neglected. After an autopistol is well broken in, maintenance of sliding parts with a light oil or LSA (teflon suspension) is adequate. Heavy lubricants tend to attract and hold dirt and residues.

Breech face corners and crevices need to be toothbrushed regularly and extractors should be kept free of residues and brass shavings that can limit cartridge rim engagement and interrupt proper cartridge feeding. Firing pin holes collect residues that can soften primer ignition.

The flush of solvents with compressed air followed with visual inspection with a magnifying glass will be needed periodically to get at areas that routine cleaning does not reach. Many of those "I don't know why it happened" stoppages can be traced to lack of thorough cleaning procedures in autopistols. Match guns particularly need this more detailed attention before a shoot.

COMBAT CONDITIONING REVOLVERS

Reworking handguns for flawless functioning requires gunsmithing skills. It takes hours of trial and error work to perfect techniques, observing closely and thinking ahead for each step in a modification to avoid a serious blunder. The specific details of these operations are beyond the scope of this book, but a discussion of the various modifications needed will serve as a guide to the able craftsman who can do the work himself. For anyone undertaking these projects, the watch word is patience and common sense. As a rule, expert hands can spend as much as four hours perfecting the action on a revolver.

For simplicity, the routines described here assume the use of the Smith & Wesson K frame action. Procedures, however, are applicable to any other revolvers, differing only in the names of parts or in some unique design functions. The S&W trigger pull has made this revolver the nearly universal choice of League wheel gun shooters in the Southwest. Colt has a loyal following in the eastern states and where the PPC dominates courses of fire The Ruger Security Six, recently tested and accepted by the U. S. Border Patrol is

Many common points of design relate to all revolver lock work. The basic principles for timing actions likewise are applicable to any DA revolver. Specific techniques for timing each kind of gun willlvary, however. Deburring, smoothing of all sliding surfaces and regulation of coil springs are the basic steps for combat conditioning of wheel guns. Actions are identified above as S&W K-frame (A), Colt I-frame (B), a Ruger Security Six (C), Dan Wesson/High Standard (D).

catching on with the shooting public. This is a gun that is easy to condition and maintain. It's trigger can be improved to rival that of the S&W Model 19. The Dan Wesson Model 15 and High Standard MK III respond favorable to match conditioning, having large, simple, easily manipulated lock parts.

Before attempting a detailed breakdown of any firearm, the shooter should study the illustrated parts breakdown (IPB) furnished with the gun. These documents can be obtained through a large dealer or by writing to the manufacturer.

To inspect for timing, check the release, rotation, and relocking of the cylinder relative to hammer movement.

To avoid mutilated screw slots, appropriate size screwdrivers (or Allen wrenches) should be used to loosen side plate screws. Do not pry up the side plate, merely hold the gun frame in the flat of the hand with the side plate up and smartly rap the handle straps with a mallet. This procedure will loosen the side plate so finger pressure can lift it out.

Inspect with 5X or greater magnification all surfaces where parts rub, noting any scratch marks or irregular contact points. Deburring is the first operation and it must be done thoroughly to eliminate any superfluous sources of drag and irregular tension in the operation of the gun. Hammers may touch lightly on the frame, side plate, or cylinder latch. Edge burrs on the hand can drag on the sides of its slot in the frame. Burrs can be removed with fine Swiss files, #600 emery cloth, and with hard Arkansas stones. Soft metal brushes on hand grinders are also effective for this operation. Care should be taken so that only edge and surface burrs are removed that interfere with parts movement. Do not reshape parts or remove metal other than the burr itself. Areas for burr inspection include the hammer, hammer channel, trigger, hand, cylinder stop, rebound mechanism (if applicable), ratchet, cylinder latch, breech face, recoil plate, extractor star, and the yoke/frame union.

CHECKING BASIC LOCK FUNCTIONS

Timing of the action should be checked. Holding the gun in profile, observe the following sequence as the hammer is slowly cocked.

Alignment of the bore to each cylinder is checked with the bore rod. Misalignment can indicate whether or not a gun will shoot tight groups.

First, the cylinder stop should disengage completely, before the hand engages the ratchet to start cylinder rotation. The stop should release as the trigger retracts; the stop will drop on the cylinder a little over halfway to the next stop notch on S&W revolvers (Colts should drop the bolt in the long, tapered lead, a little later than on the Smith). Cylinder rotation should be completed with the stop in the next notch just before the hammer is fully cocked. If rotation is not complete chances are the hand is too short or worn. If the cylinder turns before the stop retracts, or if the hammer binds after cylinder rotation is complete, the hand may be too long or too thick. Timing problems are best taken care of at the factory or by a pistolsmith who has access to an assortment of parts for fitting. Alteration of a single part can throw off timing sequences elsewhere in the action. Timing functions are interrelated and it requires a thorough understanding of the mechanism to expertly regulate revolver lock work.

A check with a bore gage will show if any cylinders fail to align with the barrel. Correcting any misalignments calls for an experienced eye and proper tools and parts. Again, this is work for an experienced pistolsmith. This check should be made by a prudent pistoleer before purchase of new or used guns, however.

Next, observe the cylinder/barrel gap as the action is cycled several times. If the yoke is aligned and square to the frame, the gap should be constant. Otherwise, the cylinder or yoke bearings could be bent, causing eccentricity of cylinder rotation. If a revolver is in this condition, it will be hard to maintain consistent accuracy.

INTERNAL LOCK FINISH

Polishing comes next, where key interfaces of the mechanism are dressed smooth and finished to minimize sliding resistance. One most important place is the underside of the DA fly (Sear) as it contacts the trigger lobe.

Both surfaces must be completely and patiently stoned and dressed with crocus cloth in the direction of the sliding motion. A final polishing with jewelers rouge may be applied, or the parts can be lapped with J-B® bore cleaning compound. Care must be taken not to remove metal, only tool marks. Action parts are hardened on Smith revolvers, and any penetration of this surface will destroy the part for use in the gun. Alteration of part shapes can cause timing problems in any revolver. The rebound slide (where applicable) needs the same polishing treatment. Those surfaces that carry heavy spring loading need to maintain flat contact with the mating sliding surfaces. These surfaces should be finished to a glassy smoothness to reduce intermittent drag and maintain low sliding resistance.

SPRING TENSIONS

Revolver mainsprings can be lightened to ease pressure on a DA contact surface. However, reduced striking energy of the hammer can cause misfires. As a rule, only coil-type mainsprings should be shortened on an empirical basis. Cut one-half coil at a time until a misfire occurs using primed empty cases for testing. After this, cut another spring adding 1 to 2 full coils for reliable ignition and then install the second spring. Leaf type springs can be softened by reducing the width and polishing the flat sides. Properly conditioned, S&W flat springs have a soft action and do not need modification to render an excellent DA pull. Reliability takes precedence over all other considerations.

Colt DA actions (pre-Mark III) can be altered without lightening hammer striking force. The trick is to change trigger lifting action by welding and rounding the lobe of the trigger nose. This is similar to the Officer's Model "short" action modifications. The change should be done by an experienced pistolsmith and the whole action has to be retimed after installation. The effect is to shorten the action slightly, eliminating up to the last 3 to 5 degrees of hammer arc where the characteristic Colt spring tension gain is experienced just before letoff.

Paul Blazejowski (pistolsmith at Krasne's Inc., 568 Sixth Avenue, San Diego, CA, 92101) does this short-action alteration on Colt revolvers. "Ski" is an ex-Marine Corps armorer who was factory trained at Colt's, Smith & Wesson, and High Standard. For a good part of his service career, he was an armorer for the Marine Corps pistol team; he knows precision handgun fitting like few other gunsmiths. One important feature of this short action job is that spring sets are not altered. The finished handgun is fully reliable as to ignition and DA recovery. Loss of mainspring impetus due to shortening the hammer arc is offset by lightening the hammer to reduce inertia. Once this alteration is completed, the main objection to using Colt DA

Colt Detective Special Lock Work

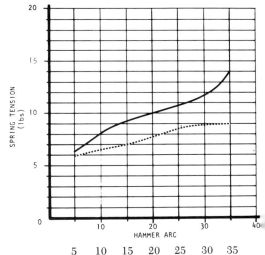

	5	10	15	20	25	30	35
Factory	6.5	8.5	9.25	10	10.75	11.75	14
Blazejowski Alterations	6	6.5	7	7.75	8.5	8.75	9

Blazejowski's technique can shorten hammer arc by up to five degrees, alters the trigger lobe so that it "rolls-off" the strut. These changes eliminate the spring tension gain inherent in Colt double action locks. The whole action has to be retimed following alterations.

Paul Blazejowski does an excellent trigger job on the old Colt revolver actions. These are the most difficult guns to condition for competitive DA shooting. Ski's job is well worth the effort, making Colt's measure up to DA standards set for combat performance.

revolvers for combat shooting is overcome and the many other fine features of these guns can be appreciated.

Graph above shows the trigger pull profile of a Detective Special revolver before and after the Blazejowski treatment. Two basic changes enhance DA trigger operation. Smoothing of the articulating parts reduces irregular drag in the factory pull. Threshold tension needed to initiate trigger movement is reduced along with the maximum peak tension. The tension profile levels out 10 degrees before hammer release. Trigger lobe alterations allow the DA fly (strut) to "roll-off" rather than to "lift-off," eliminating one source of the Colt spring tension gain. This is a major improvement for DA combat shooting.

On Smith revolvers, the rebound slide spring can be shortened by one-half coil to moderate high-end trigger pull tension. Too much shortening of the spring is counterproductive, however, since the recovery action will be weakened. The hammer block can be removed to satisfy purists, but prudent shooters will leave it in as a safety precaution. None of these rebound or hammer block details need attention on revolvers that feature transfer bar ignition. The Colt Mark III, Ruger Security Six, Dan Wesson and High Standard revolvers use this design.

Single-action let-offs can be altered to eliminate creep by decreasing sear engagement and very lightly stoning the engagement surfaces. This is a job that must be done with great finesse, since shortening the trigger nose can destroy timing. Bobbing the SA sear hook on the hammer can result in a stub, where the DA fly bumps the trigger nose as the hammer falls off of SA cock.

MISCELLANEOUS REFINEMENTS

Further detailed polishing is called for on the tip-end of the center pin where it engages the frame. Both the pin channel and the round end need to be polished. The front of the extractor rod should be polished where it engages the locking bolt in the barrel shroud. Locking bolt engagement can be increased to stabilize a loose yoke. By filing the retaining pin flat to make it longer, the locking bolt protrudes farther from its housing. The locking

bolt cone then draws in the extractor rod, reducing looseness in the yoke. These techniques work on Smith and Ruger revolvers but are unnecessary on Colt or Dan Wesson guns that do not secure the front end of the extractor rod.

Occasionally, gun screws work loose and cause stoppages or lost parts. The micrometer sight screw on Smith revolvers is one such item. Colt's extractor rod may loosen up after several hundred rounds. A drop of Loc-Tite©, a resinous liquid that increases thread friction, followed by setting the screw tightly will eliminate this problem.

One last detail finishes the revolver for combat match shooting. The sharp edges of the chamber opening should be eased and slightly radiused to eliminate hangups of bullet noses during reloading. This procedure must be done with a piloted cutter for best results. Most tool makers will provide one or a multi-fluted chamfering tool (90 degrees) will work in a pinch. Care must be taken to cut all easements to the same, slight depth. The very slight radius has no ill affect on case head support and provides positive improvement on cylinder loading time and reliability. One wonders why such a simple operation could not be performed at the factory.

Any revolver that cannot deliver three to four inch groups from a machine rest at 50 yards should be checked thoroughly by a competent pistolsmith. Misalignments, or misfit parts may very well be the cause of the difficulty. Other than this, nothing much can be done to improve revolver accuracy outside of expert and careful fitting. Occasionally, the crown of a barrel becomes damaged and can adversely affect accuracy of the gun. Recrowning the muzzle will correct this condition.

COMBAT CONDITIONING AUTO PISTOLS

The possibilities for improving autopistol performance nearly stagger the imagination. Over the years, various pistolsmiths have perfected techniques to bring the normal 9 to 10-inch fifty-yard machine rest groups shot with the Government Model down to 1/5th that size. In addition, various modifications

Surface smoothness is necessary for friction surfaces that slide over one another. The spring loaded center pin in the cylinder assembly and its frame channel need stoning.

The tip end of the ejector rod must ride up over the locking bolt on S&W and Ruger models. Polishing these engaging surfaces enhances revolver operation.

and refinements have been worked out to make the self-loader function more effectively for combat shooting.

The discussion here is limited to the Government Model and its variations, for these are about the only self-loading guns seen at combat shooting events. The principles illustrated will apply as well to nearly all autopistols, although techniques may differ as to how modifications are done.

ACCURACY STANDARDS

Accuracy in a combat gun is a broad, open subject. Most autopistols shoot well enough for defense purposes as they come from the factory. Indeed while reworking increases autopistol accuracy, the methods called for to accomplish the improvement tend to work against reliable functioning. Within limits, though, accuracy can be increased without unduly jeopardizing reliability. Many combat shooters install a National Match barrel and a trigger job on the .45 ACP. The result shoots 2 to 3 inch groups at 25 yards and is fully reliable.

But eight to twelve minutes of angle accuracy will not hack it on long range shots such as on Stage I of the Advanced Military. All first stage shots must be grouped inside the 8 inch, round bullseye of the 50 yard NRA target. Combined human and mechanical errors of the handgun demand a piece that can deliver 2 to 3 inch 50 yard machine rest groups. Fitting techniques and replacement parts systems have been developed that will produce this result with no apparent reduction in functional reliability of the arm.

INHERENT DEFICIENCIES

The basic problem of accuracy arises from the Browning recoil mechanism of the ACP. The barrel moves inside the slide, while sights are affixed to the slide. On firing, the barrel disengages from the slide during cycling then reengages on to battery. The barrel can reposition in a slightly different place vis-a-vis the sight plane. This action causes inconsistent grouping because the barrel is never pointing at the same spot from one shot to the next. Movement at the breech end is most important since very small displacements are magnified by the length of the barrel. Muzzle displacements at the bushing are less important and slide fit is least important, unless it is so bad that it affects breech-end movement.

Lateral and vertical displacements of the barrel breech are possible. Lateral movement is controlled mostly by the fit of the barrel hood in the slot of the standing breech. Anywhere from .006 to .010-inch play is normal. Each .001-inch movement will cause 1/4 mil bullet impact shift at the target. This amounts to slightly less than 1/2 inch at 50 yards. Barrel legs ride up on the slide stop pin to raise the barrel into locking position. Vertical barrel play between the top of the slide and the slide stop pin can be as much as .020-inch in a particular gun. Fitting the barrel hood and legs are the two most important areas for accuracy in the ACP. Reducing fitted tolerances in these two areas will have the greatest single effect on accuracy improvement and the least effect on reliability. Standard GI and commercial barrels can be custom fitted by building up the sides of the hood and barrel legs with heliarc welding. Match barrels are manufactured with over sized hood and leg dimensions making hard fitting necessary.

A Match-Grade barrel bushing can be added to stabilize muzzle displacement. One of the best precision bushings on the market is made by Sportsmen's Equipment Company. Manufactured to Naval Ordnance specs for Match bushings, this unit is machined from normalized SAE 4350 steel. They are hard and wear resistant, and take a marvelous lap fit to the barrel that will last as long as the gun. Soft bushings tend to wear egg-shaped after several thousand rounds. Bushings have to be fitted carefully to provide the correct zero-play fit in battery without causing binding during cycling that can result in malfunctions.

Slide tightening by squeezing the sides of the slide in a vise can take up lateral play. Slides sometimes pitch up and down excessively, too, and this can be reduced by carefully peening the guide rails. The resulting

Locking bolt engagement in the end of the ejector rod may need adjustment if crane looseness is evident. Filing the retaining pin flat allows the bolt to protrude more from its housing; this tightens up crane looseness.

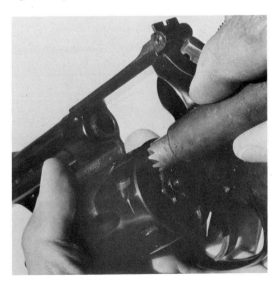

Radiusing chamber openings is important for smooth, consistent speed loadings. Burrs on sharp edges cause lead bullet noses to hang up, adding time to reloading operations.

Complete disassembly of parts is the way to start combat conditioning of an autopistol. Deburr edges and channels on all parts in the frame. Close inspection of bright spots indicates areas for stoning to reduce drag and roughness in the action.

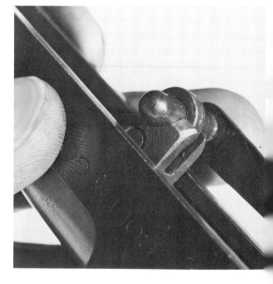

Check for breech-end barrel play on ACP's. This procedure tells whether or not the barrel is well fitted. This is a critical area that affects accuracy and gives a general indication of how well the gun will shoot.

Breech-end barrel-to-slide fitting depends on precision tolerances between the barrel legs and the slide stop pin. Match conditioning requires the fit to be close at this point as well as at the barrel hood. Hood dimensions control lateral play at the barrel breech.

The barrel hood should fit closely to the channel and the standing breech of the slide. This dimension controls lateral play of the barrel breech that limits horizontal group dispersions. This is the second most important dimension for match conditioning an ACP.

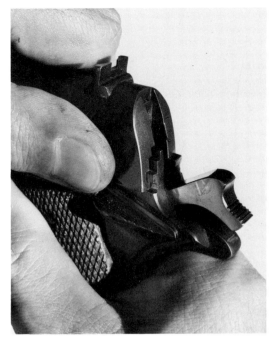

Tight slide fit contributes the least to accuracy and the most to unreliable operation. Refitting of the slide may be required if this part is terribly loose on the frame rails. Check for pitch displacement as well as yaw and roll.

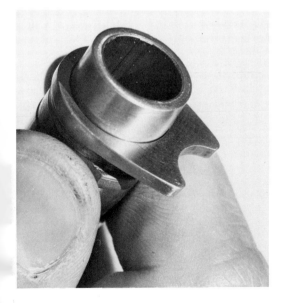

The third critical area for accuracy is the muzzle fit to the barrel bushing. A zero play fit can be carefully and expertly lapped to control muzzle play while still not affecting reliable slide operation.

The Group Gripper provides a simple, reliable way to accurize a .45 ACP. The special link and spring guide replace these regular parts in the gun.

fit is tight and needs to be lapped to provide the proper degree of looseness, so as not to hamper reliable operation. A tight slide has the least effect on accuracy improvement, while it is the chief cause of most reliability problems with accurized autopistols. Unless the shooter wants a super-accurate gun, or the slide is grossly loose, slide tightening may not be worth the effort on a combat gun. If great care is taken with the job, it need not make the gun unreliable. However, this is one area of improvements that is consistently botched by amateur gunsmiths.

ACCURACY SYSTEMS

There are two easy ways to accurize the ACP without resorting to complicated hand fitting techniques. The Group Gripper,® available from Sportsmen's Equipment Company, was the first device made available for

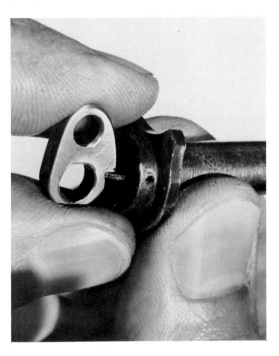

Spring bias applied to the Group Gripper link raises the barrel uniformly into engagement with the slide. As the barrel goes into battery, the notch in the link engages the flat leaf spring in the spring guide to exert upward pressure.

this purpose. Group Gripper essentially applies spring biasing to the link to set the barrel up consistently into the locking abutments. By eliminating the vertical breech-end play, the biggest single source of inaccuracy, group sizes can be reduced from 10 to 40 percent depending on the original relative looseness of the gun. By placing the barrel high up in the locking recesses, the geometry of the barrel-to-slide fit reduces a good deal of lateral play, also, but may require some sight elevation.

The Group Gripper kit consists of a special link with a notch on the front edge that engages a flat leaf spring mounted in a special operating spring guide. Only the link and spring guide need replacement to convert the gun, no special tools or fitting is required. Sometimes, a special long link is required where lug recesses are unusually high. After Group Gripper is installed, 40 to 60 rounds are required to effectively seat the parts. A bit of light oil on the locking lugs helps the break-in process. Machine rest groups will shrink steadily in size to an expected 4 to 5 inches at 50 yards. Addition of a precision bushing will give near-match accuracy for about $28.00 ($12.95 for the Group Gripper; $7.50 for the bushing and $7.50 for installation). The Group Gripper alone is one of the best cost-effective solutions to achieving good combat accuracy with reliability in the ACP.

BAR-STO BARRELS

Another very satisfactory solution to the problem is the installation of a stainless steel barrel system from Bar-Sto Precision. This unit consists of a stainless steel barrel and bushing system that can be installed in any GI or Commercial ACP without tools. Barrels are of exceptionally high quality, made to near maximum dimensions and held to close tolerances to fit issue guns. Hood and leg dimensions are more generous than on standard barrels. Bore quality is superb and this contributes to accuracy along with closely held near maximum external tolerances.

Bar-Sto stainless steel barrel systems are available for both regular Government Model slides and the shorter Commander. Spring fingers on the collet bushing engage the barrel swell near the muzzle. Combined with close tolerance field dimensions in barrel legs and the hood, these barrels provide match accuracy with completely reliable functioning.

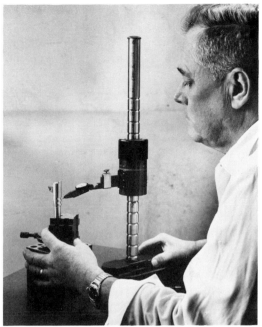

Irv Stone, proprietor of Bar-Sto, checks locking rings for concentricity, one of many quality checks in the making of his barrels. This skilled Texan is a life-long pistol shooter, spent his early career as a jig bore and prototype builder for the aerospace industry.

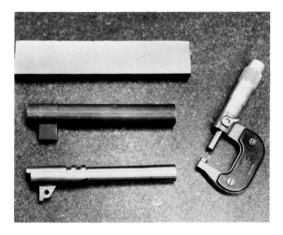

Bar-Sto barrels start life as a bar of 416 stainless steel. The blank is machine formed, then drilled, reamed, and rifled. Final outside dimensions are precision machined to close, consistent tolerances. Final heat treatment brings the barrels up to 38 Rockwell C for durability and long service.

On the standard barrel, outside diameter is reduced from .580 to .560-inch about 1.075-inch back from the muzzle. The transition to the smaller diameter is a slope that engages five spring fingers on the collet-bushing. Four of these fingers apply spring pressure on the barrel slope to center it in the slide and press the barrel against the fifth wide, stationary finger on the bottom of the bushing

The combination of long, wide hood, long barrel legs with full locking engagement and self-centering collet-bushing results in 50 percent or more normal reduction of groups with issue guns. No tools or modifications are needed for installation of the Bar-Sto barrel. Using match ammunition, machine rest tests with the Bar-Sto system produced 2 to 3.5-inch groups at fifty yards. Hard fit match barrels, also furnished by Bar-Sto, print 1 to 2.5-inch groups under the same conditions. The same performance is available from the short Commander guns; this is the only collet-bushing system available for the Commander. Barrels are available in .45 ACP, .38 Super, and 9mm Parabellum calibers.

Irving Stone, owner of Bar-Sto Precision and designer of this barrel system, is a rare

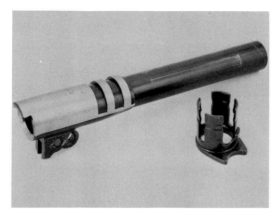

Colt's Mark IV barrel looks like the Bar-Sto system, but differs in its basic principle of operation. The Mark IV bushing fingers bind the barrel at the muzzle swell to effect centering of the barrel in the slide.

kind of person. The impeccable quality of his product reflects the integrity of the man. He offers a quality product without production compromises and sells it at a reasonable price. At $45.00, the Bar-Sto barrel is not out of line with comparable quality replacement parts that require gunsmithing services for a hard fit. It is a good value, giving match accuracy with carefree maintainence and durability of stainless steel.

Colt has offered the Mark IV bushing system in their commercial Government Model pistols for the past several years. The collet bushing system used in these guns is effective in reducing group size to 4 to 5 inches. Its performance is about equal to the Group Gripper compared with standard ACP's. The principle of operation differs from the collet design used in the Bar-Sto system, however. The Bar-Sto collet fingers apply spring tension to press the barrel against the stationary bottom collet finger, maintaining center and uniform muzzle height. On the other hand, the Colt collet binds the fingers between the barrel slope and the slide, drawing the barrel forward and helping to lift it into battery. Pressures at the collet finger contact points on the barrel slope are rather high, and effective life of the parts is dependent on heat treatment of the

bushing. Design of the Colt collet is such that it cannot be used in the Short Commander. Some combat shooters have complained that the Mark IV system will not sustain its accuracy after several thousand rounds. These shooters have switched over to hard fit Match barrels, or one of the accuracy systems mentioned above.

TRIGGER ADJUSTMENTS

A good trigger job is necessary for Match use of an ACP. Limiting the sear engagement and lightening the pull tension are accomplished with a few exacting steps. First, breakdown the gun, and clean the trigger channel of any burrs or roughness with a 1/4 inch fine-cut draw file. Heavy mainspring pressure is a chief cause of poor trigger pull. Cut up to 2 1/2 coils off the mainspring to reduce contact pressure between the sear and the hammer notch. The gun fires from an inertia firing pin and

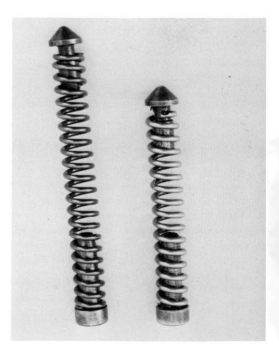

Taking up to three coils off the mainspring of an autopistol improves trigger pull dramatically. Autopistol ignition is not nearly as sensitive to mainspring tension as revolvers.

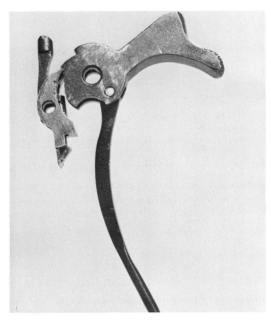

This alignment of ACP ignition parts is critical to a good trigger pull. Sear engagement on the hammer must be limited to make a crisp, single-motion pull. Reducing this engagement too much can result in malfunctioning of the trigger.

An over-travel stop can be installed on a standard ACP trigger by drilling and tapping the solid steel portion of the shoe. Using an undersized tap or a nyloc set screw keeps the threads tight so the Allen-head screw will hold a depth setting. The screw bottoms on the magazine catch body.

This close-up compares altered hammer hooks (right) with a factory new hammer. Great skill must be used to avoid too much metal stock removal, making the trigger too light and/or having the sear intercept the safety notch.

mainspring pressure is not too critical, unlike revolver mainsprings.

The depth of sear contact with the hammer hooks is exaggerated as a safety precaution on commercial and GI guns. Limiting this engagement will aid the pull, making it break crisply without creep. Some of the hammer hook projections can be ground off to limit engagement. This often results in the sear intercepting the safety notch as the hammer falls. Rounding the outside edge of the safety notch may be called for.

Another technique for limiting sear engagement involves drilling a small diameter hole just beneath the sear notch on the hammer; a short piece of rod is press fit and soldered in place. Filing down the pin projection can regulate the amount of sear engagement without running the danger of safety notch interference. Also, if too much is removed by grinding the hammer hook projections, the pull can become too light. Often, guns in this state will drop the hammer as the slide slams home to battery. In this situation the hammer must be discarded or the sear notch can be ground deeper in some cases. The pin method allows for considerable latitude in adjustment without the danger of failure.

The sear nose and hammer hooks should be stoned lightly on their interface. This operation can be done also with J-B bore cleaning paste used as a light lapping compound. A little of this operation goes a long way, since the pull can be made too light. Strive for a 4 1/2 pound pull for safe operation in defensive shooting and combat matches. A very light trigger on a combat autoloader is dangerous. The finishing touch on a trigger job is the installation of an overtravel stop. Target triggers have built-in stops, but their wide tread is not advisable for use in combat shooting. The regular short commercial trigger can be drilled and tapped for a Nyloc® allenhead set screw. The screw should be positioned to contact the magazine catch body as its arresting point.

FEEDING RELIABILITY

Other details condition the ACP for combat service. Feed ramp and barrel throat areas have to be polished with #600 emery, crocus cloth, and/or rubber burnishers. This process eliminates possible drag or stemming of short rounds during the feeding process. Be careful not to extend the front edge of the ramp farther forward than its original profile in the frame. Remember to polish; do not reshape. After polishing the ramp, the barrel is placed on the frame in its lower rearward position. Check to see that there is no ledge formed by barrel overlap of the ramp. Such a ledge will cause feeding hang-ups. The ledge must be removed so that the barrel throat blends with the ramp profile. The throat refers to the incline leading to the chamber opening. On GI barrels there is a narrow throat channel designed to feed hardball ammunition. Lead bullets, and especially semi-wadcutters used in combat match work, will not feed reliably with an issue barrel throat.

ACP barrels should be throated as shown to assure reliable feeding of lead bullet reloads. The edge formed by the intersection of chamber walls and the lower half of the feed ramp should be eased very slightly to avoid stemming of feeding cartridges.

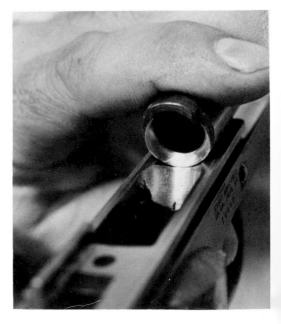

After polishing the feed ramp in the magazine well, the throated barrel should be mated to the frame to check for override. A slight edge produced by the barrel will interrupt smooth cartridge feeding and must be removed.

Target barrels are fully throated so as to feed lead bullets. Properly formed, the throat incline should extend around the full 180 degrees of the bottom half of the barrel breech end. GI or old commercial barrels must have the throats opened for reliable feeding. Use care to see that grinding does not undercut chamber wall support of the case head. Polish to finish the job, then carefully ease the transitional edge from the throat into the chamber proper. Short, fat .45 ACP rounds are especially vunerable to hangups on the bottom edge of the chamber entrance.

EXTRACTION AND EJECTION

ACP ejectors and extractors have a significant influence on flawless functioning. The ejectors must have sharp, well defined faces to assure proper ejection of fired cases. A notched or blunt face will not "bite" the brass, resulting in stove pipes, where the case is caught mouth-up with the rim between the

The front facets of the ejector face should be square and smooth; the juncture of the facets should be sharp and clean to pinion the brass and pivot it out of the ejection port.

standing breech and the hood of the barrel. Extractors must have enough spring tension to hold a case against the breech face. Weak extractors will not hold fired cases securely enough for pivoting out of the ejection port. Double feeding or crushing of fired case mouths into the barrel hood can result. Weak extractors should be replaced. The lower inside edge of the extractor must be gently relieved and deburred so as not to shave brass cartridge rims during feeding. This shaving can cause stemming and/or insufficient closing energy for the slide. Any brass shavings can drop into the action or collect around the extractor to cause malfunctions. The sharp edges on the slide at the bottom of the standing breech should be eased slightly, too.

MISCELANEOUS DETAILS

The opening of the magazine well should be chamfered to allow easy, quick insertion of magazines. Chamfers can be made using a safe-edge warding file. Maintain even and consistent 45 degree slopes on the chamfer until they are at least 1/16 inch wide. Magazines should be inspected closely for burrs on the inside of feed lips, dents and cracks in the upper portion. The engagement with the magazine catch should give about 1/32 inch vertical free play to assure positive engagement and release. Lightly file the upper ledge of the catch notch on the leading edge of the magazine. A fine cut, safe-edge file will do with careful strokes; do not overdo this operation and check as you go. Flush magazines with solvent after filing. Magazines jettisoned during firing usually get dirty and should be flushed in solvent before reuse. Any magazine with a history of faulty operation should be discarded or marked for practice only. Do not use select-grade magazines for general shooting. This practice increases the chances for damage that can cause a malfunction during competition of a defensive shootout.

After the gun has fired several hundred rounds, the slide stop pin tends to turn freely. So, occasionally bullet noses of feeding

Worn ejectors and/or weak extractors can contribute to the "stove-pipe" stoppages. This failure can be corrected easily by "wiping" the case out of the port, but the interruption plays hob with rapid fire scores. A weak or sloppy one-hand hold can also contribute to this phenomenon.

The ACP functions normally when the ejector and extractor are in proper condition. Rim damage results from multiple firings with a rough or damaged extractor claw. Dirty chambers or corroded brass can put extra strain on the extractor, also. Autopistols respond favorably to proper cleaning and servicing. With minimum reasonable care, self-loaders fire flawlessly for thousands of rounds.

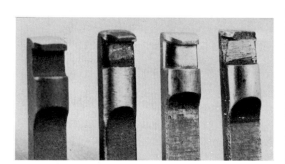

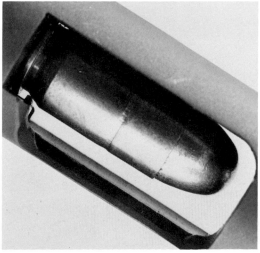

The ACP extractor requires attention to assure perfect functioning. On the left is a new GI extractor showing the square cut rim slot that gouges feeding case rims. Next, the new commercial version has a chamfered bottom edge on the slot. An altered and polished slot on the next unit is ideal. The fourth example shows a broken extractor hook which resulted from firing corroded brass.

Test the ACP extractor for adequate tension by inserting a cartridge in the extractor claw. The cartridge should not fall out of the slide when tilted at any angle.

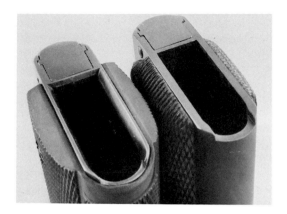

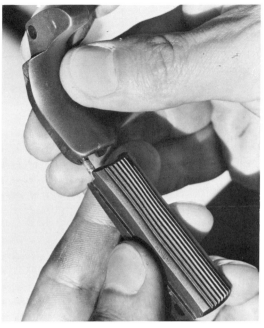

Chamfering the magazine well opening (left) facilitates quick and easy magazine insertion. The radius of the front of the well is edge-relieved but not chamfered. This is an area where bullets can hang up. Magazines should be introduced on a 20 to 30° angle to the well, spine-first to avoid bullet nose contact with the frame.

A small pin mounted in the grip safety slides into a mating hole in the mainspring housing to lock the grip safety in the down position. This detail aids in acquiring a firm, consistent griphold on the autopistol.

Slide stop pins loosen and will allow feeding rounds to raise the stop during a firing string. Drilling a detent for the slide stop plunger eliminates this possible malfunction.

Most combat guns shoot only one load, so a fixed sight is quite serviceable. Some shooters opt for micrometer sights, and a popular solution is the mounting of a S&W K-frame adjustable sight. The latter makes a trim, functional installation if expertly done.

Conditioned to peak efficiency, the combat automatic is highly reliable. This picture sequence shows the rearward slide cycle of a normal functioning ACP. Routine maintenance alone will keep the gun shooting once it has been expertly combat conditioned.

rounds will raise the slide stop to engage the slide. It is disconcerting and disasterous to have the slide stay open in the middle of a shot string. To avoid this embarrassment, cut a detent with a small carbide drill where the slide stop plunger presses against the slide stop in its normal downward position. Take care not to make the detent too deep, since it will neutralize slide stop action. The purpose is to avoid inadvertent slide stop engagement. Normally combat shooters do not shoot clean, leaving a loaded round in the chamber during magazine changes. Because of this the slide stop is applied manually only for safety precautions, locking the slide in its rear position between shooting stages and when off the firing line.

The ACP grip safety is an anachronism on combat guns. It gives a mushy handhold and has little function for match purposes. It is usually pinned solidly out of engagement. This can be done by a pin in the mainspring housing that engages a channel in the base of the grip safety. The safety can also be held neutral by a transverse pin through the frame.

Issue sights on ACP's are not adequate for

match shooting. Two points of view dominate current philosophy on sights. One school installs the S&W K-frame adjustable micrometer sight by milling a slot atop the slide, extending from ejection port to the rear. The regular dovetail slot is filled, welded, and refinished to slide contours. The rear end of the slide is transverse milled to create an aperture body slot for the adjustable sight. This conversion gives a reliable, adjustable sight many shooters prefer for zeroing a variety of loads. The other school does not trust micrometer sights on reciprocating, vibrating autopistol slides. Instead, a high, fixed rear sight is installed on the regular dovetail; it is filed according to front blade height so bullet impact will be zeroed at a given range. Windage is adjusted by drifting the sight in the dovetail for the standard load; elevation is zeroed by filing front or rear sights appropriately.

With handguns combat conditioned and maintained at peak efficiency, the shooter can be confident his equipment is not likely to fail. The challenge of equipment readiness is part of the whole sport to some shooters; top-grade equipment is an inspiration for all shooters. Knowing the handgun can perform puts a competitive onus on the individual to sharpen his human skills. As skills improve the quest for perfection in equipment is renewed and never really ends. In shooting, the mechanical and human systems are inseparable.

CHAPTER XV

HANDLOADING FOR COMBAT HANDGUNS

MOST ROUNDS FIRED BY combat shooters are reloads. Cost of factory ammunition is a foremost consideration, but also, quality and power levels are equally important reasons to reload. The whole activity is not overly complicated, and since match shooting consumes a great deal of ammunition, production techniques are of interest, too.

Load levels for combat ammunition are set by force factors prescribed in League match rules. Few, if any, shooters exceed these minimum limits, since it increases recoil disturbance with no increase in scoring advantages. More powerful defensive loads and maximum loads for combat guns shall be explored, also. These hotter loads are important for real-time defensive situations, where greater terminal ballistic effects are desired. While the loads and techniques will be described in this chapter, the technicalities of terminal effects are given attention in Chapter sixteen.

Load schedules will be predominantly influenced by .38 Special, 9X19mm (Luger) and .45 ACP. Because of power rating ad-vantages, among other things, more .45 ACP's appear on League firing lines than any other caliber. A number of career peace officers shoot with combat groups and prefer to use their duty guns with .38 Special cartridges. A few competitors show up with 9mm guns in certain events, either to experiment or out of devotion to the caliber. 9mm brass is hard to come by, and commercial cases cost a fortune. Ready availability of low cost brass favors .45 ACP and .38 Special. Occasionally, a .38 Super is used in competition but, again, for the same reasons 9mm appears.

CARTRIDGE CASES

A collection of 2000 brass cases will serve as a starter. Autoloaders are hard on brass, both as to feeding and extraction, and loss on the shooting grounds. Handpicked match cases can be kissed goodbye, since they comingle with other empties on the firing line. Revolvers are easier on brass in this regard. However, cold working of long .38 Special cases during reloading operations tends to produce cracks at case mouths and longitudinal body splits. Short, fat autopistol cases are not crimped and tend to last longer regarding cold working factors; case rims and bases are another story, however. No sane pistol loads are so hot that primer pockets enlarge, and case head integrity is no problem either. Any loads that expand extraction grooves on autopistol cases had better be backed off.

It is a good idea to obtain cases of the same make if possible and all of the same reloading age, preferably virgin or once fired. If possible, keep these cases together and reload all at the same time. This kind of uniformity will pay in terms of reload quality and accuracy performance. It also eliminates sorting problems when it comes time to retire the lot; early signs of deterioration usually indicate symptoms characteristic of the whole lot. Combat loads are stiffer than mid-range ammunition used in formal target shooting; com-

bat load cases cannot be expected to last as long. But, autopistol cases expecially are rugged and will withstand 20 to 50 reloadings, if they don't get lost or stepped on in the interim.

It is a good idea to purchase or select high-grade commercial cases for match shooting. Some pistoleers buy match grade ammunition and then save the brass. These cases will get lost in competition and represent an expendable item of expense. The need for highly uniform match ammo is of particular importance. Otherwise, once fired GI or commercial cases are available for the stock of practice ammunition hulls.

Cases should be deprimed and cleaned. For best results, a drum case tumbler should be used (Thumbler's Tumbler® is available from J&G Rifle Ranch, Turner, Montana 59542). Walnut shells with brass polish or iron oxide polishing compound, provides a good tumbling medium. This apparatus will brighten up the brass and can even be used to tumble clean, finished rounds. Without a tumbler, use of a detergent water solution is

Tumbling fired, deprimed cases in walnut shells or ground corn cobs saturated with rouge or Brasso® solution cleans the brass efficiently. This Tumbler's Tumbler is available from J&G Rifle Ranch, Turner, Montana.

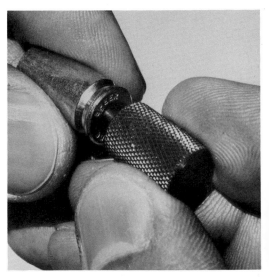

Match ammunition should have primer pockets cleaned before repriming. Use a spade-type tool, such as this Lee Pocket Cleaner or a wire brush type offered by RCBS is quick and efficient.

an effective way of cleaning fired brass, followed by a hot, clear, rinse. The hot cases will air dry after rolling inside a terry cloth towel. Cases should dry for 24 hours to assure no moisture contamination of priming compound when new loads are assembled. Do not force dry cases in an oven; this leads to oxidation and possible change in relative hardness of case heads and rims.

Primer pockets normally will clean out with tumbling or vigorous washing. Some caked residues may remain, but will fall out with the next firing/cleaning cycle. Generally match cases should have primer pockets cleaned by a chisel point tool such as the Lee Pocket Cleaner® or a wire brush type made by RCBS. This is a precaution against primer failure and erratic ignition. For practice ammunition, it is not worth the effort to individually clean primer pockets.

PRIMERS

Primers can be a problem in revolvers, particularly if the shooter has lightened the main spring. Thin cups, sensitive priming compound are called for; Remington and Federal primers can be recommended in this regard. Occasional irregularities in primer cup hardness can cause a misfire. The few small pistol primers that have ever failed in the author's experience were during a match. Murphy's Law always strikes when you can least afford it! The reliability of ignition inherent in most autopistols eliminates the consideration for primer cup hardness. CCI large pistol primers have worked well. And, shooters can thank CCI for making high-quality primers available at competitive prices. Not too many years back, major ammunition firms were not overly eager to sell reloading components at competitive prices. No match level loads will require the hot primer pulse of Magnum caps. Some maximum loads using hard to ignite spherical powders will call for hot primers. Unless specified, Magnum priming is uncalled for in most pistol loads.

PROPELLANTS

Propellants for combat loads pose no big problem. Nearly all shooters who "roll their own" ammunition, reload with Bullseye®. This powder has the advantages of low cost and a reputation for inherently accurate reloads in nearly every caliber. It is not as flexible as other propellants, but accounts for midrange up to threshold combat loads in nearly all center-fire pistol calibers.

Dupont 700-X® affords considerably more loading flexibility, extending into the full-power range in both .38 Special and .45 ACP cases. This powder burns cleaner (without the oily residue) than Bullseye and cooler; it will not lead as badly on hot loads. Cost is higher than Bullseye but not by much when purchased in bulk. 700-X will not produce as small groups as Bullseye in some guns. But this factor has to be determined by testing. Winchester 230® ball powder has somewhat slower burning rate than Bullseye. Its application in maximum loads for small pocket auto cartridges has been notable. Red Dot® is an inexpensive, efficient powder for many calibers, but accuracy is erratic within different guns of the same caliber and with different loads.

Loads used in combat matches may not be the same ones used for defensive shooting, although they would be adequate in most situations. The middle-range of shotshell propellents provide efficient handgun loads. Such powders as Unique®, Herco®, AL-5®, AL-7®, SR7625®, PB®, or HS-5® provide more powerful loads especially in 9mm/.357 bores, where the faster burning powders are limited. Due to its high expansion ratio, .45 ACP works very well in maximum loadings with Bullseye and, especially 700-X. The fastest loads in the smaller bore size are produced from Magnum shotshell powders loaded to produce optimum average chamber pressures within peak pressure limits for the gun. These powders include SR4756, N1020, HS-6, AL-8, 296 and 630.

INTERNAL BALLISTICS

Velocity is a function of chamber pressure. The average pressure x time (barrel length) determines the bullets' velocity. Peak chamber pressures (the figures most often quoted) do not indicate average pressures. The load peak relates to the gun's capacity to contain pressure without bursting. In conventional guns these maximums run to around 20,000 psi in regular cartridges to about 35,000 psi nominal for Magnum handguns and 9mm. The systems will shoot heavier loads, but not without shortening handgun service life, particularly in small size or alloy frame guns. Powder burning rates can be adjusted so the pressure curve peak does not exceed the maximums while increased total energy is released.

In Graph XV-I we see three representative pressure curves. Curve A demonstrates fast burning powders. In this curve pressure rises rapidly to maximum with a steep fall off as the powder charge is burned out and bullet travel opens bore volume. Curve B shows what happens when the powder burning rate is delayed, or made more *progressive*. Pressure builds up more slowly to maximum. As bullet travel accelerates, all the powder is not burned out. Additional burning produces gas and heat expansion to fill the volume opened by bullet travel. The net effect is to extend the peak of the curve to the right and make the down slope more gradual. The result: more area under the curve and a higher average pressure, with more velocity and energy for the projectile in any given barrel length. Curve C illustrates powders that burn too slowly to create enough gas and heat to raise peak pressure to maximum.

It is possible to load handgun cartridges to performance levels that exceed usable, applicable limits for combat shooting. In most combat handguns, loads exceeding 350 to 400 foot pounds of energy do so at some cost of control, accuracy, and handgun service life. The shooter may be enthralled with the idea of carrying elephant loads around in his handgun, but shooting performance and mechanical integrity of the gun are going to suffer. Loads so heavy as to seriously affect the scores on basic courses of fire should be reduced. Field and hunting applications are different. The combat shooter has to perform predictably and consistently well with multiple shot strings. Approaching the defensive load business with an eye to practical maximum levels is prudent and mature.

BULLETS

Again, the choice of bullets for combat match shooting is fairly straight forward. A standard .45 ACP projectile used by most combat shooters is the 200 grain, Hensley and Gibbs #68 semi-wadcutter. This bullet has an impeccable performance record in all match shooting activity whether combat or NRA style. Several slightly different versions are available from other mold makers. Some of the variations will not feed as reliably as the #68. Normally, one would think the truncated conical nose section of the semi-wadcutter would have a hard time making it up the feed ramp. To the contrary, the front edge of the #68 nose cone matches the ramp contact diameter of the profile on a regular hardball jacketed bullet. This can be seen

Propellant Variations

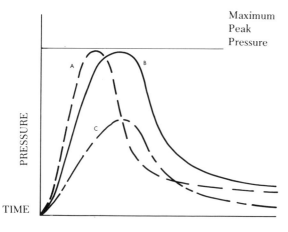

A broad selection of cast and swaged lead bullets are available in combat calibers. These are some of the exceptional performing projectiles. (Top Row) Left to right—.358-inch diameter—the (A) 142 grain Lee RN, (B) 145 grain Markell SWC, (C) 148 grain Speer HBWC, (D) 150 grain Lee SWC, (E) 158 grain Hornady RN, (F) 158 grain Speer RN, (G) 160 grain Lee RN,(H) 160 grain H&G #7 two-band spire point. (Bottom row) Left to right—9mm (I) 107 grain Markell RN, (J) 125 grain Markell RN, (K) 125 grain H&G #7 spire point, (L) 124 grain Lyman Conical, (M) .45 ACP all 200 grain-Speer swaged SWC, (N) H&G #68 SWC, (O) Adams RNWC, (P) .452 Nichols RN (experimental), (Q) .452 Nichols Spire Point.

by standing a loaded #68 round up against a standard GI hardball cartridge. Rates of bullet elevation and lift angles of the feeding round are the same even though the bullet shape differs radically. Seating depth of the #68 must be watched to assure proper feeding, however. Speer, Incorporated makes a very reliable 200 grain swaged lead SWC that is virtually the same bullet as the #68 H&G. Swaged lead bullets maintain quite uniform weight and density.

Other very effective bullets for the ACP are the Lyman #452374, a 225 grain replica of the GI hardball bullet. The .452 Nichols (H&G #249) is a scaled-up version of the H&G #7 125 grain 9mm spire point design. Al Nichols has recently made a 200 grain experimental cast version of the standard round nose hardball bullet. Unfortunately, molds are not ready as of this writing. John Adams, a Los Angeles combat shooter, designed a

200 grain .452 bullet that incorporates a round nose section for feeding reliability, with a slight square shoulder to cut nice clean holes in targets. A number of L.A. competitors have adopted this design.

In .38 caliber, the 148 grain wadcutter is used in police PPC firing. Inexpensive reloading, low recoil, and inherent accuracy recommend this choice. However, the bullet is poorly adapted to multiple cylinder reloading because of its flat nose. The standard round nose 158 grain service bullet is hard to beat; with the case mouth crimped deep enough to hide the wall, these rounds chamber smoothly in a multiple loading device. One of the most accurate .38 bullets is a spire point 160 grain stretched version of the 9mm 125 grain H&G spire. This bullet (H&G #7 two-band) has two lube grooves. Crimping the case mouth into the top lube groove makes a slick, flawless chambering cartridge. The spire point and long straight body of this 160 grain bullet evidently stabilizes perfectly out of 18-twist S&W barrels. Bullet precession rates must be very uniform over long distances to produce the exceptionally tight 50 yard groups shot with this bullet.

The lighter weight (less than 158 grains) .38 bullets usually are not loaded in combat match ammunition. However, an excellent all around bullet is the Lee #358-150-SWC. This is a 150 grain semi-wadcutter that has performed wonderfully well in a number of .357 bore guns. Lee's 142 grain round nose configuration (#358-142-RN) also has performed well, giving very consistent, tight groups in slow twist revolver barrels. This 142 grain weight is a bit light to meet minimum load requirements without leading. The power factors seriously limit light weight

The Hensley and Gibbs #68 bullet is a 200 grain semi-wadcutter design, the nose of which closely approximates the tangent radius dimension of the standard hardball ogive. When carefully seated, this H&G projectile will duplicate feeding reliability of hardball ammo in a throated barrel.

bullets because of the premiums put on bullet momentum as against kinetic energy.

For 9mm match loads, the H&G #7 125 grain spire point bullet is most commonly seen (the actual cast weight may be lower than specified). Lyman's #356402 is a classic, truncated spire point, a design that was popular in the early part of the century for the 9mm Luger. Again, the lighter bullet weights are severely handicapped with the power factors and ratings based on momentum theory of ballistic performance. 9mm combat loads are much more effective with light bullets that take full advantage of the high-intensity interior ballistics of this limited capacity cartridge. With heavy bullets, 9mm is little better than .38 Special service loads.

Lead bullets are most commonly used in match shooting because of low cost and ease of production. Home grown jacketed bullets can be made, but the cost of jackets prohibits their mass use for combat shooting. Early half-jacketed rounds also left pure lead exposed to the barrel walls. Special lubricants cut down the amount of leading by lowering barrel wall friction. Soft pure lead in the core also tended to set back during firing of stiff loads. Random deformation of bullet shapes caused inaccuracy.

Availability of 3/4 jackets has eliminated the exposed lead problem. Bullet dies are available that can form jackets into the nose ogive to support the lead core during acceleration. The idea for using jacketed bullets is to provide gilding metal covering to eliminate leading and support the pure lead core. Much hotter loads are possible with this arrangement. While the jacket supports the core and protects it from pressure and heat, on terminal impact the soft core deforms, mushrooming the nose section more readily than with harder, cast lead alloys. This idea works well except when jackets resist deformation. Any significant resistance to deformation in a high-velocity load delays mushrooming until after the bullet has passed through the terminal target.

Some high-speed jacketed bullets go clear through the target before expansion takes place. The design of jackets, their shape, thickness, and nose structure affect performance. The best bullets resist (1) inertial deformation in the bore, and (2) centrifugal deformation from over stabilization on the way to the target. But, on terminal impact, the jackets must (3) quickly deform at the nose to achieve expansion at the earliest possible time. Meeting all these performance criteria is a tall order for any bullet design. The best bullets do a good job, making com-promises that favor one performance factor slightly over another. Specialized designs that overly favor one performance aspect do poorly in the other two.

Lead bullets must be cast from a reasonably hard alloy to work well. Hot propellant gases, especially in high pressure loads, transfer convectional heat to the bullet base. Barrel wall friction also heats the contact surfaces of the bullet. The most vulnerable place is the bullet base rim; heated from both sides and the bottom, the thin edge section melts and smears on the bore. Mild leading can

For personal defense, heavier than minimum match loads are called for. Use of jacketed projectiles eliminates the possibility of leading, while pure lead cores allow mushrooming on terminal contact. These are some representative bullets from a wide variety of projectiles available from several suppliers.

(Top row) Left to right — .357 caliber — (A) 110 Hornady JHP, (B) 125 grain Remington SJHP, (C) Super Vel 137 grain JSP, (D) 140 grain Speer JHP, (E) 146 grain Speer JHP, (F) 158 grain Hornady JHP.

(Middle row) Left to right — 9mm — (G) 90 grain Super Vel JHP, (H) 95 grain Remington FMJ, (I) 100 grain Speer HBHP, (J) 108 grain Super Vel JSP, (K) 115 grain Hornady JHP, (L) 116 grain Norma FMJ, (M) 125 grain Speer JSP, (N) 130 grain Remington FMJ.

(Bottom row) Left to right — (O) .45 ACP — 185 grain Hornady JHP, (P) 200 Speer JHP, (Q) 230 grain Remington JMJ.

be controlled by using an Alox lubricant and with effective cleaning with Rice's solvents and lubes. Choice of alloys is important in limiting leading. Wheel weight metal has adequate hardness; so has #2 Lyman alloy or equivalent as well as Linotype metal. One criticism on Lino metal is its tendency to leave bubbles in the interior of the bullet. Bubbles affect the dynamic balance of the bullet as it spins to the target, makes precession erratic, increases yaw and air resistance. Accuracy suffers. Solid swaged lead bullets have the most uniform density, close weight variations, and freedom from internal voids.

Bevel based bullets eliminate the chief cause of leading, the base edge. Bevel basing is an aid to rapid reloading and consistent bullet seating. The amount of case mouth belling can be reduced, extending case life. Really hot loads should be gas checked, although this practice is not as popular today as it was in the past due to current availability of first-quality jacketed bullets.

Bullet casting operations can be streamlined with two or more people cooperating for high volume output. Up to ten cavity molds are available. These large molds require a lot of arm and hand strength to

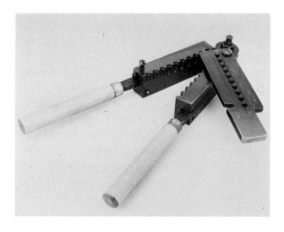

A ten-cavity mold is heavy to manipulate, but it is capable of producing volume output for serious shooters. A four-cavity mold is about the minimum size for high volume output.

manipulate. A large, open lead pot is needed with an amply large ladle to charge the cavities. Mold temperatures can be modulated by touching the bottom of the mold block on a wet towel after each casting. Any apparatus that can support the mold while it is opened and emptied will conserve strength for long casting operations. Bullets should fall on a soft pad to avoid deformation.

Large, gravity fed lead melters eliminate ladling; most designs come with a support rack to hold large molds. As convenient and safe as these melters are, they will not reach the output levels of a good multicavity mold with open lead pot setup.

Lee Precision, Inc. has introduced a line of aluminum bullet casting molds that have a number of advantages. Low cost, light weight, and cavity uniformity recommend these products. Lee's four cavity molds have the same weight as a single cavity semi-steel block. Cavity uniformity is especially important in volume production. Many of the best made iron molds have significant variations between cavities. For uniform match grade bullets, all projectiles should be taken from a single, selected cavity. Lee molds are made by a hobbing process that cuts the cavity to a near finished size. Then a carbide bullet form is inserted and the paired blocks are squeezed in a hydraulic press. The resulting cavity is very uniform in size and smooth in finish. Because of the light weight and rapid heat dissipation of Lee's four cavity molds the number of castings are almost doubled, making it function like an eight cavity iron mold. Aluminum's high specific heat means that the Lee molds need little if any warm up time. They also tend to "freeze" the lead sooner, and dissipate heat faster than iron. The tendency is to achieve and maintain an even working level temperature. Bullet finish and dimensional tolerances are exceptionally good.

For defensive loads, properly designed jacketed bullets expand at lower velocity than cast bullets of comparable weight. How-

The Lee Production Melter is a good size for moderate bullet casting. The relatively large size of the melter maintains adequate lead temperature for continuous output while more lead ingots are melting. Large open lead pots run with hand ladles are

This unique Lee aluminum bullet mold is lightweight, highly efficient. Ease of production with a four cavity model just about doubles the output obtainable with a semi-steel four-cavity mold. The aluminum four-cavity mold weighs about the same as a steel single cavity mold.

ever, loads with lead bullets attain velocities up to 15 percent higher than jacketed bullets of the same weight using the same powder charge. Lubricated lead has a considerably lower friction coefficient than gilding metal jackets. The resulting increase in ballistic efficiency is useful with some kinds of loads, particularly in autopistol loads that traditionally shoot nonexpanding FMJ bullets. In pocket autos, lead bullets are more efficient than the usual FMJ nonexpanding factory ammunition. In really hot combat loads, gas checks should be used with lead bullets.

The loading tables (XV-I, XV-II, XV-III) give a breakdown into three classifications for combat ammunition. Minimum combat loads are given that satisfy power factors and requirements for league accuracy standards. The next class of loads are those in

the moderately heavy group, representing maximum effective defensive loads that are more powerful than League minimum for serious defensive work. They are controllable within scoring standards for regular combat courses of fire. The last group represents maximum loads for the caliber given. These loads are not necessarily recommended for use, although they will be safe in modern guns in good condition. Recoil, muzzle blast, and excessive energy levels do not make them well balanced for all around use. Included in the tables for comparisons and reference are selected commercial loads.

SPECIAL PURPOSE LOADS

Special purpose loads fill some of the gaps in performance with regular ammunition. Also, they can provide unique performance

TABLE XV-I

COMBAT MATCH LOADS*

Cartridge	Powder	/	Wt.	Bullet	/	Wt.	MV	ME	Threshold Velocity
.45 ACP	Bullseye		4.3gr	#68 H&G		200gr	816	294	800
.357 Mag.	W-W296		16.5	#7 H&G		160	1355	651	1345
.38 Special	Bullseye		3.6	Speer RN		158	860	259	848
9x19mm	700X		4	#7 H&G		125	1085	326	1072
.38 Super	700X		4.2	#7 H&G		125	1075	321	1072

*Loads fired in 4-inch barrel revolvers or 5-inch autopistols. The loads are designed to meet Southwest Pistol League minimum standards, which is why energy/ velocity figures are so distorted in some cases. Power rating rules favor the .45 ACP. Leading problems may occur with the .357 Mag load given; see Chapter 14 for bore care tips. Gas checks may be required for this load.

TABLE XV-II

DEFENSE LOADS*

Cartridge	Powder	/	Wt.	Bullet	/	Wt.	MV	ME
.45 ACP	700X		5.2gr	Speer JHP		200gr	889	352
.357 Mag	AL-5		9.5	Horn. JHP		158	1011	357
.357 Mag	Unique		8	Speer JHP		140	1068	354
.38 Special	AL-7		9	Speer JHP		140	1072	357
.38 Special	Herco		8	RemgtnJHP		125	1150	366
.38 Special	AL-7		8	Horn. JHP		110	1198	350
9x19mm	Herco		7.2	SpeerHBHP		100	1263	353
9x19mm	Herco		6	RemgtnJHP		115	1175	352
.38 Super	Unique		6.5	RemgtnJHP		115	1180	355

*Other jacketed bullets of the same weights can be substituted with comparable performance.

TABLE XV-III

MAXIMUM LOADS*

Cartridge	Powder	/	Wt.	Bullet	/	Wt.	MV	ME
.45 ACP	Unique		7.7gr	Speer JHP		200gr	1010	452
.357 Mag	N1020		14	Horn JHP		158	1202	504
.38 Special	4756		12	RemgtnJHP		125	1312	478
9x19mm	Herco		7	RemgtnJHP		115	1301	431
.38 Super	Unique		7	RemgtnJHP		115	1330	451

*These loads are not recommended for regular use, although they should be safe in modern guns in good condition. Approach maximum powder weights from 2 grains below indicated amounts and increase by increments of ½ grains.

The variety and quality of factory handgun ammunition has increased in recent years. Virtually all representative loads from mid-range target to full-bore magnum power are available. Only a few of the many effective commercial rounds are shown here.

Group A — 9mm — 90 grain Super Vel JHP; 100 grain S&W JHP; 115 grain JSWC; 115 grain Remington JHP.

Group B — .45 ACP — 173 grain Remington Hi-Way Master; 190 grain Super Vel JHP; 230 grain GI Hardball Winchester-Western.

Group C — .38 Special — 110 grain Norma JHP; 125 grain Remington JHP; 158 grain Super Vel SWC International Police.

Group D — .357 Magnum — 137 grain Super Vel JSP; 158 grain Remington SJHP; 158 grain Winchester lead SWC.

of their own. In defensive shooting, there is a need for loads of moderate power and low penetration that provide wounding capacity out of proportion to loading levels. Three such loads can be discussed here. These include reversed hollow base swaged lead wadcutter bullets, three piece buckshot charges, and plastic bullet loads.

Using .358-inch Speer, Hornady, Super Vel swaged lead hollow base wadcutter bullets, very effective low velocity expanding loads can be made. By reversing the hollow base, the ultimate in hollow point design is possible. The large, full caliber open end,

blossoms to nearly double bore diameter on impact. Velocity levels should be kept under 850 fps, since at this point, the bullet starts to disintegrate on impact. With the case crimped into the upper most lube groove, usual target loads of Bullseye or 700-X in .38 Special and .357 Magnum cases give adequate zap for these special loads. Terminal transfer of energy to the target exceeds 50 percent. This same loading technique can be used with any caliber wadcutter by hollow basing the bullets in a lathe collet.

Three pieces of #1 buckshot (.30-inch diameter) can be assembled in a Speer plas-

Light target load powder charges are all that is needed to propel these 148 grain hollow based wadcutters to cause mushrooming to nearly double the caliber size. Inverting the hollow base of this Speer HPWC bullet produces defensive ammunition with wounding efficiency out of proportion to kinetic energy.

Buckshot loads are made up for .357 brass using three pieces of .30-inch #1 buckshot loaded into a Speer plastic shot sleeve. Effective range is limited to short distances presently, due to erratic centers of impact.

The three-ball "pawnshop" loads leave an efficient "footprint." By spreading the shot over a sizeable area, terminal ballistic effects are enhanced relative to the total striking energy.

tic shot capsule. A .357 Magnum case loaded with 10 grains of Unique with a heavy crimp into the plastic sleeve gives a lethal defensive load. Shot patterns with the buckshot produce 3 hole "footprints" that enhance terminal effectiveness. These loads are suitable only at very short ranges, due to erratic release of the buckshot from the capsule; any shots beyond 50 feet range might miss a silhouette target. Each 39 grain shot pellet has about the energy of a .22 LR bullet, but in a low sectional density ball. Very nearly all the kinetic energy is transferred on the terminal end. More predictable patterns can be made using BB shot, which can be just as lethal as the buckshot at close range. Use of these loads for home defense would reduce the possibility of wall penetration of projectiles that miss the mark. For police work, shooting of mad dogs or other dangerous animals in civilized areas is a possible application of the loads.

Red Jet plastic bullets, designed for indoor pistol practice with primer ignition, can make some unique ammunition. These light 11 grain .358-inch projectiles are seated all the way down on top of 9 grains of Bullseye powder in a .357 Magnum case. The loads clock in at 2403 fps with energy of 141 foot pounds. Muzzle flash is considerable. Transfer of energy to the target is complete with shallow penetration. These loads need more experimentation for complete evalua-

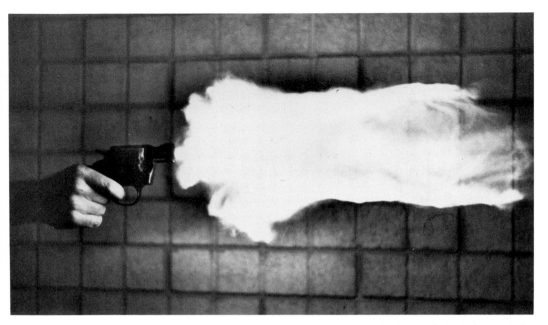

This load took its own picture! With the shutter open, the brilliant muzzle flash was all the light needed to make the photo. This was a special Red Jet plastic bullet load using 9 grains of bullseye behind the 11-grain plastic projectile; muzzle velocity was slightly over 2400 fps.

tion, however. Designed by the author originally to provide anti-hijacking loads in aircraft in flight, further testing revealed that they would not penetrate standard residential double drywall construction. They may also be quite effective for court room use by bailiffs and for home defense. The full effects of heavy clothing, belts, or buckles, etc. on penetration is not known. The sudden, violent, and complete energy transfer from the light plastic bullets provides this load's chief recommendation.

Primer powered wax bullets can be loaded for practice of draw and fire and point shooting fundamentals. A standard primed case is pushed down into a cake of paraffin to cut out and insert the bullet. Primer ignition is enough to drive the paraffin slug. If primers set back due to low pocket pressure, drill out the primer flash hole about 1/32-inch. Special wood block holders can be made to position 30 to 50 cases at a time, so paraffin blocks can be gang-punched in a vise or flat press. This technique gives high produc-

tion where a lot of wax bullet loads will be fired. Impact of the wax projectiles on a plywood silhouette is sufficient to stop an impact clock for use in basic shooting drills.

Red Jet bullets are easy to load. Bullets must be seated fully down on the powder charge to assure efficient burning of the propellant. A more dense plastic/wax composition undoubtedly would enhance ballistic efficiency.

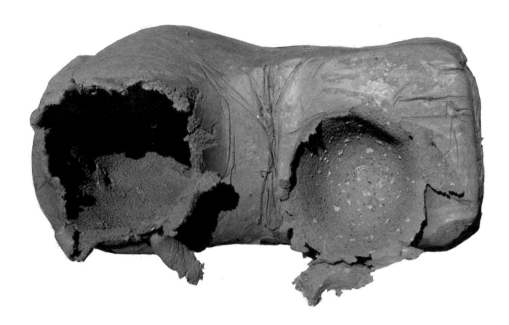

Complete terminal energy transfer of Red Jet bullets is shown here on a clay impact block. The effects are compared to a Super Vel 110 grain .357 load. The Red Jet left a 4-inch diameter by 2½ -inch deep crater. The JHP bullet penetrated the 6x6-inch block, leaving a 5½-inch turnip-shaped cavity.

PRODUCTION TECHNIQUES

Two kinds of production techniques are needed to produce ammunition for combat handgunning. High output of good quality practice ammunition is one thing, assembly of precise match ammunition is another. Only those courses of fire that require long range small group shooting will need precision assembled ammunition. In these situations, the difference in going clean or scoring down in a match can be entirely due to the ammunition. Otherwise, a good grade of practice ammunition is okay for most fast, short range stages.

Precision match cartridges need to be made from selected cases and bullets. Assembly should be on individual loading presses. If an analytical balance is available, use it. Otherwise, a high quality reloading scale such as the Ohaus Model 1110® is best. De-

primed and cleaned cases should be weighed; select a group from plus or minus one grain weight difference off of a median weight for the lot. These cases should then be checked for length against standard cases that have performed well in a particular gun. Do not load special match rounds; merely assemble to very close specifications the usual standard loads. Analytic balances are useful for measuring powder charges that are right on the money. All these procedures take time, and some people may think its like carrying coals to New Castle; but, they are not usually the people who carry home first place positions, especially in demanding long-range matches.

Sized bullets should be weighed and kept to within plus or minus .5-grain weight if possible. By grouping bullets as the batch is measured, the modal weights within the tolerance will cluster. It doesn't matter which weight is chosen, just use a uniform group. Assemble these loads giving careful attention to uniform crimps (rolled or tapered, heavy or light) and overall length for the cartridge. Autoloaders are especially sensitive to feeding reliably cartridges that are shorter or longer than a particular length. Case neck tension must be ample to assure bullets will not be driven back into cases when they feed up the ramp.

Purchase of a progressive loading tool for production work is a good investment. Charging five dollars an hour for one's reloading time soon adds up to the price of the tool for an active combat pistoleer. Tools can be purchased by small groups where members can rotate their use during a given time. Standardized loads eliminate the need for individual changeovers and readjustments within a given caliber. One of the finest and oldest progressive tools on the market is the Star. It has decades of proven performance by target shooters who are critical and demanding. Reloads assembled on a properly adjusted Star will satisfy all but the most exacting demands. Complete with the Hulme case feeding attachment, nominally 500 rounds per hour can be loaded with ease on the Star. This kind of a setup is a must for serious combat shooters who want to develop into top grade performers.

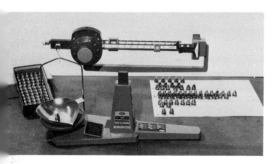

The Ohaus Model 1110 scale is one of the finest devices available to the handloader. Its reliability was checked against an analytical balance. Precise measurement of match ammunition components is vital to consistently high performance in competition, especially for long-range events.

Firing of up to 500 rounds a week is necessary to attain and keep peak proficiency in competitive circles.

Once loads are assembled, testing should be a part of the routine. Two approaches to this task are useful. One is to use a machine rest to objectively check ammunition and the gun. But shooters do not compete with machine rests. So, the best deliberate prone technique is needed to see how ammunition groups in the hands of the shooter using sight alignment.

The Ransom Machine Rest® is highly recommended as one of the finest tools available for precision testing. This rest should be securely anchored to a solid mounting. The author uses a 30 pound steel plate bolted to an 18-inch diameter concrete caisson. This mount represents stability in the extreme; inadequate machine rest mountings can introduce errors not attributable to the gun or ammunition.

Lee Precision also makes an effective, inexpensive pistol rest. The shooter has to get the hang of using it for best results. Uniformity of handhold on the gun is required to achieve valid group testing. The base is a reference frame for the carriage assembly to which the gun is attached. Firing is done with the hand on the gun handle in the usual way. Recoil lifts the gun and carriage slightly off the base. This system more nearly simulates actual shooting conditions than clamped down rests, and offers some advantages not found in the more rigid kind of rest.

As part of a complete evaluation program, revolvers should always be tested for accuracy with each individual cylinder. Five or ten shot groups will soon show which chambers group best. A small scratch or indentation can be made to indicate the most accurate chamber, so it alone will be used to fire precise, long-range deliberate groups.

An electronic chronograph is useful to test loads from particular guns to check for

For convenient production of quality reloads in high volume, the Star Progressive Reloader is essentia
Proven after decades of reliable service in reloading for critical target ammunition, the Star is unsurpassed

Precision handguns and custom loads must be tested to prove performance. Long-range events necessarily need tested components that deliver 1 to 2.5-inch machine rest groups at 50 yards. This Ransom Master Rest is one of the very best devices of its kind available on the market.

A less expensive rest is made by Lee Precision, which allows accuracy testing that very nearly reflects conditions of actual shooting. Installation and operation of this apparatus is simple and reliable.

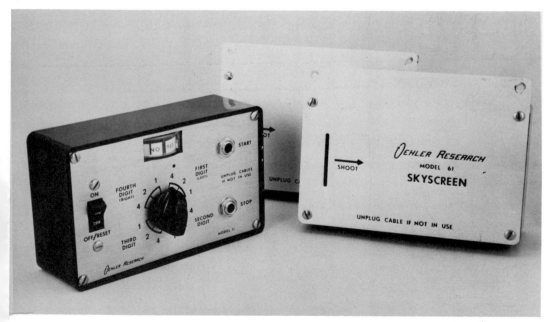

It is useful for experimental loads to know if they meet velocity standards for competition. The Oehler Model 1161 offers a precision, small, and lightweight instrument with the convenience of photoscreens, all for a modest cost.

de facto velocities. Published velocity figures often differ considerably from what a load does in another gun. On loads that are borderline for minimum League requirements, a particular gun may qualify with a load while another one may not. For any detailed analysis of new loads, muzzle velocity data is primary. Today, excellent counter chronographs are available for just over $150. One of the best units available for basic, portable work is the Oehler Model 1161® that comes complete with photo electric screens and operates on self-contained dry cell batteries.

Simple and direct in use, it probably combines more desirable features per dollar than any other unit currently available. Photoscreens eliminate time consuming screen changes, and accuracy of the unit allows discrimination among load variations.

For more detailed loading information and techniques, the shooter should collect several of the better known loading manuals put out by bullet and accessory manufacturers. Speer, Hornady, Sierra, Lyman, and Hodgdon offer some of the most valuable and authoritative manuals for the reloader.

TABLE XV-IV

COMMERCIAL LOADS°

Caliber	Brand	Bullet /	Wt.	MV	ME	Bbl
.45 ACP	Super Vel	JHP	190gr	1010	429	5″
	Remington	JHP	185	952	372	5
.357 Mag	Super Vel	JHP	110	1346	441	4
	Remington	JHP	125	1304	471	4
	Speer	JHP	140	1258	491	4
	Speer	JSP	158	1152	465	4
.38 Special	Norma	JHP	110	1221	364	4
	Remington	JHP	125	1067	316	4
	Speer	JHP	140	1036	331	4
	Super Vel	SWC	158	1002	351	4
9x19mm	Remington	JHP	115	1208	373	4
	Super Vel	JHP	90	1388	385	4
	Speer	JHP	100	1280	363	4

°MV data taken on an Avtron K233 with K101 photoscreens. Figures may vary from advertised velocities taken from special test barrels.

Note: Divide 4-inch revolver data by .9 to approximate velocities from 6-inch barrels.

Load testing is an integral part of preparing custom ammunition for precision combat matches, such as the Advanced Military. Here, a Ransom Master rest is used mounted on a 30-pound steel adaptor plate. The whole unit sits atop a solid concrete caisson. Such an installation gives highly reliable firing data at 50 yards, so useful in analyzing handload and pistol performance.

CHAPTER **XVI**

BALLISTIC PERFORMANCE
OF COMBAT LOADS

THE JARGON OF ballistics is fortified by such technical abbreviations as MV (muzzle velocity), ME (muzzle energy), and RSP (relative stopping power). It is also sprinkled with considerable BS, contributed by individuals who wish to "prove" points using naive or polemical discussions. The amount of practical information related to combat loads and ballistics needed by the shooter is relatively simple. But the overall field of handgun ballistics is quite complex and controversial, demanding a more thorough analysis and understanding.

Because of the defensive nature of combat shooting, the emphasis in handgun loads centers on terminal performance. Interior ballistics is a concern as it affects terminal efficiency. The short ranges at which pistols are fired precludes any detailed consideration of exterior ballistics. Operating pressures, recoil effects, and the linear internal ballistic characteristics of most pistol cartridges hold operating efficiencies within rather narrow limits. While almost any pistol ammunition *can* be used defensively, there are four main cartridges and some alternates

that are used for combat purposes. These choices correspond to the same cartridges that are available for use by law enforcement and military agencies; these are the .45 ACP, 9mm Parabellum, .357 Magnum and the .38 Special. The .38 Super is seen rarely with .45 ACP and .38 Special virtually the only two calibers represented. In the South West Pistol League, the .45 ACP dominates all other calibers.

MINIMUM LOAD PERFORMANCE

Combat shooting League doctrine prescribes power factors for the various bore sizes. These factors relate to the nominal ballistic power deemed necessary for defensive use and to the relative recoil disturbance developed by the loads. This latter standard can be used to determine some scale of difficulty in shooting given loads. The more recoil, the more difficult it is to score well, so the more points are given for scores in determining placements within the various shooting classes. While the author does not wholly subscribe to this doctrine, it has been established for more than a decade and it provides a rationale for comparisons and combat loading thresholds.

The formula for determining minimum load factors is

$$F = \frac{MV}{1000}$$

where F equals force factor, M is the bullet weight in grains and V is the velocity in feet per second.

In addition, League rules prescribe minimum load factors for each bore size and load level as follows:

Caliber	Force Factor	Power and Rating
9mm	134	1
.38	134	1
.38-40	167	1.3
.45	160	1.3
.44	195	1.3
.357 Magnum	213	1.3
.41 Magnum	285	1.3
.44 Magnum	335	1.5
.45 Magnum	355	1.5

Given the force factor for the bore size and loading level, the shooter may choose his bullet weight and solve for V. In .45 ACP with a bullet weight of 200 grains, V is solved for:

$$160 = \frac{200 \times V}{1000}$$

$$V = \frac{160 \times 1000}{200}$$

$$V = 800$$

A load must be selected that produces at least 800 feet per second in the chosen gun. Obviously, the velocity is easier to achieve with a given load in a longer barrel. If that load is fired from a shorter barrel, it will require more powder to meet the specifications. Short barrels usually mean lighter weight and a heavier propellant charge develops more free recoil for the same bullet weight. As a practical matter, the prescribed force factor will subtly influence the bullet weight/handgun choice in order to optimize performance. With a force of 160, the .45 ACP cartridge, firing a 200 grain bullet in the Colt Government Model is optimal.

The list below gives the threshold velocities needed to meet load specs for league shooters. The listing is given by bore size with the usual available bullet weights.

It is interesting to note the effect of the momentum-basis factor formula on bullet weight as it compares to kinetic energy. Even with the smaller force factor required for 9mm bullets, velocities generated by a minimum combat load produced 56 percent more kinetic energy than the usual 200 grain .45 ACP match load. In all cases, heavier bullets in each caliber generate lower kinetic energy.

The basis for calculation of the competitive power factor should be recoil. Some individuals maintain that the standard should be killing power, but some of these fallacies are discussed fully later in this chapter. With .38 Special 158 grain loads shot in a 35 ounce revolver, free recoil is 2.86 fp. With this as a basis, the usual .45 ACP 200 grain competition load fired in a 39 ounce autopistol develops free recoil of 3.69 fp. This figure is 1.29 times the .38 Special level. This would justify the 1.3 power rating assigned to the .45 Government Model. However, a 43 ounce .44 Special revolver firing a 200 grain bullet is required to have a force factor of 195. Firing an appropriate threshold load, the gun would develop 5.04 fp of free recoil or 1.75 times as much as the .38 Special load. Yet this revolver receives a power rating of 1.3 just the same as the .45 ACP!

Going the other way, a shooter who fires an aluminum frame Commander in .45 ACP would have to cope with 5.44 fp of recoil or 1.9 times the .38 Special, yet he will receive a 1.3 power rating. A shooter of the Model 39, firing 115 grain threshold loads will experience 4.05 fp recoil or 1.42 times the .38 Special. Yet the 9mm shooter receives the power rating of 1. The power rating is used

TABLE XVI-I

THRESHOLD COMBAT VELOCITIES

9mm/.38 Super (F=134)	MV	ME	Sectional Density
90 grains	1489 fps	443 fp	.097
100	1340	398	.107
115	1165	347	.123
125	1072	319	.134
.38 Special (F=134)			
110	1218	362	.123
125	1072	319	.139
140	957	284	.156
150	893	266	.167
158	848	251	.176
.357 Magnum (F=213)			
110	1936	915	.123
125	1704	806	.139
140	1521	719	.156
150	1420	671	.167
158	1348	637	.176
200	1065	504	.224
.45 ACP (F=160)			
185	865	307	.129
200	800	284	.140
220	727	257	.154
230	696	246	.161

The terminal ballistic controversy rages mainly over these two caliber sizes: the 230 grain .45 ACP bullet (left) and the 158 grain .38 Special bullet (right). Momentum theory favors loads in .45 ACP, and power ratings further subsidize this bullet/ load. Kinetic energy theory favors lighter weight projectiles from the .38 Special.

as a factor to determine championship points in all league classes of shooting. Score for score, the shooter of the Government Model .45 ACP receives 1.3 times his scores in the match. Is there any doubt as to why the .45 Government Model dominates league competition?

A .357 Magnum gets the 1.3 power rating. A threshold load in a large frame (41 ounce) Smith Magnum wheelgun will develop 6.86 fp of recoil or 2.40 times the .38 Special to earn an equivalent power rating to the .45 ACP. To say that the system is biased in favor of the Colt Government Model is a gross understatement! Shooting the same threshold .357 load in the Model 19 (35 ounces), produces a hand stinging, 8.04 fp of recoil, 2.81 times the level of the .38 Special. If recoil comparisons are to be used as the criteria for competition, the power factor and power rating systems should be overhauled. Other-

League power ratings favor the Government Model, even over other guns in .45 caliber. The lightweight aluminum framed Commander in .45 ACP (left) has a recoil index of 1.9 vs. 1.3 for the same load in the 39 ounce Government Model, yet the power rating is the same for both guns (1.3).

wise, have no ratings and just require any registered league shooter to use the .45 Government Model with a designated load; the effect would be just about the same as it now exists.

MOMENTUM vs. KINETIC ENERGY

This brings us to the old controversy over momentum versus kinetic energy that has bent out of shape many writers and analysts over the decades. It reduces itself to the slow, heavy, large bullet diameter school, and the supporters of light, fast, high energy projectiles. Which is the "correct" point of view?

Is the .45 ACP "better" than the modern 9x19mm (Parabellum) loadings? Is the .38 Special hopelessly obsolete? Systems for terminal ballistics are not comparable to the Golden Tablets. They are merely a means of explaining and measuring relative effectiveness of observed ballistic phenomena. This area of investigation is far from being an exact or absolute science, regardless of how many formulae or equations can be run for calculating performance.

It is very hard to collect exact empirical data in this area, since the terminal object in a defensive shootout is a live human body. Experiments on anesthetized livestock and

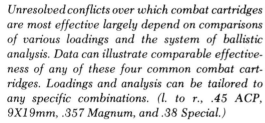

Unresolved conflicts over which combat cartridges are most effective largely depend on comparisons of various loadings and the system of ballistic analysis. Data can illustrate comparable effectiveness of any of these four common combat cartridges. Loadings and analysis can be tailored to any specific combinations. (l. to r., .45 ACP, 9X19mm, .357 Magnum, and .38 Special.)

Distortions created by comparative ballistic systems can be laughable. By using Hatcher's scale procedures, it can be illustrated that a Big League fast ball has 41 times the "stopping power" of the .45 ACP hardball bullet. Ballistic performance measurement systems that cannot be demonstrated empirically should be viewed skeptically.

human cadavers along with detailed autopsies of gunshot victims have given a set of references as to what makes handgun projectiles produce effective terminal ballistics. Relationships in the Hatcher System have been drawn directly to the functions of bullet momentum, cross sectional area of the projectile, and to the form factor representing bullet nose shape. Much of the basic information came out of the Thompson-LaGarde investigations early in this century. The credibility and validity of this method must be considered in light of the limited loadings of pistol cartridges of the day.

Taken in context of the time, development of the Hatcher System for comparative terminal ballistics makes sense. Nearly all commercial and military handgun cartridges in the early part of the century were loaded within the same subsonic velocity ranges; roughly 850 to 950 fps. The common bullet construction was a round nosed lead configuration. Under these circumstances, it follows that a greater cross sectional area of the bullet would cause greater tissue displacement. Coincidentally, these larger diameter

bullets would also weigh more and carry greater momentum than smaller diameter bullets. At subsonic velocities, blunt projectiles would also create considerably more observed tissue damage than smooth, round nosed bullets. At elevated velocities (above 1000 fps) bullet nose shape becomes increasingly less critical regarding wounding capacity.

The Hatcher System indicates that the standard .38 Special service round has half the "stopping power" of the .45 ACP. There is no real definition, measurable or demonstrable, of what "stopping power" really is. Most people with any shooting experience would accept this basic difference in terminal effectiveness between the standard .38 and .45 caliber rounds, however. But, according to the momentum basis of the Hatcher analysis, the Super Vel 90 grain 9mm load traveling at 1485 fps has the same stopping power rating as the standard .38 Special 158 grain service load. Most any knowledgeable shooter is going to challenge that conclusion! Carried to a ridiculous extreme it can be demonstrated that a baseball hurled by a big league fastball pitcher is 41 times superior in "stopping power" to the .45 ACP. All any nation needs to be dominant in defensive tactics is several divisions of Dizzy Deans and an inexhaustable supply of horsehide! Unfortunately, without empirical evidence, most calculated ballistic systems are just so much conjecture.

Within the narrowly defined load ballistics available prior to two decades ago, the Hatcher System has some merits. It is interesting to note that present day defenders of the Hatcher System are also boosters of the .45 ACP. And no wonder! This is not to discredit Hatcher, the .45 ACP, or proponents of heavy bullets; but, realistically, the situation must be reviewed in perspective and with a look at handgun ballistics advances of the past two decades.

FALLACIES OF BALLISTIC SYSTEMS

One fallacy of the Hatcher System (used to calculate the relative stopping power factor) is the use of momentum concepts to define "stopping" or "knockdown" power. The connotation carries the idea of mass colliding with another mass. Bullets do not "knockdown" targets in the way that an automobile would run down a pedestrian. Bullet impact is not transferred to the total mass of the body. Research has shown that the transfer takes place along the wound channel in a radial pattern perpendicular to the center of the channel. The faster the bullet, the more radial the effects. Furthermore, transfer must take place within the first 15 centimeters (approximately 6 inches) of travel in order for the bullet to have any decisive wounding effect on human targets.

The disruption of homeostatic processes of the body is what causes death or unconsciousness. The effect of a striking bullet must cause trauma in vital organs and/or circulatory and nervous systems to instantly incapacitate an adversary. It takes energy, not momentum, to achieve this effect. The effectiveness of a bullet is measured by the terminal energy it transfers. The more stable the bullet is as it passes through tissue the less energy it transfers. Cross sectional area is an important element in energy transfer, whether the bullet is large in diameter to start with or expands its diameter after impact. Bullets traveling at supersonic speeds ride through the wound channel in back of the shock wave created by its passage. Actual damage is done by hyperextravastation of tissues caused by the hydrostatic pressure rise in the wound channel. As velocities exceed 1000 fps, the bullet nose shape has no particular effect on energy transfer from empirical experiments. Unstable bullets that tumble or yaw as they pass through tissues create considerably more damage than stable projectiles. Stable, low velocity projectiles create a narrow, cone-shaped channel ahead of the bullet nose.

KINETIC ENERGY THEORY

The kinetic energy theory of terminal ballistics offers a means by which actual dynamic performance can be measured. This is in contrast to the Hatcher System, where results are measured in terms of a calculated coefficient. With the kinetic method, results are measured by the amount of energy lost when the bullet travels through a medium. Ballistic gelatin or Duxseal compound can be used. Velocity is measured as the bullet enters and after it exits the impact target. Standard procedures use a 16x16x15 centimeter block of material. Differences in kinetic energy (with compensation for bullet weight loss) show how much work was done on the target by the bullet. This is a good relative indication of wounding capacity of the ammunition. This system yields an empirical, comparative quantity that can be measured consistently regardless of other factors. Theoretical speculations need not be made, since measured results will speak for themselves.

With this terminal ballistic measurement

system, specific loads must be compared. Generalizations such as the ".45 ACP is superior to the 9x19mm" are invalid. One must specify particular loads, since, today, there are great and surprising variations in ammunition performance. A hot .357 Magnum load that penetrates the target before bullet expansion begins may be a dud compared to lighter, more unstable bullet loaded down in the .38 Special.

The sectional density of the projectile influences internal, external, and terminal ballistic performance of particular loads. Sectional density is calculated by dividing the bullet weight in pounds by the square of the bullet diameter in inches. As data, sectional density is a ratio of bullet weight per cross section of the bullet. The smaller the ratio, the less weight there is relative to the cross section. The less weight in a given cross section (bullet diameter), the faster the bullet accelerates with a given mean chamber pressure. This phenomenon is due to (a) lighter weight means less bullet inertia (resistance to movement), (b) lower barrel wall friction, plus (c) more "push" per unit of weight.

Lightweight projectiles tend to show increased internal ballistic efficiency in terms of kinetic energy per weight of propellants. Using appropriate slow burning propellants, loads can be assembled also to produce maximum energy per peak pressure (piezometric efficiency). In effect, handguns are engines for converting potential chemical energy into mechanical energy. Their capacity to act in this regard is enhanced by lighter weight; low sectional density also works the same way on the terminal end. Fast internal acceleration and efficient energy transfer inside the barrel indicates quick transfer of energy upon impact with the target. This also means faster energy loss in the atmosphere, where low sectional density projectiles have relatively poor ballistic coefficients. Light bullet loads are meant to be used at short distances, under 50 yards.

The low mass and high velocity of most light combat pistol bullets means deforma-tion on target impact is greater, especially on collision with bony body processes or other solid terminal material. This greater deformation of low mass projectiles plus the shorter overall length, contributes to instability within terminal body media. Instability increases hydrostatic disturbance in the wound cavity with greater wounding capacity. Ricochet potential is greatly reduced for low sectional density bullets, but penetration in depth is also considerably inferior to heavier bullets in any given caliber. The best load combinations depend on performance standards set for the ammunition, followed by empirical testing to verify performance with any combination of caliber, bullets, and load levels. There are no "perfect" loads except in terms of narrow, specialized performance criteria. Comparisons for load efficiencies have to be made in terms of specific, measured ballistic performances.

During investigations made by Di Maio, Jones, and Petty, using the method mentioned above, it was found that the Norma FMJ 116 grain commercial 9mm Luger load transferred the same kinetic energy to the gelatin test blocks as the Winchester-Western 230 grain FMJ .45 ACP cartridge (102 fp vs. 108 fp). Their investigations also determined that the Remington 9mm 115 grain JHP and the Super Vel 90 grain JHP rounds were superior to the Super Vel .45 ACP 190 grain JHP (344 and 378 fp vs. 313 fp). So we see a considerably altered point of view from this kind of research. While the standard .38 Special combat round is bested by commercial .45 ACP (GI hardball equivalent), it comes up to about three quarters effectiveness instead of half-way as in the Hatcher analysis; on the other hand, Super Vel and Winchester full bore .38 Specials better than double the energy transfer of the .45 ACP hardball load!

Who is right? Remember that any terminal ballistic comparisons are only a means of estimating relative wounding capacity. "Knock down power" is a myth! If the wound is in the wrong place and the target is re-

The key to combat effectiveness is the shooter. Trained in bullet placement and gun handling skills, appropriate loads in any of the basic combat calibers will serve equally well. Those loads that exceed basic thresholds of power and do not distract from shooting scores are adequate for effective combat use.

sistant enough, there will be combat failures with any kind of ammunition. Marksmanship and gun handling ability are at least as important as kingsize ballistics in defensive combat shooting. The lost kinetic energy method gives us a considerably more rational and objective method of comparison than Hatcher calculations.

The retracing of police shooting records for references that support one kind of ammunition over another seems fruitless. Without detailed autopsy evaluations and specific terminal ballistic data of the ammunition used, such generalized references as "solid torso hits" or "strikes in vital areas" mean absolutely nothing. There are not going to be any pat answers to all the questions about handgun effectiveness; so the unending

stream of polemics will continue from advocates and detractors of the various cartridges. However, as more objective data is collected and correlated, better terminal ballistic standards are being established.

Meanwhile, one of the best things that can happen to improve overall handgun effectiveness is to redesign combat targets to have "K" zones correspond to "lights out" portions of the human physiology. Such targets should provide a method of point differentiation for K hits that creates real scoring incentives. Modified silhouette targets of the California Combat Association have made a good start. Even the lowly .38 Special service load has ample "stopping power" if the bullet is placed where it will have maximum effect.

These four targets reflect "X" zones related to "lights out" areas of the body. Not all "K" zone areas offer proper shooter incentives which assure tight bullet placement that decreases chances of terminal ballistic failures with any ammunition. Shown above is the combat league silhouette (A), San Diego County Sheriff's silhouette (B), Colt's T-8 silhouette (C), and the California Combat Association team silhouette (D).

XVII

EPILOGUE:
THE POLICE HANDGUN

SINCE THE PEACE officer's sidearm has been declared an item of safety equipment, there has been a massive purchase of handguns by law enforcement agencies. These agencies must now furnish individual duty weapons. There have been several new influences in the past decade that affect handgun choices. As in all decision making processes, there are opportunities for naive, normative, and irrational thinking that arise on both sides of the issue. Senior administrators are aware of these factors and seek to weigh evidence and motivations of supporters and detractors of the various options.

There are no really new facets to the problem of choosing a police handgun. Ballistic developments of the past two decades have made the choice less critical regarding effective cartridges. Today, any of the four most likely cartridge choices (.38 Special, .357 Magnum, 9mm Luger, and .45 ACP) can be loaded to adequate defensive performance levels. The same goes for possible alternate choices such as the .38 Super. Momentum theory based on the Hatcher System is largely polemical in its rationale for heavy bullet superiority. No convincing empirical evidence has been offered to prove the "relative stopping power" theory. No one denies the effectiveness of the "200 grain, 1000 feet per second" rule of thumb for combat loads. But, the lost kinetic energy analysis demonstrates empirically that loads of equal or superior wounding capacity to the .45 ACP can be had from the .38 Special, .357 Magnum or the 9mm Parabellum. It appears that criteria other than wounding capacity must be considered regarding choices for effective combat ammunition. Recoil control and recovery is largely a function of gun weight and projectile weight in terms of a given load level. Expense for an ammunition change-over can be quite significant for many law enforcement organizations. Public relations issues in some areas of the country also may limit the kind of ammunition issued to police.

THE PROBLEM OF CHOICE

Any analysis in depth reveals that there are no clearly "right" or "wrong" decisions

Although there are four basic choices for commercial police cartridges (five, counting .38 Super) load variations in each design must be carefully considered. Any of these cartridges can be loaded to provide adequate police ballistics.

regarding choices from among the leading cartridge/handgun combinations. Structuring of these choices may serve to illustrate this point. The majority of considerations relate to either Colt's Government Model and .45 ACP, four basic service DA revolvers in .38 Special of .357 Magnum, the 9mm Parabellum in either the S&W Model 39/59, Colt's Commander (steel or aluminum frames), or Browning's Hi-Power. These choices fall into the old classic dichotomy of DA revolvers versus autopistols. Analysis of the alternatives may not reveal clearcut choices; final decisions will have to be based on the particular emphasis given to factors for or against possible gun/cartridge alternatives.

AUTOPISTOL CHOICES

Colt's Government Model is a 39 ounce sidearm. Even its proponents recognize this as a disadvantage, coupled with the need for extraordinary training of police officers for its safe and efficient use. Weight in the handgun is a good factor regarding recoil control, but it is a disadvantage for carrying as a duty sidearm. Two distinct advantages of the ACP are convenience of magazine changes (fire power) and speed of operation, especially for the first shot. Quick magazine changes are an advantage where more than six rounds are fired. Statistics show that most fire fights are settled one way or the other with fewer than six rounds exchanged. If multiple assailants are engaged, the peace officer will have to find cover before six rounds are expended or run a high risk of being shot.

The speed of operation of the Government Model depends on the gun being carried cocked and locked. This is potentially the most dangerous condition for any handgun. Even well trained shooters can blast off a round inadvertently when coordination goes

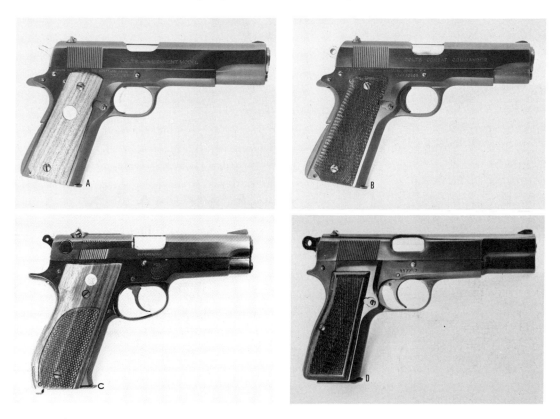

Autopistol choices for police duty are limited by availability and appropriate design configurations. Four self-loaders meet the qualifications: the Colt Government Model (A), the Commander (both in alloy and in steel frames) (B), S&W Model 39/59 (C) and Browning's Hi-Power (D). The Colt handguns are chambered for .45 ACP, .38 Super, and 9mm Parabellum; the Browning and S&W guns are offered only in 9mm.

"spastic." It is not merely a coincidence that military procedures require the autopistol to be carried with the chamber empty and the hammer down.

The many coordinations and routines for controlling the .45 ACP are never mastered thoroughly by some people. The relatively complicated routines of autopistol manipulation invite errors. People experienced in handgun training programs are leary of self-loading guns. Proponents take human coordination for granted when they preach for mass adoption of autopistols. It is not uncommon to have rounds go off while charging the chamber, due to faulty lockwork or miscoordination of the trigger finger. Safety in a police duty gun is of great importance. Carried cocked and locked and used in ex-

pert hands, a properly conditioned .45 ACP can be regarded as the foremost combat handgun. In mediocre hands, and in factory condition it leaves much to be desired regarding both safety and effectiveness. Requiring the gun to be carried hammer down on an empty chamber greatly reduces first shot speed and neutralizes one key advantage of the big automatic.

Double action features of the S&W Models 39 and 59 do away with certain first shot safety problems in self-loading pistols. However, it raises concern over second shot recovery. Training techniques can get around this dual-mode trigger transition, but there is no first shot speed advantage over the DA revolver. Safety procedures and lock design of the Model 39/59 overcomes most possible

The current interest in DA autopistols and big magazine capacity brings considerable focus on the S&W Model 39 and 59 (top). Magazines are shown with eight and fourteen rounds capacity. These handguns are among the finest DA autopistols available.

dangers regarding chambering the first round. Placement of the safety lever on the slide is awkward for speed manipulation. After the first round is fired, the DA auto is as dangerous as any other self-loader, being subject to inadvertent discharge by over-controlling the trigger. The dual-mode trigger has many unique problems of its own regarding effective delivered fire and safety.

BIG MAGAZINE CAPACITY

The 14 round magazine of the Model 59 (13 rounds in Browning's Hi-Power) has enormous appeal. Unfortunately, much of the appeal is in terms of the naive assumption that a lawman becomes less vulnerable in a fire fight. Policemen who figure they can "shoot it out" with impunity against multiple assailants because of big magazine capacity, may be lying in the street clutching nine to ten unfired rounds in their dead fist. Big

magazine capacity is primarily a convenience for volume fire in military or counter-insurgent conditions. It is no substitute for precise, controlled fire. Facing multiple assailants, a peace officer must seek cover; with single assailants he must deliver the first disabling shot. The large magazine philosophy is out of phase with these real time combat needs. *The big magazine will not help deliver effective fire any faster.* There are few situations for urban police where the fifteen round feature is usable. Under stress, an untrained officer might be prone to spray with those extra rounds, rather than to deliver effective aimed fire. In a prolonged fire fight, it becomes more difficult to keep track of remaining rounds with a large magazine. Otherwise there is no reason not to have the extra capacity. The weight of extra cartridges helps stabilize the gun in recoil, and many shooters report the grip shape is better on the Model 59 compared to the original Model 39. Large magazines provide more ammunition carried on each individual officer; or, fewer magazines need be carried for the same deliverable number of rounds.

ALUMINUM FRAMES

The aluminum frame of M59 and Commander autopistols comes under criticism. Realistically, police sidearms are carried a lot and shot relatively little. The low volume of fire over the service life of the gun should not cause concern regarding durability. Proper cleaning and lubrication will eliminate most all causes of abrasion that would unduly wear the soft metal frame. Magazine wells can become worn in time, so smooth chrome plating of magazine bodies will help. Shiny objects attract attention, however, so magazine floor plates should be left blue. While the light guns develop more free recoil than all-steel equivalent models, the light frames keep down total gun weight for easy carrying. Efficient 9mm combat ammunition does not create undue free recoil when light bullets are used, so the guns are not difficult to recover after firing. This factor holds for the S&W Model 39/59 as well as the 9mm Colt Commander. Lightweight further emphasizes the need for precise handholds on autopistols for effective shooting. In .45 ACP, the aluminum Commander has quite noticeable recoil energy. The 33 ounce Browning Hi-Power and Colt's steel Combat Commander are quite pleasant guns to shoot in 9mm.

Functional reliability of self-loading pistols is often questioned. Ammunition variations in handloads and/or magazine problems are most often at fault. A specified commercial ammunition can eliminate the former problem. But the magazine remains as the vulnerable component of autopistols issued in mass. A magazine can be dropped and damaged and then carried for months before the gun is fired again. This particular circumstance would be unusual, however.

REVOLVER CHOICES

Revolvers have been the traditional police handgun all during this century when autopistols were available for adoption, too. Numerous prestigous agencies (FBI, U. S. Border Patrol) have examined both types of guns over the years and remained with the DA revolver for official duty purposes.

The chief recommendation for the DA revolver is safety and simplicity of operation. Some departments have modified issue guns to fire DA only to avoid the possibility that a revolver, cocked on optional SA, could be discharged accidentally. A well tuned DA can be fired with considerable precision. Training techniques have been developed to condition officers to shoot in this mode, but some people never master the finer points of control. Miscoordination during the DA pull serves to open the cone of fire. Beyond 15 yards range, group dispersions can become so wide as to result in serious loss of discretionary fire control.

The revolver's six round capacity has been criticized. Practical experience has not shown this to be a handicap in usual shooting encounters. Speed loading techniques are necessary to use a revolver effectively. Reloading processes are more complicated than those required for Colt or S&W autoloaders, but the practical time differences are not significant. When under fire, any handgun should be reloaded from behind cover, since if the officer remains exposed without dispatching the assailant, he could be down before six rounds are used. The revolver promotes precision use of rounds; there are not enough cartridges in the cylinder to spray indiscriminately, but this is no real problem. The .45 ACP is at no particular disadvantage, either, with only six rounds to fire before reloading.

The DA revolver is not a particularly exciting gun. It does not receive much of a "press" in shooting journals, while autopistols garner rather lavish praise and plenty of space these days. Proponents of autopistols are made to feel they are part of the shooting *Avant-Garde*. Surely the revolver reflects more traditional, conservative values. These two value systems, as irrational as they may seem, play a big role in the choosing of police handguns.

NO IDEAL CHOICE

Probably, there is no ideal police handgun. The decision process in choosing the gun has to consider weighted evidence, that which represents the most influential policies of given law enforcement administrations. The autopistol is King in on-going military campaign actions where fire power carries a decisive advantage. On the combat shooting range, where the shooter's attention is continuously directed toward the awareness of the sidearm, match rules and standard practices strongly favor the self-loader. But for the duty officer, the sidearm is an appendage, a symbol of authority that rarely plays a direct part in his daily routine. For this purpose, the revolver is more carefree, requiring none of the practiced coordinations needed to put an autopistol into action. The DA auto may

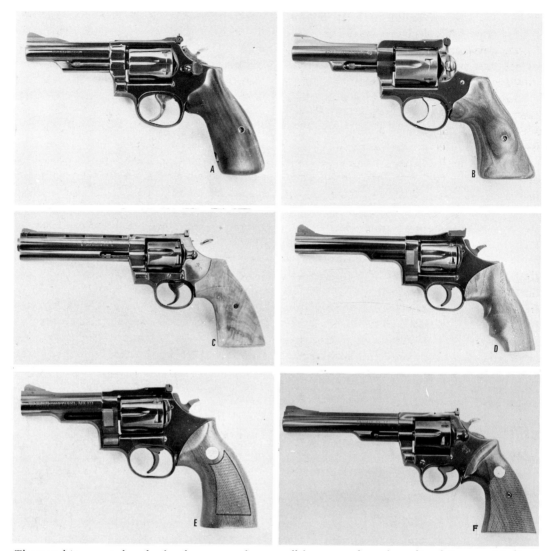

The trend in recent decades has been away from small-frame revolvers for police duty guns. Medium-frame models provide adequate size and weight for shooting stability, while not being outsized and too heavy for carrying. Current choices include such favorites as the S&W Model 19 (A), Ruger's Security Six (B), Colt's Python (C), the Dan Wesson Model 15 (D), and High Standard's Mark III Centennial (E), and Colt's Mark III Trooper (F).

appear to be an effective compromise between the regular automatics and the DA revolver. In reality it creates its own unique set of control problems with the dual-mode triggering.

RATIONALES

Speculation may turn up some typical choices for police departments. Avant–Garde groups go for the latest trends; this would be the Model 59 S&W using one of the hard hitting 9mm loads such as Super Vel 90 grain JHP or the Remington 115 grain JHP. The rationale behind this thinking is fire power and security in military oriented tactical situations against possible mass assaults in civic insurgencies. The threat of such actions may prompt many departments to look for large magazine capacity. In contrast, the traditional choice would be a .38 Special revolver, chosen probably for reasons of economy and possibly using one of the newer loadings for that staid cartridge.

Moderate viewpoints may favor .357 Magnum revolvers, since load flexibility is possible. Full-bore .357's have more power than is needed for effective defensive fire. Loads for the .357 can be tailored to provide more efficient terminal ballistics while not unduly increasing recoil reaction over hot .38 Special loads. Much attention is given to stainless steel guns because of the low maintenance factors. Since Smith & Wesson and Ruger are the only current makers of such guns, they get the nod. Ruger provides black sights on their stainless steel model; this is a revolver that is relatively unsung. The lock work cleans up simply to provide a combat revolver that is the equal of S&W performance. Ruger is also qualified to bid for U. S. Government revolver contracts along with Colt and Smith & Wesson. These are the only three Federally qualified revolver makers in the U. S. at this time. The Ruger Security Six has been adopted for bids and purchased in quantity by the U. S. Border Patrol.

Believers in the ballistic superiority of the .45 ACP will tend to choose the .45 Government Model for the cartridge as well as handling speed. The big, slab-sided handgun makes an imposing authority symbol. Safety conscious departments will go to revolvers or adopt DA automatics because of the first shot safety feature. The saving grace for many autopistol adoptions will be (1) adequate training programs for the autopistol and (2) the fact that few police handguns are drawn in the line of duty. The absolute number of accidents should be small. Being a good police officer does not guarantee above average coordination, however. The few poorly coordinated individuals are generally well known in a department; issuing .45 ACP's to these individuals is going to make a lot of other people bug-eyed around the stationhouse. On the other hand, revolver adoption is no assurance of accident free operations, but it cuts the odds considerably.

Regardless of the choices made, the effective use of police sidearms depends on peace officer proficiency. It is hoped that this book will serve to improve the training of all combat marksmen.

Woodworth, and Schlosberg: *Experimental Psychology.*
    New York, HR&W, 1954.
U.S. Army: *Fundamentals of Ballistics,* (ST 9-153).

Aberdeen Proving Ground, Maryland, 1964.
U.S. Army: *Fundamentals of Small Arms,* (TM 9-2205).
    GPO, 1952.

BIBLIOGRAPHY

Bristow, Allen: *Search For an Effective Police Handgun.* Springfield, Thomas, 1973.

Byrne, John J.: *Hand.* Springfield, Thomas, 1959.

Candland, Douglas: *Psychology — The Experimental Approach.* New York, McGraw-Hill, 1968.

Cooper, Jeff: *Complete Book of Modern Handgunning.* Englewood Cliffs, Prentice-Hall, 1961.

Decker, Ruby: *Motor Integration.* Springfield, Thomas, 1962.

Hall, Michael: *Locomoter System — Functional Anatomy.* Springfield, Thomas, 1965.

Hatcher, Julian S.: *Textbook of Pistols and Revolvers.* Plantersville, Small Arms Technical Publications, 1935.

Hatcher, Julian S.: *Hatcher's Notebook.* Harrisburg, Stackpole, 1962.

Johnson, Melvin, and Haven, Charles T.: *Ammunition.* New York, Morrow,,1943.

Johnson, Melvin, and Haven, Charles T.: *Automatic Weapons of the World.* New York, Morrow, 1945.

Jordan, W.H.: *No Second Place Winner.* Shreveport, 1965.

Lowry, E.D.: *Interior Ballistics.* New York, Doubleday, 1968.

Mann, Franklin W.: *Bullets Flight.* Philadelphia, Riling Books, 1965.

Moses, Robert A.: *Adler's Physiology of the Eye.* St. Louis, Mosby, 1970.

Quick, John: *Dictionary of Weapons and Military Arms.* New York, McGraw-Hill, 1973.

Rubin, and Walls: *Studies in Physiological Optics.* Springfield, Thomas, 1965.

Shepard, Roy: *Alive Man! The Physiology of Physical Activity.* Springfield, Thomas, 1972.

Slovenko, Ralph, and Knight, James: *Motivation in Play, Games, and Sports.* Springfield, Thomas, 1967.

Smith, W.H.B., and Smith, Joseph: *Book of Pistols and Revolvers.* Harrisburg, Stackpole, 1968.

Steindler, Arthur: *Kinesiology of the Human Body.* Springfield, Thomas, 1973.

Taylerson, A.W.F.: *Revolver — 1889-1914.* New York, Crown, 1971.

Weston, Paul: *Combat Shooting for Police.* Springfield, Thomas, 1972.

Woodworth, and Schlosberg: *Experimental Psychology.* New York, HR&W, 1954.

U.S. Army: *Fundamentals of Ballistics,* (ST 9-153). Aberdeen Proving Ground, Maryland, 1964.

U.S. Army: *Fundamentals of Small Arms,* (TM 9-2205). GPO, 1952.

INDEX

INDEX

Note: Italicized numerals represent captioned illustrations.

MY